**Rhetoric & Composition**
PhD Program

PROGRAM
Pioneering program honoring the rhetorical tradition through scholarly innovation, excellent job placement record, well-endowed library, state-of-the-art New Media Writing Studio, and graduate certificates in new media and women's studies.

TEACHING
1-1 teaching loads, small classes, extensive pedagogy and technology training, and administrative fellowships in writing program administration and new media.

FACULTY
Nationally recognized teacher-scholars in history of rhetoric, modern rhetoric, women's rhetoric, digital rhetoric, composition studies, and writing program administration.

FUNDING
Generous four-year graduate instructorships, competitive stipends, travel support, and several prestigious fellowship opportunities.

EXPERIENCE
Mid-sized liberal arts university setting nestled in the vibrant, culturally-rich Dallas-Fort Worth metroplex.

English
DEPARTMENT

Contact Dr. Mona Narain
m.narain@tcu.edu
eng.tcu.edu

Reviewers from March 2018 through March 2019

A journal is only as good as its reviewers. We acknowledge and celebrate the dedication, good will, and expertise of our generous reviewers:

Sheila Carter-Tod, Virginia Tech University
Sidney Dobrin, University of Florida
Abby Dubisar, Iowa State University
Bryna Siegel Finer, Indiana University of Pennsylvania
Laurie Grobman, Penn State Berks
Bruce Horner, University of Louisville
Lynée Lewis Gaillet, Georgia State University
Kristine Johnson, Calvin College
Steve Lamos, University of Colorado Boulder
Christina LaVecchia, Mayo Clinic
Loren Marquez, Hampden-Sydney College
Christine Mok, University of Rhode Island
Kelly Moreland, Bowling Green State University
Jessica Nastal-Dema, Prairie State College
Annette Powell, Bellarmine University
Andrea Riley-Mukavetz, Grand Valley State University
Shyam Sharma, Stony Brook University
Steve Sherwood, Texas Christian University

composition STUDIES

Volume 47, Number 1
Spring 2019

Editor
Laura R. Micciche

Editorial Consultant
Bob Mayberry

Book Review Editor
Bryna Siegel Finer

Editorial Assistants
Kelly Blewett
Christiane Boehr
Ian Golding
Christina M. LaVecchia

Former Editors
Gary Tate
Robert Mayberry
Christina Murphy
Peter Vandenberg
Ann George
Carrie Leverenz
Brad E. Lucas
Jennifer Clary-Lemon

Advisory Board
Sheila Carter-Tod
  Virginia Tech University

Elías Dominguez Barajas
  University of Arkansas

Qwo-Li Driskill
  Oregon State University

Susan Martens
  Missouri Western State University

Aja Y. Martinez
  Syracuse University

Michael McCamley
  University of Delaware

Jessica Nastal-Dema
  Prairie State College

Annette Harris Powell
  Bellarmine University

Melissa Berry Pearson
  Northeastern University

Margaret Price
  The Ohio State University

Jessica Restaino
  Montclair State University

Donnie Sackey
  Wayne State University

Christopher Schroeder
  Northeastern Illinois University

Darci Thoune
  University of Wisconsin-La Crosse

SUBSCRIPTIONS

Composition Studies is published twice each year (May and November). Annual subscription rates: Individuals $25 (Domestic), $30 (International), and $15 (Students). To subsccribe online, please visit http://www.uc.edu/journals/composition-studies/subscriptions.html.

BACK ISSUES

Back issues, five years prior to the present, are freely accessible on our website at http://www.uc.edu/journals/composition-studies/issues/archives.html. If you don't see what you're looking for, contact us. Also, recent back issues are now available through Amazon.com. To find issues, use the advanced search feature and search on "Composition Studies" (title) and "Parlor Press" (publisher).

BOOK REVIEWS

Assignments are made from a file of potential book reviewers. If you are interested in writing a review, please contact our book review editor at brynasf@iup.edu.

JOURNAL SCOPE

The oldest independent periodical in the field, *Composition Studies* publishes original articles relevant to rhetoric and composition, including those that address teaching college writing; theorizing rhetoric and composing; administering writing programs; and, among other topics, preparing the field's future teacher-scholars. All perspectives and topics of general interest to the profession are welcome. We also publish Course Designs, which contextualize, theorize, and reflect on the content and pedagogy of a course. Contributions to Composing With are invited by the editor, though queries are welcome (send to compstudies@uc.edu). Cfps, announcements, and letters to the editor are most welcome. *Composition Studies* does not consider previously published manuscripts, unrevised conference papers, or unrevised dissertation chapters.

SUBMISSIONS

For submission information and guidelines, see http://www.uc.edu/journals/composition-studies/submissions/overview.html.

Direct all correspondence to:

> Laura Micciche, Editor
> Department of English
> University of Cincinnati
> PO Box 210069
> Cincinnati, OH 45221–0069
> compstudies@uc.edu

Composition Studies is grateful for the support of the University of Cincinnati.

© 2019 by Laura Micciche, Editor
Production and distribution is managed by Parlor Press, www.parlorpress.com.
ISSN 1534–9322.
Cover art by Giovanni Weissman and design by Gary Weissman.

http://www.uc.edu/journals/composition-studies.html

composition STUDIES

Volume 47, Number 1
Spring 2019

Contents

Reviewers from March 2018 through March 2019	4
From the Editorial Assistants: An Interview with Laura R. Micciche	9

Composing With   13

Adventures in Collaborative Documentary Editing Across
Continents, or How I Learned to Make Better Movies   13
Alexandra Hidalgo

Articles   16

Approaching the (Re)Design of Writing Majors: Contexts of Research,
Forms of Inquiry, and Recommendations for Faculty   16
*Kara Alexander, Michael-John DePalma,
Lisa Shaver, and Danielle M. Williams*

Encouraging Languages other than English in First-Year
Writing Courses: Experiences from Linguistically Diverse Writers   38
Alyssa G. Cavazos

"Nameless, Faceless People": How Other Teachers' Expectations
Influence Our Pedagogy   57
Brooke R. Schreiber and Dorothy Worden

Decolonial Potential in a Multilingual FYC   73
Cruz Medina

The Reader in the Textbook: Embodied Materiality and
Reading in the Writing Classroom   95
Carolyne M. King

To Ensure Warfighting Function: Writing Inside a
U.S. Army Brigade Headquarters   116
J. Michael Rifenburg

Beginning at the End: Reimagining the Dissertation
Committee, Reimagining Careers   135
Amy J. Lueck and Beth Boehm

Good Things in Threes: Long-Term Effects of Literate Dwelling   154
Steve Lamos

Where We Are 175

Where We Are: My Mundane Professional Life 175

Book Reviews 181

Composition Studies, Public-Facing Activism, and
Our Continued Social Turn: A Review Essay 181

> *Performing Antiracist Pedagogy in Rhetoric, Writing, and Communication,* edited by Frankie Condon and Vershawn Ashanti Young
> *Writing for Engagement: Responsive Practice for Social Action,* edited by Mary P. Sheridan, Megan J. Bardolph, Megan Faver Hartline, and Drew Holladay
>
> Reviewed by Darin Jensen

Retention, Persistence, and Writing Programs, edited by Todd Ruecker, Dawn Shepherd, Heidi Estrem, and Beth Brunk-Chavez 188

> Reviewed by James Clifford Swider

Bad Ideas about Writing, edited by Cheryl E. Ball and Drew M. Loewe 191

> Reviewed by Jenn Fishman with Alli Bernard, Jessica Brown, Grace Chambers, Lorena Dulce, Ryan Higgins, Brian Huback, Saúl López, Aishah Mahmood, Shane Martin, Beth Michalewski, Madi Moster, Carly Ogletree, Alyssa Paulus, Lily Regan, Anna Story, and Haley Wasserman

Assembling Composition, edited by
Kathleen Blake Yancey and Stephen J. McElroy 198
> Reviewed by Sara Austin

Composition, Rhetoric, and Disciplinarity, edited by
Rita Malenczyk, Susan Miller-Cochran, Elizabeth Wardle,
and Kathleen Blake Yancey 202
> Reviewed by Jacob Babb

Retroactivism in the Lesbian Archives: Composing Pasts and Futures, by Jean Bessette 205
> Reviewed by Katie Brooks

How Writing Faculty Write: Strategies for Process, Product, and Productivity, by Christine E. Tulley 209
> Reviewed by Emily Carson

Public Pedagogy in Composition Studies: Studies in Writing and Rhetoric, by Ashley J. Holmes 213
> Reviewed by Erin Cromer Twal

Contributors 217

From the Editorial Assistants: An Interview with Laura R. Micciche

As editorial assistants, we invited outgoing *Composition Studies* editor Laura R. Micciche to participate in an interview about her time with the journal. Micciche became editor of *Composition Studies* in 2013, bringing it to the University of Cincinnati. She is currently working with incoming editors Matt Davis (University of Massachusetts Boston) and Kara Taczak (University of Denver) on the journal's transition. As Micciche was wrapping up the spring 2019 issue, we asked her about working on the final issue, hiring graduate students, and developing inclusive editorial practices. Call this an exit interview, but we're calling it a celebration of her achievements.

So, it's your last issue. How are you feeling?

Proud of the work accomplished by the whole editorial team, David Blakesley at Parlor Press, the authors, reviewers, and review board. Definitely takes a village to do this work. I'm also feeling hopeful about the future of the journal because incoming editors Matt Davis and Kara Taczak bring a lot of experience from their time working as editorial assistants for *CCC* and a good dose of enthusiasm too. I'll definitely miss working with authors so closely, as that has been one of the great joys of this position, but I'm still in the editing game. With Chris Carter, I'm co-editing the WPA book series for Parlor Press.

You became *Composition Studies* editor in 2013. What do you remember about that first year and the work involved?

I remember thinking that I wasn't ready for the job. An independent journal like *CS* has no host organization to streamline the transition process. There's no training manual, only what the previous editor relays and recommends. Jennifer Clary-Lemon, who was editor before me, created an excellent guide for me that helped orient me to the many tasks involved with small-scale academic journal publishing. I had never before thought about how the work I read in JSTOR or ProQuest got there. Now I know that, for an independent journal, the editorial team sends the issue via email to a contact at one of these subscription companies. I also had to learn how to navigate our submission manager, Open Journal Systems (OJS), a platform that makes the editorial process streamlined, for sure, but isn't what I'd call transparent for a new user. Speaking of that, I had to figure out who at my university could help me figure out how to host OJS on a local server.

Another first thing I remember about becoming editor is reading through the many files that Clary-Lemon shared with me via Dropbox. I looked at everything from decades-old correspondence between editors and authors to feedback on manuscripts from editorial team members. And then I read the first five or so years of the journal, beginning with the first pamphlet in 1972 when the journal was called *Freshman English News*. Interesting how much of the content from those early issues returns in different forms—in the first issue, for instance, Thomas W. Wilcox wrote about "The Trend Towards Freshman Seminars," and several contributions argued over what "freshman composition" should teach, a topic that re-emerges in early issues addressing teaching "minority" students and teaching with multimedia. You can see historical grooves when you look back at publishing in the pre-professional age of composition studies. Gave me a more expansive understanding of how we got to the present moment.

During your editorship, what experiences stand out?

Working with advanced graduate students and junior scholars on their first publication. Affirming that an author's work is important and needs to be shared. Meeting authors and talking with prospective authors at CCCC about their work. Getting into the weeds while copyediting and, along the way, figuring out something new about a piece. Worrying about the sustainability of print journals and the fiscal health of *CS*—not wanting to be the person who drove it into the red. Collaborating on the production process with you two and other editorial assistants over the years: Kelly Blewett, Christiane Boehr, Christina LaVecchia, and Janine Morris. Impossible without a team!

How has your research or writing been changed by your time as editor?

I've learned so much about the field, the kinds of questions people are asking, methods they are using, pressing issues for contemporary readers and scholars. Yes, I've been changed. One definite takeaway is that I've expanded the methods I use to do research. For a long time, I relied on textual analysis, which probably reflects my training in an English department during the height of poststructuralism. The more I learned from authors about methodological diversity, the more I felt a shortcoming in my own work. During my editorship, I attended the Dartmouth Summer Seminar on Research where I got a very challenging and exciting crash course in qualitative and quantitative research methods. Soon after, I conducted qualitative research for *Acknowledging Writing Partners* (WAC and University of Colorado Press 2017). During the same period, I integrated more qualitative research in the courses I teach, aiming to prepare students to be versatile researchers with a repertoire of methods to suit the questions they want to study.

Under your direction, *Composition Studies* was the winner of the 2017 Outstanding Composition and Rhetoric Journal Award in Recognition of Inclusive Editorial Practices. Congrats again! What are some inclusive editorial practices that you value?

This gets more attention by Kelly Blewett, Christina LaVecchia, Janine Morris, and me in the March 2019 special issue of *College English* devoted to editing, so I'll keep this brief. Some of what we've tried: attending presentations by recipients of Scholars for the Dream awards and inviting panelists to submit their work to *CS*, doing the same at special interest group sessions, recruiting for diverse representation on the editorial board and within the reviewer pool, developing sections of the journal that allow for submissions other than long-form articles, welcoming plural methodologies, and intervening at the level of citation when an argument requires engagement with more robust source material. There's a lot more to do, but this is some of what we've been working on over the past six years.

Tell us about your next editorial or research project. Or both!

As I mentioned, I'm co-editing a WPA book series and look forward to working with authors in that capacity (people of writing studies, send your work: https://www.parlorpress.com/wpa.html). Aside from that, I'm at the beginning stages of a project that studies "the mundane" stuff of faculty life in writing studies. My idea is that by tracking writing faculty's everyday experiences within academic institutions, I will be able to show how small actions, behaviors, feelings, and experiences accumulate and form larger systemic patterns. I hope the data I ultimately collect will form a varied portrait of rituals and routines, institutional social orders, place-based practices, and taken-for-granted realities in workplaces differentiated by location, status, resource availability, student and faculty populations, and intersectional identities. I'm thinking this will be a longitudinal cross-institutional research study, which I've never done before. Perfect time to do something new since 2019 marks my 20th year of faculty life!

You've hired graduate students to assist with copyediting, proofreading and archiving. What advice would you give graduate students who are interested in editorial work?

Approach editors—especially editors of independent journals—to ask if they could use some help. You might be surprised by their answers! When you go to conferences or other professional gatherings, talk to editors. Ask them how they found their way to this work and what pathways they might recommend to you. When your writing is edited for publication, pay attention to editor marks and comments so that you can understand what decisions the editor is making. And, if you like resource guides, pick up *The Copyeditor's Handbook: A Guide for Book Publishing and Corporate Communications*, 3rd edition, by Amy Einsohn. It's surprisingly readable and packed with useful information.

What can we look forward to in the spring 2019 issue?

This issue is a blockbuster. We've got a Composing With by Alexandra Hidalgo about composing independent documentary films. Next, we feature eight articles focused on an impressive range of topics: designing a writing major, encouraging linguistically diverse student writers in fyw, understanding influences on L2 writing instructors' pedagogical decision-making, teaching fyc with a Spanish-English approach, tracking constructions of reading and readers in writing textbooks, writing in military contexts, reimagining dissertation committees, and reflecting on literate dwellings. The Where We Are section consists of 116 six-word sentences on the topic of "My Mundane Professional Life." The unattributed entries are compiled in poetic form, generating a collective portrait of what writing faculty encounter, do, and feel on a daily basis. Funny, touching, maddening—this piece has a little bit of everything. Finally, we round out this issue with seven book reviews and one review essay. If you're like me and can't keep up with scholarship in writing studies, start here! And thanks for reading, sharing, and submitting your work (yes, that means YOU, dear reader).

Ian Golding, University of Cincinnati
Rich Shivener, University of Cincinnati
March 2019

Composing With

Adventures in Collaborative Documentary Editing Across Continents, or How I Learned to Make Better Movies

Alexandra Hidalgo

Since 2012 I've coauthored a number of academic publications with peers and students. I love the process of dividing up the research and figuring out who will write which sections. Although it usually becomes clear that some of us are better at big picture thinking and others are more detail oriented, my coauthors and I bring comparable skills to the table. Collaborations in filmmaking, on the other hand, work differently because of the very nature of the production process. From its inception, film has been an art form that depends on multiple crewmembers performing their specialty. The cinematographer is in charge of capturing the film's visuals with their camera, the sound person is the only one who can hear how voices and ambient sounds are picked up by microphones. Through the instruments they wield and the formal and informal education they've received, crewmembers deliver heterogeneous pieces of a hopefully cohesive whole.

While for a decade I've worked with crews when filming my documentaries in what's called the production stage, it wasn't until last year that I began sharing the postproduction process with someone. After I have shot all—or at least most—of my footage, I begin to shape it into a narrative. Unlike in alphabetic writing when the editing process comes after some kind of a draft has been written, film editors put together every draft of the film. Being a filmmaker who doesn't work within the studio system and whose funding is tight, I edit my own films. When I began working on *The Weeping Season*, a feature documentary about my father's 1983 disappearance in the Venezuelan Amazon, I decided to tell the story with higher production values than I had used in my previous work. In order to do so, I am applying for film industry grants to cover the significant cost of making a documentary, even an independent one.

As I began applying for grants, I learned from film mentors and from a grant workshop I attended that chances of getting funded are slim if you're editing your own film that tells a personal story. The idea is that you don't have enough distance from the characters and events in order to make the at-times harrowing narrative decisions that are necessary for a good film. After spending years crafting video essays that are based on my and my family's experiences and having edited *Pixelating the Self: Digital Feminist Memoirs,* a book composed of multiple authors' explorations of their personal lives, it seemed questionable that I had to work with an outside editor to tell my own story. However, I've learned that the rules of filmmaking make sense once you try them, so I set out to hire an editor.

I found Cristina Carrasco, a Venezuelan editor living in Argentina, through a childhood friend. I needed someone who spoke English and Spanish, the two languages in which the film unfolds, and someone who understood the current political situation in Venezuela. When I began filming the documentary in 2004, we were focusing on my father's story, but since Venezuela is currently undergoing a stark political and economic crisis, we need to address that situation in the film. Cristina has a strong understanding of the situation in Venezuela and a decade of experience editing fiction and documentaries that play on TV, in cinemas, and at A-list film festivals. She can see things that I cannot see, just like with my academic training I can see things that she can't.

We work through Skype marathons that sometimes last up to seven hours. We pass the Adobe Premiere version of the film back and forth, with me leaving her extensive notes on our shared Google documents to which she responds using track-change comments. It is an elaborate apparatus that makes up for the fact that we live in different continents but are birthing a project together. And having birthed films (and two children) on my own, I don't want to work on a documentary without an editor again.

Cristina is trained in how narrative, in particular film narrative, needs to evolve. We've divided the story in three acts, and she's taught me that the end of each act needs to feature a moment in which the rules of the game change and there's no way to turn back. We are constantly moving the events of the story's various timelines around like chess pieces. Here my scholarly brain comes in handy and I'm able to think through the most logical ways in which events can unfold while retaining their emotional punch. I can think through all the variables that will be altered by each potential reordering. I've always shown drafts to smart and generous friends and colleagues for feedback. My husband Nate, the film's cinematographer, is my constant creative companion in any project I embark on. However, the level of creative and intellectual engagement with Cristina is new and has pushed the story in daring directions it would have never gone had I been editing the film on my own.

As for working with an outside editor for personal pieces, the rules turned out to make absolute sense. Without any personal attachment to scenes, plot lines, and characters, Cristina is able to pinpoint the moments that, while deeply meaningful to me, won't connect with audiences who haven't lived through my experiences or don't share my memories. She is also able to explain how scenes that I thought should never end up in the film bring something new into the narrative. After the film is complete, I want to think more carefully and at length about how this kind of collaboration can become a model for academic scholarship. Until then, I will enjoy this intricate cross-continental creative journey and be thankful for not taking it alone.

Works Cited

Hidalgo, Alexandra. *Pixelating the Self: Digital Feminist Memoirs. intermezzo*, 2018, http://intermezzo.enculturation.net/08-hidalgo-et-al.htm.

Articles

Approaching the (Re)Design of Writing Majors: Contexts of Research, Forms of Inquiry, and Recommendations for Faculty

*Kara Alexander, Michael-John DePalma,
Lisa Shaver, and Danielle M. Williams*

In this article, we discuss the three-year process of redesigning our writing major at Baylor University. In tracing our process, we discuss the decisions we made with regard to the redesign of our major and contextualize our decision-making process in relation to existing scholarship on the writing major. Additionally, we highlight the range of sources we examined in our efforts to understand how the various dimensions of each context might influence the redesign process. Finally, we distill key insights from our redesign process and provide practical guidance for writing scholars who plan to undertake similar redesign efforts. Through this essay, we aim to provide writing scholars with an approach for navigating—in thought and in practice—the complex processes of decision-making and research central to (re)designing a writing major. On the whole, we hope our article will be a useful tool for helping others in their major-building efforts and serve as one possible response to an exigent and perennial question in writing major (re) design: How is a writing major developed or redesigned?

Over the last twenty years, the field of rhetoric and composition has produced an abundance of scholarship on the formation, aims, and value of the undergraduate writing major (e.g., Giberson and Moriarty; Olson and Drew; O'Neill, Crow, and Burton; Shamoon, Howard, Jamieson, and Schwegler). This research offers a range of theoretical and pedagogical approaches that serve as a basis for defining what the writing major is and what it might be. This research also offers program profiles, an invaluable resource for scholars who are considering developing or redesigning writing majors (e.g., Giberson, Nugent, and Ostergaard; Program Profiles section of *Composition Forum*).

Program profiles are important for several reasons. First, they prompt imaginative possibilities for the writing major in various institutional settings. Second, they provide insight into the creative thinking and disciplinary priorities that undergird the development and redesign of writing majors.[1] They can also help to advance knowledge in our field. One of the most important functions of program profiles is that they can provide flexible roadmaps that writing specialists can use and adapt as they consider *what* a writing major might look like in their particular institutional context. Another important consideration is *why* a writing major might take one shape or another based on the hierarchy of disciplinary values privileged by those (re)designing the major—questions that are central concerns in writing major scholarship (e.g., Balzhiser and McLeod; Giberson).

Yet program profiles often insufficiently capture the *how* of writing major (re)design. In fact, they fail to adequately address the complex decision-making and rigorous research processes in which writing specialists engage during program (re)design. Operating with limited knowledge of the decision-making and research processes through which existing writing majors have been (re)designed leaves programs that are attempting to (re)design writing majors at a significant disadvantage. As Greg A. Giberson notes in his afterword to *Writing Majors: Eighteen Program Profiles*, "Most of the programs I am familiar with struggled through the process in a very nonlinear, haphazard way, unaware of the internal and external forces that would come into play at different stages during their development" (242). Without sufficient knowledge of decision-making and research processes in writing major (re)design, programs must devise heuristics for decision-making and approach research through trial and error, which is inefficient and frustrating.

Functioning in this haphazard way contributes in part to another key concern raised in recent writing major scholarship, namely the ever-shifting identity of the undergraduate writing major. According to Deborah Balzhiser and Susan McLeod, the writing major "is growing at an impressive rate" and "a significant amount of institutional change is underway" (416), yet there is "little consensus about what a writing major should look like" (422). Andrea Lunsford similarly observes that "new majors, programs, and departments seem to be proliferating without. . . a center of gravity" (qtd. in Balzhiser and McLeod 422). In light of this reality, Balzhiser and McLeod suggest the need to articulate common aims for the writing major while still accounting for differences in institutional and departmental contexts (425).

In response to these challenges, Giberson identifies "some shared, important parameters that all program developers work within during the conception and implementation of their programs" and offers a heuristic for thinking through common concerns related to such work (242). Giberson's approach encourages writing specialists engaged in (re)design efforts to consider questions concerning departmental support, departmental and institutional resources, program foci, program goals, student learning outcomes, and disciplinary values. Along with a shared method for thinking through limitations and opportunities for (re)designing writing majors, Giberson's heuristic provides a tool for considering the broader disciplinary implications of major (re)design decisions. Ultimately, Giberson's tool offers writing scholars a flexible and adaptable approach to decision-making and research related to writing major (re)design, and it also makes these processes more transparent.

In this article, we discuss the concrete ways that we adapted Giberson's heuristic in the redesign of our writing major at Baylor University—a nationally ranked private Christian research institution located in Waco, Texas, with an undergraduate student body of 14,000. Sharing our redesign builds upon Giberson's contribution by offering an extended discussion of the processes we used in our local context, along with recommendations for how others can adapt our approach to suit their specific local contexts. Ultimately, our article encourages those interested in (re)designing writing majors to be more intentional and forward-thinking in their processes of program development (242). In short, we hope our article will be a useful tool for helping others in their major-building efforts and address the exigent and perennial questions: What does a writing major look like? How is a writing major developed or redesigned?

In what follows, we highlight the approach we employed for navigating—in thought and in practice—the complex processes of decision-making and research central to (re)designing our writing major. The inductive and multilayered approach we discuss employs textual analysis, rhetorical analysis, interviews, and self- and group-reflection. To capture the complex situatedness of a writing major, the approach we discuss analyzes the overlapping and dynamic contexts in which many writing majors operate. This approach includes:

1. determining key decisions related to the (re)design of writing majors;
2. defining the purposes for examining each context in which a writing major operates;
3. deciding on the kinds of research to conduct in each context;
4. generating questions to analyze the data collected from each context in order to determine the strengths, weaknesses, gaps, and needs in a writing major;
5. mining the findings from the analyses carried out in relation to each context to propose courses of action for building on strengths, addressing weaknesses, filling gaps, and responding to needs of a writing major; and
6. developing arguments that draw from the analyses of the data collected to provide justification for proposed curricular changes.

In discussing the ways this approach was employed in redesigning our writing major, we articulate the purposes, questions, and motives that guided our analysis of four contexts: the field of rhetoric and composition; our writing major; our writing faculty; and our department. Throughout our essay, we discuss the decisions we made in our redesign efforts and contextualize our decision-making process in relation to existing scholarship on the writing major. Additionally, we highlight the range of sources we examined in our efforts to understand how each context might have bearing on the redesign of our writing major. Finally, we distill key insights from our redesign process and provide practical guidance to others doing similar work.

Our article contributes to scholarship on the writing major in several regards: First, it provides a concrete model of how Giberson's valuable heuristic might be adapted to inform the processes of program (re)design in a local context. In extending Giberson's contribution, this article demonstrates the ways in which the parameters and considerations he offers may be utilized in practice. As Sanford Tweedie, Jennifer Courtney, and William Wolff assert, localized accounts of redesigned majors are significant but such "stories must be relevant to others by speaking to local and global issues" (261). Writing specialists sharing approaches to (re)design must attempt, in other words, to "provide information to others [in the field] who may find themselves in similar situations," as Peggy O'Neil, Angela Crow, and Larry Burton suggest in *Field of Dreams* (2). In sharing our redesign process here, we aim to give readers an approach that is contextualized within our local circumstances but also adaptable to a range of other contexts.

Second, by making our decision-making and research processes visible, our article provides a window into vital but often hidden dimensions of writing major (re)design work. Thus, writing scholars can keep these key considerations in mind when negotiating similar challenges in their institutional contexts. As Tim Peeples, Paula Rosinski, and Michael Strickland note, "Building a storehouse of knowledge, which includes stories or 'cases,' is one powerful way to help agents more consciously develop their local, institution-specific programs" (73).

Scholarship of the kind we share here is also important to the field because as several scholars note, "Our field has not come to a consensus on the shape, content, or focus of our majors" (Giberson and Moriarty 3). Thus, as we work to (re)design writing majors suited to local contexts, it is important to share the ways in which our context-specific decisions also grow out of scholarly conversations and knowledge-making in the field as a whole. In sharing the ways our process stemmed both from our local circumstances and from ongoing scholarly work on the writing major, we aim to contribute to Giberson and Moriarty's vision for scholarship that helps to "secure [the] place of [the writing major] on our campuses, and in our discipline, for years to come" (3).

Background

The professional writing (PW) major at Baylor University was established in the mid-1980s in the English Department. The major emerged out of a need for students to be prepared to write in their professions and to secure professional-level employment. Classes in the major, originally designed by English literature and journalism faculty, drew heavily from existing English literature courses. PW majors were required to take three upper-level literature courses and a grammar course taught by linguistics faculty. Depending on their choice of electives within the major, students might take only 9-12 hours of professional writing (PW) courses. This curriculum remained the same for three decades. Figure 1 outlines this original PW degree plan.

The Professional Writing major requires students to complete thirty hours of "3000" or "4000" level courses distributed among language, writing, and literature:

1. **Writing** (fifteen hours):
    a. Required
        i. ENG 3300 (Technical and Professional Writing)
        ii. 4318 (Writing for the Workplace)
        iii. 4377 (Writing Internship)
    b. Electives: Two courses selected from:
        i. 3303 (Expository Writing)
        ii. 3307 (Screenplay and Scriptwriting)
        iii. 3309 (Writing for the Popular Market)
        iv. 4309 (Advanced Argumentative Writing)
        v. 4311 (Advanced Writing for the Popular Market)
        vi. 4375 (Special Topics in Writing)

2. **Literature** (nine hours): Nine hours of "3000" or "4000" level literature courses

3. **Linguistics** (three hours): ENG 3302 (Modern English Grammar)

4. **Elective** (three hours): An additional "3000" or "4000" level English course (may include professional writing, creative writing, literature, or linguistics).

Fig. 1. Professional Writing Degree Plan (original major)

About fifteen years ago, the English Department began hiring faculty trained in rhetoric and composition to teach in the PW major. Although we each recognized a pressing need to update the PW curriculum when we were first hired and even initiated a few efforts to make changes, we ultimately decided to put off a major curriculum revision until multiple PW faculty members were tenured. In the interim years, we adjusted our approaches for teaching existing courses and regularly offered special topics courses to enhance the curriculum.

In 2012, Kara attended the Conference of the Council for Programs in Technical and Scientific Communication (CPTSC). In a session on the status of undergraduate writing majors in the U.S., the presenters reviewed data on trends in undergraduate writing programs, including core courses, program names, number of faculty, and number of required writing courses. Baylor's PW major was not on this list. When Kara inquired about why our major was not listed, the presenters stated that Baylor's program did not meet one of the main criteria for a major: at least 18 hours of required writing courses. While we knew the PW major did not include enough writing courses, we now had confirmation that our program was not considered to be a writing major by professional standards. This moment was a turning point for us: We suddenly had a compelling argument and powerful evidence to support a program revision. With this exigence, and with several of our PW faculty now tenured, we approached our department chair about revising our curriculum.

To spearhead and organize our program redesign efforts, though, we thought it necessary to create a PW Coordinator position. In the fall of 2013, Kara was named PW Coordinator, and she initiated meetings with the PW faculty about how to revise the major in order to meet professional standards. We concluded that the PW major should be redesigned to include more writing courses, to better serve the needs of PW students, and to take advantage of PW faculty's areas of scholarly expertise. Our initial conversations also led us to see the need for more in-depth research and laid the foundation for the approach we employed throughout our redesign process.

Define the Identity of a Writing Major: Studying the Field of Rhetoric and Composition

One of the first critical tasks in redesigning our writing major was making decisions about how to define the major. In pursuit of this goal, we examined the field of rhetoric and composition to understand what an undergraduate writing major looks like by the field's standards. We first researched statements by professional organizations (CCCC, CWPA, CPTSC, and NCTE) to collect information on standards, outcomes, goals, and practices for writing majors. In addition to professional statements, we read scholarship related to the writing major (e.g., Allen and Benninghoff; Balzhiser and McLeod; Estrem; Giberson and Moriarty; Grobman and Kinkead; McCormick and Jones). Finally, we researched over seventy-five undergraduate writing programs in U.S. universities. We compiled data on degree plans, curricular requirements, mission statements, program names, and types of degrees offered. We then narrowed our focus to thirty programs that seemed to best align with our program goals and aspirations. In this more focused stage, we researched program descriptions, program objectives, core courses, elective courses, course titles and descriptions, and the number of full-time faculty. We also tried to get a sense of the available resources, such as whether institutions had a graduate program in writing that offered masters or doctorates. We examined these data sets by asking questions such as the following: What does the field recognize as a writing major? What are the standards and outcomes of a writing major? What are the theoretical, methodological, historical, and curricular frames undergirding writing majors? What do programs call themselves?

Important decisions regarding how to define the identity of our writing major grew out of this research. Given that the writing major is "an amorphous and still-developing construction that has varied missions, purposes, and course requirements" (Carpini 16), processes of major development and redesign challenge writing specialists to define what we mean by "writing" and to determine the scope of our writing majors. In the absence of clearly defined models, this process requires difficult and complex judgments. We began our process by considering the variety of majors that Dominic Delli Carpini outlines in "Re-Writing the Humanities"—ranging from praxis-focused, career-oriented models to liberal arts-focused models that emphasize learning common in humanities-based programs. Based on our students' interests and career aspirations and our faculty's expertise, we determined that our writing major should fuse professional preparation with humanistic inquiry and scholarship, much like the writing major that Carpini describes at York College. Like Carpini, our faculty believe that "liberal inquiry need not be mutually exclusive with profession-based goals" (31-32). We thus sought to design a writing major that has the potential to prepare students to write professionally, think rhetorically, and "enac[t] reflective, humanist practices" (32).

Recommendations

Based on our experience, we recommend the following to define the identity of your writing major:

- Conduct research on undergraduate writing majors and explore definitions of the writing major accepted in the field using data

from the CCCC Committee on the Major in Writing and Rhetoric (ncte.org/cccc/committees/majorrhetcomp) and the CPTSC program list (cptsc.org/programlist.html).
- Examine statements by major professional organizations (CCCC, CWPA, CPTSC, and NCTE) about the professional standards and practices of writing programs and writing majors, and evaluate the outcomes, goals, and practices in your writing major against these standards.
- Read the rich and ever-growing body of literature on the writing major in order to gauge strengths and weakness of your major and to imagine the possible shape that your writing major might take. Consult, for example, sources such as Giberson, Nugent, and Ostergaard, and essays featured in the Program Profiles section of *Composition Forum*.
- Compare the curriculum of your writing major with the writing majors at peer-aspirant universities and select innovative and award-winning models.

Articulate the Aims of a Writing Major: Reflecting on Students' Perspectives

Another crucial phase of our redesign process was a self-study we conducted to determine the central learning objectives for our major. This procedure was based on the WPA self-study guidelines currently available online (Council). Through our self-study, we drafted aspirations that delineated our goals for a major and outlined student outcomes. As we worked to determine the goals of our writing major in the context of our self-study, an important part of the process involved reflecting on students' perspectives. Specifically, feedback from students in our courses, ideas students shared in exit interviews, students' comments on course evaluations, interests and needs expressed by current students, and the professional paths pursued by many of our graduates played an integral role in shaping our decision-making process concerning the aims of our major. To use Hill Taylor's terms, the aims of our writing major were crafted in many respects as responses to "the places our students inhabit and come from, the places they hope to go, and especially the worlds they aim to create" (100). As TJ Geiger and Erin Bradley, et al. recommend, we considered students' perspectives and experiences, which elicited the following questions: What do students need to learn? What are students gaining from the present curriculum? Where are the gaps? What are the graduates of our program doing? What feedback do our alumni have? What outcomes do we as writing faculty want to achieve?

These student perspectives helped us arrive at the overarching goal for our redesigned writing major: to cultivate versatile writers who have the knowledge, experience, and rhetorical facility to adapt to the rhetorical demands of academic, professional, and civic contexts. In line with this broad goal, we articulated three learning outcomes. We aim for our majors to become

- *Versatile communicators* who have the writing knowledge, analytical capabilities, and technological facility needed to adapt to a range of audiences, purposes, genres, media, and situations.
- *Creative professionals* who have the collaborative writing skills, project leadership experience, and workplace practices to thrive in writing-centered and writing-related careers.
- *Innovative problem-solvers* who have the writing expertise, research skills, and design abilities needed to address complex problems in professional, academic, and civic settings.

Much like Bradley, et al., we worked to design a major that gives writers a strong foundation in rhetorical theory, experience studying and using a wide range of genres, and opportunities to develop imaginative capacities through writing and reading a range of text types. In addition, we wanted students to gain knowledge of and facility with design, and offer various occasions to examine questions of ethics, morality, and justice in relation to the work of rhetoric and the practice of writing. And like the nonfiction writing program that Beth Taylor describes at Brown University, we aimed to design a major that serves the academic needs of our students and prepares them to succeed in their future professional aspirations. Likewise, our major was redesigned with "a concern for empowering people in different spheres of human activity, different spheres in which training in the arts of rhetoric and writing will prepare a person to use language to participate effectively in one endeavor or another, to participate in different aspects of their lives" (Moriarty and Giberson 213). Articulating these student-oriented outcomes also better prepares us to talk to prospective students, and often their parents, about our major.

In an effort to better reflect these aims and based on feedback from students and our research of the field, we decided to change the name of our major. We felt that "Professional Writing" did not effectively capture our major's depth. As a specialization within the field of rhetoric and composition, the title felt limiting, incomplete, and even misleading. The name itself expresses professional preparation and encapsulates only a segment of what we do or how we want to be known. For example, it carries the connotation of a vocational major in which the "basic skills" of writing are being taught for the narrowly drawn purpose of career preparation. We, therefore, decided to add the term

"Rhetoric" to our name to become "Professional Writing and Rhetoric" (PWR). The addition of "Rhetoric" indicates the theoretical underpinning of how we teach writing and highlights that our majors are equipped to be versatile and adaptive writers who use their talents to intervene strategically in a range of writing contexts. We also believe this name more clearly aligns us as a rhetoric and composition major within our field's professional organizations. Additionally, we believe the name more accurately reflects our faculty's training, research areas, and expertise.

Recommendations

Based on our experience, we recommend the following to determine the aims of your writing major:

- Consider students' perspectives, interests, and career aspirations using exit interviews, student feedback, and course evaluations.
- Interview students, alumni, faculty, advisory boards, internship site supervisors, and other stakeholders in your major.
- Base core aims on essential competencies, skills, literacies, and experiences you want students to have.
- Name your major in ways that reflect the kinds of rich learning and disciplinary expertise that students will gain.

Construct a Vision of the Discipline: Mining Faculty Perspectives

Another facet of our process was reflecting on how the redesign of our major could contribute to a more robust vision of writing and of our discipline at Baylor. We have six full-time PWR faculty members (four tenured, one tenure-track, and one lecturer). All of our faculty have been trained in rhetoric and composition and have varied research and teaching interests including literacy studies, multimodal composition, community based-writing, African American rhetorical cultures, transfer, the writing major, religious rhetoric, and women's rhetoric. Our central purpose in examining our writing faculty was to take stock of our individual areas of expertise, interests, aspirations for the major, and vision for the discipline of rhetoric and writing studies. The questions guiding our process were: What expertise do our faculty have? What courses are our faculty excited to teach? Which courses align with faculty expertise? Which do not? How can we use the redesign of our major to expand perceptions of writing and the discipline of rhetoric and composition at our institution? How will our local redesign contribute to a more expansive vision of writing and the writing major in our field?

To examine these questions, our research consisted of informal focus group interviews among the full-time faculty members who teach in the PWR major. We met frequently throughout the three-year redesign process and often completed brainstorming or research tasks prior to each meeting. During meetings, we examined the research we had collected, shared our perspectives, and discussed possible courses of action for redesign. There was extensive discussion throughout this process, and while we disagreed on different points, we were always able to talk our way to consensus by revisiting our objectives. One of the major turning points in our program redesign was when we decided that the expertise and interests of the faculty should be a guiding factor in our redesign. As one faculty member noted, when individuals teach courses they are passionate about, those courses attract students.

Another important turning point came as we began to think about the ways our local redesign decisions could influence perceptions of writing at our institution and expand the vision of writing in our discipline. Like Heidi Estrem, we view the development and redesign of writing majors as fertile ground for disciplinary expansion and redefinition (12). Thus, as we deliberated about our curriculum, course descriptions, and course titles, we viewed our work as an opportunity to enact what Rebecca Moore Howard calls "curricular activism"—a chance, that is, to "seize the microphone, and the stage itself, to circulate informed, nuanced, proactive visions of writing, of student writers, and of writing instruction—visions that exceed the skill-based ideology of literacy instruction" (42). Beyond creating courses that we considered important to student learning, well-suited to the expertise of our faculty, and fitting for our institutional context, we also sought essential areas of inquiry for the discipline of rhetoric and composition.

For example, our disciplinary commitment to civic rhetoric, as articulated by scholars like David Fleming and Gerald Hauser, is evident in our creation of courses like Writing for Social Change and Studies in Public and Civic Writing. We developed these courses for our major because, like Moriarty and Giberson, we see a focus on civic rhetoric as providing an "ever-evolving, dynamic set of concerns that will motivate, animate, and invigorate our work for years to come" (204). Along with these courses, we also added Spiritual Writing and Religious Rhetoric—a course we see as a vital part of preparing students for civic engagement. Adding this course makes a statement about the importance of studying religious rhetoric in the field of rhetoric and composition. Moreover, these courses align closely with our university's mission.

Creative Nonfiction is another course we considered important to the discipline of rhetoric and composition. In considering whether or not to include creative nonfiction in our curriculum, we discussed many of the questions raised by Linda Shamoon and Celest Martin in "Which Part of the Elephant is This?" Ultimately, we see creative nonfiction genres as professional writing genres—as kinds of nonfiction writing that align with the writing knowledge and experiences of scholars trained in rhetoric and composition. Like Doug Hesse, Tim Mayers, and Celest Martin, our faculty view creative nonfiction within the scholarly purview of scholar-teachers trained in rhetoric and composition and an important part of what majors in writing should be composing, reading, and analyzing. As Martin argues, creative nonfiction courses can provide students opportunities to learn about craft, the importance of audience in personal genres of writing, and the rhetorical nature of creative nonfiction genres (227). Such courses can also teach students to share their expertise in accessible ways with non-specialist readers and prepare students to write for a broader range of writing outlets.

We also sought to promote scholarly work at the undergraduate level and therefore added several courses to enhance students' disciplinary knowledge and research experience. One of the courses we added is Research in Writing and Rhetoric. Like Laurie Grobman and Joyce Kinkead, we see the writing major as a site with rich potential for undergraduate research, as well as a site in which to collaborate with undergraduates on research projects. Similar to Jennifer Clary-Lemon, we envision the writing major as a "viable space in which to 'do' composition and rhetoric—a space in which we may engage in ideas and content of the discipline, where we may think and teach, theorize and practice" (37). Our efforts to advance such a concept of the writing major as a space to engage students in the work of composition is also evident in our inclusion of courses like Women's Writing and Rhetoric, Rhetoric of Race, and New Media Writing and Rhetoric—areas of inquiry that we view as central to the field and important to students' learning. In these courses, students gain exposure to writing theories and rhetorical histories that inform scholarly work in these areas, and students are encouraged to engage with that scholarship via their own writing and research.

Recommendations

Based on our experience, we recommend the following to construct a vision of the discipline through your writing major:

- Focus on the scholarly interests and teaching expertise of your faculty.
- Consider what courses would enhance students' theoretical and disciplinary knowledge and research experience.
- Consider the ways your (re)design choices can contribute to perceptions of your discipline at your institution.

- Deliberate about disciplinary discussions surrounding key subfields in rhetoric and composition and use those arguments to think through your curricular decisions.

Design and Structure Courses: Surveying Writing Majors

Determining the design and structure of our writing major was a key facet of our decision-making and research process. A crucial resource in making decisions about the structure of our major was surveying the design of degree plans at peer institutions. Through our research, we found that writing majors at many institutions stipulate three to five required core courses. To determine our core courses, we considered specific competencies, skills, literacies, and experiences every student should possess as well as those that would provide a good foundation for other major courses.

Other factors that guided our decision-making process include the desire to grant faculty greater flexibility in the courses they teach, to give students greater flexibility in the courses they could take, and to draw students from other majors into our program. In deciding how to structure our redesigned writing major, we kept in mind many of the considerations that Kelly Lowe notes in "Against the Writing Major" (i.e., the need for adequate staffing, careful planning, and a careful assessment of our faculty's strengths and weaknesses). Given that we have only six faculty members who teach in our major, the ability to staff our courses was a chief concern for us when structuring our major. Though many of the writing majors we studied offer specific tracks or concentrations such as digital media, technical writing, editing and publishing, public writing, and even creative writing, we opted not to create specialized tracks within our major due to staffing concerns and our desire to offer students courses in a range of genres and topics. To that end, we created a major that is organized along three foci—professional, academic, and civic—and decided that all students take at least one course in each of these areas. In addition to three foundational core courses, we determined it best to structure the major so that students would have the opportunity to take courses that would enable them to develop specialized rhetorical knowledge and writing ability in the areas that best aligned with their academic interests and professional aspirations without formally defining "tracks." Structuring our major in this way gave us the flexibility needed for a faculty of our size. We also decided to keep the number of required courses low and eliminated prerequisites, which enabled majors to take courses at any point during their matriculation and encouraged non-majors to enroll as well. These decisions gave students increased flexibility to explore different areas of writing, including persuasive, civic, scientific, technical, argumentative, professional, new media, and spiritual writing.

In addition to flexibility, we wanted to ensure that students have a balance of elective and required courses. Most of the writing majors we studied offered theoretical courses, such as rhetorical theory, composition theory, rhetorical history, and research methods. We therefore organized our electives into two categories: Lecture Courses (theoretical and historical) and Workshop/Project-Based Courses (writing workshop), requiring students to take two theoretical courses and three writing workshop courses. In creating our "Lecture Courses," we considered faculty and student interests, along with the theoretical and historical knowledge that we view as essential for our graduates. Examples of courses that grew out of our process are Women's Writing and Rhetoric, Literacy Studies, and Rhetoric of Race. Based on faculty research interests, we know these are three courses faculty will regularly use to teach composition and rhetorical theory, history, and analysis, and we believe these subjects will attract students. We also consider the knowledge students will gain in these courses as essential to their learning and to our university's curriculum. While we initially created a long list of electives in our "Lecture Courses" category, our past students had expressed frustration when they did not have a chance to take courses listed in the PW curriculum. Consequently, we pared down our list of elective courses so that we could offer them regularly. The questions guiding our process during this stage of redesign were: Which courses should constitute the major's core, and which should be electives? How often will courses be taught? How will we staff these courses?

Concerns regarding balance, emphasis, and generality, as discussed in Lee Campbell and Debra Jacobs' "Toward a Description of Undergraduate Writing Majors," also came into play when deliberating about how to structure our writing major in a balanced and coherent way. In their chapter, Campbell and Jacobs offer a valuable heuristic that uses the trajectory of courses within a given major to characterize kinds of undergraduate writing majors along two continua—one from general to specific and the other from liberal to technical. As we deliberated about these concerns, we opted to create foundational courses that would give students general knowledge in three areas: professional writing, academic writing and research, and public writing. We then decided that students should have a balance of theory courses and writing workshop courses at the upper levels. In constructing balance between these courses, we determined that the highest number of credit hours should be devoted to writing workshop courses (9 hours), but that students should also develop specialized rhetorical knowledge in theoretical courses (6 hours). In distributing the subject areas of the writing workshop and theory courses, we also tried to balance course offerings in such a way that students could take a series of specialized courses in either professional, academic, or civic writing. Finally, as Randall McClure suggests in "Projecting the Shape of the Writing Major," we also considered the shape of our writing major and determined for now that our courses would be structured mainly around face-to-face instruction in a traditional classroom and remain part of an English Department.

By considering these concerns throughout our research and decision-making process, we were able to create an agile but balanced course curriculum that gave students choices while providing a firm foundation in core competencies. Figure 2 shows the curriculum we designed.

The Professional Writing and Rhetoric major requires students to complete thirty hours of "3000" or "4000" level courses within the major as indicated below:

1. **Core Requirements** (9 hours)
   - 3318 Professional and Workplace Writing
   - 4309 Research in Writing and Rhetoric
   - 4377 Writing Internship

2. **Lecture Courses** (6 hours)
   - 3313 Literacy Studies
   - 3316 Women's Writing and Rhetoric
   - 3317 Rhetoric of Race
   - 3326 Studies in Public and Civic Writing
   - 4376 Special Topics Lecture in Writing and Rhetoric

3. **Workshop or Project-Based Courses** (9 hours)
   - 3300 Technical Writing
   - 3303 Persuasive and Argumentative Writing
   - 3309 Creative Nonfiction
   - 4307 Style and Editing
   - 4308 New Media Writing and Rhetoric
   - 4311 Writing for Social Change
   - 4318 Religious and Spiritual Writing
   - 4375 Special Topics in Writing Workshop

4. **Literature Electives** (3 hours): Choose one 3000 or 4000 level literature course

5. **Non-PWR English Department Electives** (3 hours): Choose one 3000 or 4000 level literature, creative writing, or linguistics course

---

Fig. 2. New Professional Writing and Rhetoric Degree Plan

Recommendations

Based on our experience, we recommend the following to design and construct courses in your writing major:

- Gather degree plans from writing majors that fit the vision of the writing major you aim to (re)design and use them to think through a range of ways that your writing major might be structured.
- Decide how many core courses you will require and the learning objectives you see as fundamental to all students who graduate from your major.
- Consider the curricular paths you want students to take within the major. These decisions include how flexible you want the major to be, if you will have prerequisites and what those prerequisites will be, what elective courses you will offer and how you will group them, and if you will have tracks or concentrations.
- Pilot special topics courses before engaging in redesign and gather evidence on the effectiveness of those courses (e.g., course evaluations, student feedback).

Develop Arguments to Justify (Re)design Decisions: Analyzing Department Contexts

While we were in the process of researching and discussing our goals for the writing major, we also considered our department context, particularly to get a sense of the various perspectives that we would need to negotiate to gain support for our major's redesign. This process entailed gathering information about the history of the major from those who originally designed it, talking with our department chair and the director of undergraduate studies about our proposed ideas during several phases of the redesign process, and talking to our colleagues in literature, linguistics, and creative writing about proposed changes. We asked: What challenges will we face in our department while getting this curriculum approved? What concessions are we willing to make? Is it better to stay in the English Department or to rethink the model altogether? Who are our allies? What logistical and practical constraints do we need to consider?

Analyzing the department before presenting our proposed changes to the departmental faculty helped us identify potential allies, circumvent landmines, and generate arguments for change based on historical precedent within the department. Our goal was to make sure our proposal would get passed. As we knew from a previous failed attempt to add graduate courses in rhetoric and composition, we needed to be strategic in order to garner our department's support for the redesign of the PW major. We sought answers to our questions by consulting with individuals in positions of power: our chair and the director of undergraduate studies. We also interviewed the linguistics coordinator who had overseen the successful redesign of the linguistics major a few years earlier. Our research gave us a clearer sense of the English department as a context replete with its own spoken and unspoken rules and sometimes conflicting motives, and it enabled us to make persuasive arguments in response to our local constraints. Ultimately, this research informed our understanding of the English department and helped us make redesign choices and arguments that led to little resistance from our colleagues.

Although our English Department offers three undergraduate majors (English Literature, Linguistics, and Professional Writing and Rhetoric), the disciplinary emphasis of the department is weighted towards the study of literature: 75% of faculty members primarily research and teach literature; literature courses make up the majority of upper-level departmental course offerings each semester; and literature majors have traditionally made up the majority of departmental majors. Consequently, we anticipated strong pushback on any proposal to remove literature course requirements to make space in the PW curriculum for additional writing courses.

The primacy of the study of literature in an English department reflects an issue of power often faced by writing majors housed in traditional departments. Writing faculty can sometimes feel outnumbered, dismissed, or unheard in large departments with different interests, values, and methods of research. Speaking against the majority is certainly not "against the rules" in a democratic space influenced by a respect for rational debate, but there are still unspoken rules about what can and cannot be said during a departmental meeting. Would we unintentionally offend one of the creators of the original degree plan, if we noted how outdated it was? Would we cross a line, if we asked for a new tenure line to support our redesigned major? To what extent should departmental politics influence our decisions at this stage of revision? Since, for example, our idea to remove the literature requirements would affect the majority of our colleagues who teach these courses, we decided that our next step was to consider their concerns directly. In speaking with our chair and the director of undergraduate studies (both English literature faculty), we were pleased to learn that not only were they willing to hear our initial arguments, but they also supported our goals to make our writing major more writing-focused. By holding these meetings with key representatives from our department, we gained two insights: (1) we already had allies, and (2) we had a timeline for action since both of their terms would end in the next year. This stage in our research process gave us confidence and helped us reflect on the power dynamics of our department in more productive ways.

Through these conversations, we also gained historical knowledge of the PW major and began to develop arguments that would support accelerating our timeline for the redesign. The major had not been updated in over thirty years, even though dramatic changes have occurred within the field of rhetoric and composition (pedagogical methods, literacies required, distinct subfields), our university (as a result of strategic vision statements), and the people who teach writing courses in the major (we are now all trained in rhetoric and composition). Understanding the history of the major and reflecting on the myriad ways in which the social context has changed led us to consider new arguments about why we wanted to add courses or remove others. While we had been confident of the need to revise the major, these discussions confirmed the kairotic nature of why these revisions needed to happen now.

At times, our anticipation of a certain challenge led us to make preemptive concessions, which directly affected the redesign process. For example, since we knew we were asking a lot to remove four required courses (three upper-division literature and one grammar course), we sought to limit the damage by building in one required literature course and one elective option from either literature, creative writing, or linguistics courses. As a result, our proposed curriculum appeased colleagues who might have felt that we were taking away too many literature, linguistics, or creative writing courses, and it resulted in more flexible options for our majors. It also gave the writing faculty greater flexibility in staffing the additional writing courses we would be offering in the new major.

The strength of our arguments, and our willingness to compromise was rewarded: When our proposal was finally ready for the final departmental vote, we received virtually no pushback, and it passed unanimously. We were a little surprised, but we believe that carefully studying our department context helped us garner support, anticipate and forestall departmental objections, and craft more persuasive evidence-based arguments.

Recommendations

Based on our experience, we recommend the following to develop arguments to justify redesign decisions:

- Learn the history of your major.
- Assess the departmental politics, consider power dynamics among colleagues, and identify allies in your department.
- Consult faculty in positions of power in your department (e.g., department chair, undergraduate studies director), faculty with influence in your department, and other key department stakeholders.

- Identify challenges, potential roadblocks and landmines, practical considerations, and possible concessions.

What We Learned: Future Considerations for (Re)Designing Writing Majors

Although the research we conducted yielded several insights, we also made missteps during our redesign process. We share those missteps here in hopes that others engaged in program revision and (re)design will benefit by keeping these considerations in mind.

One of the major hindrances at the start of our redesign process was focusing too narrowly on our existing major. Initially, we were so locked into the major and staffing constraints that we had difficulty seeing alternative possibilities for what our major might be. Once we decided to table our existing major and look at innovative models of the writing major that others in the field were pioneering, we made great strides. Though logistical issues, such as course coverage or departmental pushback, will need to be addressed at some point, focusing on such issues at the start of the process can stifle exploration and creativity. Our advice then is to begin the process of redesign by imagining what might be possible for the major rather than focusing on what currently is.

The complexity of our institutional context also presented several unexpected challenges for us. Throughout our redesign process, we attempted to gain an understanding of the institutional complexities we would need to navigate in order to persuade the College of Arts and Sciences Curriculum Committee (CASCC), the University Undergraduate Curriculum Committee, and the Provost's Office to approve our recommended changes. For example, part of our research involved speaking with faculty who served on these committees, talking with faculty who recently redesigned majors in the College of Arts and Sciences, and gathering degree plans and course descriptions from majors with whom our courses might overlap (e.g., Journalism, Public Relations, and New Media; Communication; Film and Digital Media). We also familiarized ourselves with the materials that we needed to submit to gain approval for our redesign (e.g., proposals and syllabi). However, we didn't look as broadly as we should have in preparing to address potential challenges at the institutional level.

The members of our PW faculty had limited experience serving on university committees and no experience on curriculum committees outside the department, which impacted our relationships with other departments. In fact, we failed to fully consider other departments that had a stake in our redesign. It was only when the CASCC raised concerns that our revised degree plan included courses that overlapped too much with courses in other departments that these other departments became aware of our redesign efforts. For instance, women's rhetoric, new media writing, and editing and publishing are also taught in other departments: Communication; Film and Digital Media; and Journalism, Public Relations, and New Media. In addition, the Communication Department was concerned about us adding "rhetoric" to the title of our major. To address the CASCC's concerns about redundancy, we analyzed syllabi from similar-sounding courses in other departments, and articulated how we taught these courses and how our approach, assignments, readings, and goals differed. Although these arguments satisfied the CASCC, the departments were still concerned about possible overlap.

Thus, a major shortcoming of our process was a failure to discuss our program redesign with other departments upfront. In our research of the field, we had found that most programs include "rhetoric" in their title and many of the courses we were adding were taught in other English departments and writing programs. We included these data in our proposal, listing the schools, courses, and program names to show evidence for our argument. However, we should have also discussed these ideas and our reasoning with departments that had a stake in these changes. Even though we had collected adequate research and provided a persuasive rationale for our proposed changes, our lack of consultation with other departments beforehand led to multiple additional meetings with the dean's office and department chairs and resulted in additional delays. Moreover, not talking to the departments was a missed opportunity to gain input, build trust, establish rapport, and foster collaboration with these colleagues. We could have learned more about their disciplines and shared information about our own. We also could have garnered creative insights and directions beyond the purview of writing faculty. As faculty we would have benefited from this exchange, and our students would have benefited as well. Instead of a positive impression, we made a negative impression, one that we can only hope will not be lasting. Our advice, therefore, is to create a formally designed means of gaining the perspectives of faculty in other departments.

Through the process of redesigning our writing major, we learned a great deal. These insights will, no doubt, help us as we continue to reflect on ways in which we might continue to develop our program in response to students' needs, faculty interests, and wider exigencies in the field, workplace, and culture at large. Our hope is that readers of this article will benefit from adapting the approach offered here to suit their particular goals in the process of (re)designing writing majors and that others in the field will find value in the processes we describe and the results of our efforts. Through such scholarship, we might begin to construct a center of gravity for the undergraduate writing major that honors the particular contexts in which writing majors are situated as well as the rich insights of scholars in the field of writing studies at large.

Acknowledgments

We would like to express our gratitude to Laura Micciche, Greg A. Giberson, and one anonymous reviewer for constructive feedback on this article. We also wish to extend appreciation to our colleagues Coretta Pittman and TJ Geiger, our undergraduate students, and to Dianna Vitanza, Sarah Ford, and Jeannette Marsh for their support during the revision process.

Note

1. Hereafter we use "(re)design" to encompass the developing of new majors and the revision of existing ones.

Works Cited

Allen, Nancy, and Steve T. Benninghoff. "TPC Program Snapshots: Developing Curricula and Addressing Challenges." *Technical Communication Quarterly*, vol. 13, no. 2, 2004, pp. 157-85.

Balzhiser, Deborah, and Susan McLeod. "The Undergraduate Writing Major: What Is It? What Should It Be?" *College Composition and Communication*, vol. 61, no. 3, 2010, pp. 415-33.

Bradley, Erin, et al. "Coauthoring the Curriculum: Student Voices and the Writing Major." *Composition Studies*, vol. 43, no. 2, 2015, pp. 172-76.

Campbell, Lee, and Debra Jacobs. "Toward a Description of Undergraduate Writing Majors." Giberson and Moriarty, pp. 277-86.

Carpini, Dominic Delli. "Re-writing the Humanities: The Writing Major's Effect upon Undergraduate Studies in English Departments." *Composition Studies*, vol. 35, no. 1, 2007, pp. 15-36.

Clary-Lemon, Jennifer. "The Hot Arctic: Writing Majors as New Sites for New Hires." *Composition Studies*, vol. 35, no. 1, 2007, pp. 37-38.

Council of Writing Programs. "WPA Consultant-Evaluator Service Guidelines for Self-Study," 2016, wpacouncil.org/consultant. Accessed 14 Feb. 2016.

Estrem, Heidi, editor. "Growing Pains: The Writing Major in Composition and Rhetoric." Special issue of *Composition Studies*, vol. 35, no. 1, 2007, pp. 11-14.

Fleming, David J. "Rhetoric as a Course of Study." *College English*, vol. 61, no. 2, 1998, pp. 169-91.

Geiger, TJ II. "An Intimate Discipline: Writing Studies, Undergraduate Majors, and Relational Labor." *Composition Studies*, vol. 43, 2015, pp. 92-112.

Giberson, Greg A. "Afterword." Giberson, Nugent, Ostergaard, pp. 241-48.

Giberson, Greg A., Jim Nugent, and Lori Ostergaard, editors. *Writing Majors: Eighteen Program Profiles*. Utah State UP, 2015.

Giberson, Greg A., and Thomas A. Moriarty. "Introduction: Forging Connections Among Undergraduate Writing Majors." Giberson and Moriarty, pp. 1-10.

Giberson, Greg A., and Thomas A. Moriarty, editors. *What We Are Becoming: Developments in Undergraduate Writing Majors*. Utah State UP, 2010.

Grobman, Laurie, and Joyce Kinkead, editors. *Undergraduate Research in English Studies*. NCTE, 2010.

Hauser, Gerald A. "Teaching Rhetoric: Or Why Rhetoric Isn't Just Another Kind of Philosophy or Literary Criticism." *Rhetoric Society Quarterly*, vol. 34, no. 3, 2004, pp. 39-53.

Hesse, Douglas. "The Place of Creative Nonfiction." *College English*, vol. 65, no. 3, 2003, pp. 237-41.

Howard, Rebecca Moore. "Curricular Activism: The Writing Major as Counterdiscourse." *Composition Studies*, vol. 35, no. 1, 2007, pp. 41-52.

Lowe, Kelly. "Against the Writing Major." *Composition Studies*, vol. 35, no. 1, 2007, pp. 97-98.

Martin, Celest. "Not Just Another Pretty Classroom Genre: The Uses of Creative Nonfiction in the Writing Major." Giberson and Moriarty, pp. 225-41.

Mayers, Tim. *(Re) Writing Craft: Composition, Creative Writing, and the Future of English Studies*. U of Pittsburgh P, 2005.

McClure, Randall. "Projecting the Shape of the Writing Major." *Composition Studies*, vol. 35, no. 1, 2007, pp. 39-40.

McCormick, Kathleen, and Donald C. Jones. "Developing a Professional and Technical Writing Major that Integrates Composition Theory, Literacy Theory, and Cultural Studies." Shamoon, et al., pp. 140-52.

Olson, Gary A., and Julie Drew, editors. *Landmark Essays on Advanced Composition*. Erlbaum, 1996.

O'Neill, Peggy, Angela Crow, and Larry W. Burton, editors. *A Field of Dreams: Independent Writing Programs and the Future of Composition Studies*. Utah State UP, 2002.

Peeples, Timothy, Paula Rosinski, and Michael Strickland. "*Chronos* and *Kairos*, Strategies and Tactics: The Case of Constructing Elon University's Professional Writing and Rhetoric Concentration." *Composition Studies*, vol. 35, no. 1, 2007, pp. 57-76.

Shamoon, Linda K., and Celest Martin. "Which Part of the Elephant Is This?: Questioning Creative Non-Fiction in the Writing Major." *Composition Studies*, vol. 35, no. 1, 2007, pp. 53-54.

Shamoon, Linda K., Rebecca Moore Howard, Sandra Jamieson, and Robert A. Schwegler, editors. *Coming of Age: The Advanced Writing Curriculum*. Heinemann-Boynton/Cook, 2000.

Taylor, Beth. "On Brown University's New Nonfiction Writing Program—a 'Focus' within the English Concentration." *Composition Studies*, vol. 35, no. 1, 2007, pp. 77-78.

Taylor, Hill. "Black Spaces: Examining the Writing Major at an Urban HBCU." *Composition Studies*, vol. 35, no.1, 2017, pp. 99-112.

Tweedie, Sanford, Jennifer Courtney, and William I. Wolff. "'What Exactly is This Major?': Creating Disciplinary Identity through an Introductory Course." Giberson and Moriarty, pp. 260-76.

Encouraging Languages other than English in First-Year Writing Courses: Experiences from Linguistically Diverse Writers

Alyssa G. Cavazos

> First-Year Writing (fyw) courses are ideal writing spaces where students' diverse identities and language resources can flourish for specific rhetorical purposes. While research has focused on multilingual students' language and writing practices, little attention has focused on self-identified multilingual students' perceptions of language difference in fyw. Because fyw courses are an integral space in students' writing experiences and an ideal place to counter English-only ideologies, this article focuses on self-identified multilingual students' perceptions of how they negotiate language practices in academic contexts in higher education and how they perceive the role of languages other than English in fyw. Self-identified multilingual students' perceptions of language difference can inform pedagogical practices in fyw that align with students' identities as linguistically diverse writers.

Language difference in first-year writing (fyw) has been an issue of discussion since before the creation of the *Students' Rights to Their Own Language* policy statement, published in 1974. As Geneva Smitherman notes, composition scholars either expressed concern or hope for the implications of the statement on the teaching of writing. While acknowledging language difference in fyw would hopefully be the norm rather than the exception, the reality is that English-only ideologies continue to exist, especially in relation to the learning objectives of fyw. As the current anti-immigrant political rhetoric continues, fyw educators have an opportune moment to collaborate with linguistically diverse writers to resist discriminatory rhetoric through inclusive writing practices.

As a college writing educator at a Hispanic-Serving Institution (HSI) on the Mexico/U.S. border, I work with students from linguistically and culturally diverse backgrounds. My pedagogical approach reflects social justice and equity by encouraging all writers to draw on their writing and language histories. Juan Guerra reminds us that "anyone who is going to ask students to use their lived experience to write themselves into being in college classrooms and other communities of belonging must be willing to do the same" (2-3). To make sense of my students' experiences, I examine my linguistic and pedagogical background since my lived experiences with translingual writing shape how

I conduct research and teach writing. When I was in my writing course as a first-year college student at an HSI on the Mexico/U.S. border in fall 2002, the writing instructor assigned an essay that asked us to describe a space. I decided to describe Ruben's Grocery in McAllen, Texas, where my parents worked. Mi mami, the secretary of the store, manages payroll and billing responsibilities, and mi papi was responsible for organizing the produce section. The store carries products from Mexico and other Latin American countries. Naturally, el español is the norm in this espacio, and in my essay, I used Spanish words, such as cabrito, aguacates, agua fresca, and colorido, among others to represent the meaning I was making as an active participant in this space. My writing teacher's feedback focused on how I should write in English only. As a first-year college student, I didn't question her motives, as it was an English class, but I see now that I was instructed to assimilate into the dominant discourse regardless of my purposeful attempts to merge languages in my writing. My attempt to write while illustrating what Gloria Anzaldúa refers to as a "tolerance for ambiguity" through the coexistence of languages failed. If my writing teacher would have encouraged me to reflect on my translingual attempts to make meaning of a nuanced environment that directly opposes the university space, I could have further developed critical thoughts on the implications of living, studying, and using language in a border region. While the teacher shunned my use of Spanish, the essay nonetheless represents my desire to develop a healthy dialogue between the bordered and translingual spaces I was attempting to negotiate—my home and academic communities.

The teacher's feedback was a critical moment in my college experience, especially as a first-generation college student. My interest in developing linguistically inclusive pedagogies in fyw courses emerged, in part, from this moment. While teaching as a doctoral student at Texas Christian University, where about 70% of the students are white, I was made aware of my difference, racial and linguistic, which was a challenging realization. This experience led me to inquire about language diversity in English composition in my doctoral dissertation, for which I investigated how self-identified bilingual Latina/o academics in rhetoric and composition negotiate language difference in their profession (Cavazos, *Latina/os*). Through conversations with new and established Latina/o academics, I wanted to learn how I could succeed in the field of rhetoric and composition as a linguistically diverse writer. After earning my PhD and securing a tenure-track job at the same HSI I attended as an undergraduate and graduate student, I was committed to continue with this line of scholarly inquiry. As someone who learned English as a second language and as a bilingual academic, I was intrigued by how multilingual students experience the first-year writing space.

Scholarship in fyw has emphasized multilingual students' language and writing practices, particularly in developing pedagogical approaches and frameworks that build on students' writing and language agency (Canagarajah; Cavazos et al.; Guerra; Horner et al.; Kells, Balestar, and Villanueva; Lormier; Lovejoy, Fox, and Weeden; Shapiro et al.; Wojahn et al.; Wolfe-Quintero and Segade). However, little attention has focused on how self-identified multilingual students articulate their perceptions of diverse languages in fyw. Understanding how multilingual students perceive negotiations of language practices in higher education and the role of languages other than English in fyw is critical to developing linguistically inclusive pedagogies that align with students' language and writing realities.

University Context

According to the Office of Statistical Analysis and Institutional Reporting at The University of Texas Rio Grande Valley (UTRGV), during the academic year 2013-14 when study participants were either freshmen or sophomores, the University of Texas-Pan American (one of UTRGV's legacy institutions), an HSI located on the Mexico/U.S. border, had a student population of 20,053, 88% of which self-identified as Hispanic or Latino and 51% as being fluent in Spanish. In the same academic year, 2,532 students were enrolled in either first or second semester fyw. Of the students enrolled in fyw courses, 91% self-identified as Hispanic or Latino and 67% as being fluent in Spanish. Students' linguistic and cultural backgrounds are diverse. In any given fyw class, students might self-identify as second language learners, monolingual English speakers, bilingual and biliterate fluent writers in English and Spanish, semi-bilingual, and as fitting other "categories" of linguistic knowledge (Charlton and Charlton). In the same academic year, 38.5% of the total faculty members at the institution self-identified as Hispanic or Latino, and 51% of faculty members who taught fyw courses self-identified as Hispanic or Latino. Faculty members who taught in the fyw program during the 2013-14 academic school year included teaching assistants, lecturers, tenure-track, and tenured professors. The institution does not collect data on faculty language background.

Data Collection

After receiving Institutional Review Board (IRB) approval, I sent a call for participation e-mail to two faculty listservs and asked faculty to share the call with their students. I noted that I was interested in talking with students who had taken both fyw courses and who self-identified as bilingual or multilingual, terms I defined broadly since I was interested in students' experiences with a variety of languages. While I distributed the call on several occasions, only five students responded to my interview request. No incentives were provided. I conducted one face-to-face interview with each participant during the fall 2014 semester lasting between 45 minutes to one hour. The interview consisted of questions about their language and writing experiences at home and in the community, in their fyw courses, and in courses across academic disciplines, especially pertaining to their academic major (see appendix). The students who participated in the study were sophomores or juniors, and all had already taken and passed both of their fyw courses. To encourage recollection of memories in fyw, I asked for direct and concrete examples of class projects. All students who participated in the study self-identified as bilingual or multilingual; they all know English and use Spanish in diverse home and school contexts. Pablo was a sophomore computer science major and mathematics minor; Monica, a sophomore mass communication major; Jasmine, a sophomore Spanish major and medical Spanish minor; Sofia, a junior majoring in English with a minor in Mexican American Studies and learning Arabic as third language; and finally, Victoria, a junior and nursing major (all names are pseudonyms).

Research Questions and Researcher Positionality

Two critical questions guided my analysis of interviews: (1) How do self-identified bilingual/multilingual students describe and perceive their experiences with languages other than English in first-year writing courses? (2) How do they negotiate their knowledge of multiple languages in a variety of contexts? Once interviews were transcribed, I coded the transcripts to identify themes informed by the research questions. Three major thematic findings emerged, leading me to analyze participants' experiences, perceptions, and negotiation strategies in higher education: multilingual practices as academic linguistic resources, contextual rhetorical awareness of language difference, and language difference alertness in fyw. This approach prevented me from making broad generalizations that may not have aligned with all students' linguistic experience in higher education. Informed by the themes, I structure the findings based on the research questions, first discussing multilingual students' descriptions and perceptions of their experiences with languages other than English, and then addressing their negotiation practices in diverse linguistic contexts. Insights from these participants, though limited, can inform how fyw may function as a space where students can cultivate their linguistically diverse identities as writers.

Because I identified the themes using a grounded-theoretical approach, as Michael Quinn Patton recommends, allowing the themes to emerge directly from the analysis of personal interviews, students' perspectives are central to the current article. Additionally, as an English language learner, I recognize my positionality as a researcher. Embracing my multiple languages and identities in fluid and evolving ways influences how I ask research and interview questions and how I analyze interview transcripts. As someone who has been silenced and made to question my writing abilities and the legitimacy of my first language, I understand the importance of listening to different voices as we aim to design pedagogical approaches that respond to the linguistic and cultural realities of students in our fyw courses.

Perceptions of Language Difference

Sofia, a junior English major and Mexican American Studies minor, shares, "In [the second semester fyw course], I never encountered the option to use Spanish. Even though the class was a great course, we never spoke about that. The only time we spoke about Mexican American Studies or Spanish was in [the instructor's] introduction where she told us what she wrote for her master's [thesis]." Sofia recalled that she was unaware that a student could use Spanish or investigate Mexican American issues in a master's thesis. While the content of the course did not focus on language difference, the professor sharing her experience with Spanish provided Sofia with a new perspective on the purpose of academic writing. Monica, a sophomore mass communication major, shared that she enjoyed her first semester fyw course: "I loved my [...] class. It was modeled around the World Cup. Our projects were mostly readings and then we wrote a discourse community memo." She further shared that the use of languages other than English was "neither encouraged nor discouraged." She explained, "The professor is white. I don't think he speaks much Spanish. Some professors say, 'you can throw Spanish in there; it's okay.' He never said that but he never said, 'oh, you can't write Spanish.'" Although it is problematic to assume that a person may not know a language based on his or her appearance, Monica's assumption is not different from the image of the student as native English speaker that Paul Kei Matsuda describes. Matsuda argues the tacit policy of English monolingualism exists due to "the relative lack of attention to multilingualism in composition scholarship" (637) and a perception of college composition students as "native English speakers by default" (637). Monica's assumption may also be a result of an education system that has privileged the use of English as the dominant language in academic contexts. Most importantly, the assumption, from faculty or students, that English is the default language prevents conversations about how other languages function within fyw.

The rhetoric of deficiency, unfortunately, is prevalent in many fyw courses, especially in conversations concerning writers from traditionally underrepresented groups. Victoria, a junior and nursing major, shared, "[Professors] don't say: 'oh, you speak two languages. That's great.' They focus more on the content of the course. It's not of their interest if students know two languages." In focusing on content exclusively, professors may ignore how students might draw on other language resources to make sense of the content. Victoria shares experiences in one of her fyw courses: "I felt by myself. I felt secluded. If I would say anything in Spanish it would just be awkward to use Spanish. If I wanted to make reference in Spanish, I couldn't because they wouldn't understand." While we might assume that at an HSI students' multilingualism would be perceived as a resource, the reality is that English continues to be privileged as the language of instruction and learning in higher education, particularly in fyw courses. Subsequently, students may never see their linguistically diverse competence as a resource in academic contexts.

Due to institutional demand for academic writing, multilingual writers may perceive that their native language is discriminated against. Pablo, a sophomore computer science major and math minor, explains, "My Spanish language has been unconsciously discriminated against. [Professors] don't discourage it, but they don't encourage it. So, they just leave it there. It's just there. They assume it's there." He continued, "They don't praise it. They don't look down upon it. It's unconsciously discriminated against because you're not allowed to use it as much as compared to English." Because some of his professors do not acknowledge the presence of other languages as valuable knowledge, Pablo feels he is driven to choose one language over the other. He explains, "I discriminate against my own language even though I wouldn't want to. Sadly. In a way, I am pushed to doing that." Pablo's realization indicates that institutions of higher education subtly assume that English is the primary language all students use to make knowledge, which is evidence of what Matsuda defines as the "myth of linguistic homogeneity" (638). Pablo's perceptions of his instructors' views toward Spanish demonstrate that professors may subconsciously perceive content knowledge in English as separate from content knowledge in Spanish or any other language. Instructors may assume students' lack of knowledge based on a linguistic difference that does not align with standard English in students' written text, and in these instances, students might be driven to choose one language over another in academic contexts as Pablo experienced.

Participants' perceptions of their instructors' language background were central to how they navigated languages. Because Sofia is minoring in Mexican American Studies, she has encountered multiple opportunities where instructors encourage the use of Spanish. She reflected, "I think most professors I've had are really good at incorporating Spanish, maybe not on the assignments, not all of them on the assignments, but in conversation, in forums, in discussion, in bringing in a focus, a perspective from the Mexican American side." While Sofia's coursework focused mostly on Mexican American Studies, Sofia also acknowledges that most of the professors' monolingual backgrounds may pose challenges to using Spanish. Sofia reflected, "Our professors aren't bilingual or professors aren't from the area at times. So, how can they encourage us to speak a language they don't know or how can they encourage us to be proud of a culture they don't know?" Sofia's concern extends beyond the professors' linguistic repertoire; in fact, it has to do with instructors designing linguistically inclusive pedagogical approaches. Sofia raises another important issue, "It would be nice if we had more teachers who are from [the area] who are bilingual themselves. You want to see more people like you so you know that you can do that too." She identifies one of the most critical situations in institutions of higher education: faculty diversity, or lack thereof. Sofia's university is an HSI, but as Sofia suggests, the ethnic, racial, or linguistic background of faculty may not reflect the student population, a point that is underscored by the 38.5% of faculty who self-identified as Hispanic or Latino during the same academic year these interviews were conducted.

Negotiation of Language Difference in Diverse Rhetorical Contexts

Participants' perception of their language abilities as academic resources influences their decisions regarding when, where, and how to use diverse languages. As writing instructors, it is critical we understand and learn with our students about how they negotiate among diverse languages and cultures. Doing so will enable us to develop pedagogies that enhance students' consciousness of their multilingual writing abilities. The participants in my study demonstrated rhetorical awareness of how diverse personal or academic contexts influenced their linguistic choices. Students' high regard for their native language may facilitate their interactions with academic writing expectations. Jasmine, a sophomore Spanish major and medical Spanish minor, reflects on her experiences with Spanish and English:

> At home, it's all Spanish. My mom doesn't know any English. Now that I am taking my major classes I actually get to speak Spanish a lot more, which is something I like. I feel like my vocabulary is bigger when it comes to speaking Spanish. For essays, I'm taking a Spanish Literature class, so we get to read a lot of books in Spanish and then we discuss [and] write all in Spanish.

Because Jasmine desires to become a translator, she realizes the rhetorical value of expanding her Spanish and English vocabulary, and her ability to switch among English, academic Spanish at school, and informal Spanish at home illustrates her rhetorical astuteness. From a different perspective, Victoria acknowledges the challenges inherent in negotiating diverse languages: "[My] parents and grandma [are] very influential. Yes, speak Spanish. Yes, speak English, but don't overlap one or the other. Don't speak one language more than the other, keep it balanced. That way you don't have barriers [such as] chopped [language], so I can be smooth in both languages." Because her family encourages an equal and well-balanced use of both languages to avoid using language that may be perceived to lack fluidity, Victoria may be more prepared to engage and continue developing her knowledge of both languages equally in an fyw course that recognizes language difference. Monica, in contrast, shared, "I can't say that I have a safe language […] if I'm talking with someone [whose] Spanish is better than mine, I go back to English because that's my safe spot. [If] there's someone who doesn't know Spanish well, I speak Spanish because that's my dominant language." Monica's rhetorical assessment helps her decide what language will help her achieve a level of comfort and feel "safe." She also shared one of the primary reasons she often uses Spanish with her friends:

> At the university, I am doing a lot more English. There isn't much Spanish writing. Maybe that's why my friends and I use more Spanish because there's no longer a Spanish class where we're reading novels, so I do that on my own. I read on my own and I write Spanish on my own, so it balances it out.

If Monica did not see a value in her continued use of Spanish or would not perceive it as a safe language depending on the situation, she would simply not use it for these purposes.

Participants often found ways to incorporate the use of languages other than English in their writing projects. Jasmine learned English as a second language, and during her first year as a college student, she was placed in a remedial English course. She explained, "[I]t was a remedial class because I couldn't write in English. If I would have written in Spanish, it was pointless for the class. I just took it as we're writing in English. I guess also because in high school that's what is expected of you; I was still in that [frame] of mind." Jasmine's perception of English as the expected language in academic contexts is possibly due to the tacit English monolingual policy Bruce Horner and John Trimbur reference. Jasmine noted that she did not mind the focus on English, as she needed to learn how to write well in English to continue with her coursework. While it is crucial that we recognize students' writing and language learning goals as we create linguistically inclusive writing spaces (Shapiro et al.), we should also remain cautious and avoid privileging English as the only language students should be expected to use.

Jasmine emphasized that once she developed confidence in her written use of English, she made a conscious choice to link English and Spanish in all her courses either by translating from Spanish to English as she composed or by conducting research in Spanish. For instance, in her second semester fyw course, she conducted research on translation practices between English and Spanish for her major research project. She noted, "It was mainly written in English. The only times when I wrote things in Spanish was when I included quotations of what [interviewees] said or examples of how [Spanish] translates into English." She continued that her writing instructor's feedback on her use of Spanish was as follows: "If you're going to use another language, use quotations and explain what it means, so they can understand it." Although her project was written primarily in English, her professor's acceptance of Spanish in her essay suggests that he not only created a space for language difference in the classroom but also understood the significance of Jasmine's project for her future career as a medical translator. While the professor's actions can be perceived as reasonable considering the topic of Jasmine's project, other professors might have suggested for her to include only the translations in English without any reference to Spanish. Although this instructor asked Jasmine to translate the interviews to English, which might be perceived as perpetuating the myth of linguistic homogeneity, he not only appears concerned for all readers having an equal opportunity to understand both languages but also provides Jasmine with opportunities to practice translation.

Pablo and Victoria noted that in their first semester fyw course they were not encouraged to use languages other than English. However, they both emphasized that in their second semester writing courses, they reflected on their early literacy and language practices and thought about language usage as they identified a context, audience, and purpose for their research project. Pablo explains how the literacy projects in his second semester fyw course helped him utilize his language agilities:

> What I learned is that if you express your language, you are able to appeal to the audience that you really want to appeal. I used English and Spanish on [Facebook posts] in order to help [my classmates] practice their translation and try to understand both languages and how one translates into another. So, they can see translation is not word for word. Phrases can be translated differently.

His writing teacher not only created a space for Pablo to use Spanish comfortably, but she also ensured Pablo developed rhetorical tools, such as awareness of audience, purpose, and translation practices. Similarly, Victoria shared that

> In [first semester fyw], it was more general, writing essays. For [second semester fyw], I learned a lot more because of the projects; [they] made me think a lot more. The first project was about my language. I

start[ed] learning to speak in English in kindergarten and it was hard for me to say words in English. I started my project using words in Spanish and then in English because I was encouraged to write in Spanish by my teacher [...] I could express myself in both languages. It's important because sometimes you have thoughts in Spanish that make more sense than in English. If I wanted to express myself in Spanish, if I had more process of thoughts, I can just say it and I don't have to translate the whole thought into English.

Victoria was encouraged to explore her literacy history through a multilingual lens, which allowed her to make sense of her early literacy experiences. By beginning to write her literacy project in Spanish and subsequently incorporating English words, she illustrates for her readers her early literacy experiences, learning Spanish first and then English in kindergarten. Victoria's experience illustrates the need to offer students the freedom to communicate meaning and make new knowledge in a variety of languages. Both Pablo and Victoria articulated not only the benefits of using languages other than English in their major projects in fyw but also how they negotiated language choices as they became aware of audience and purpose.

Participants demonstrated a sense of agency over their language and writing practices. Monica reflected, "I don't think I've ever felt that I had to give up a language. Maybe I don't write in Spanish in my English essay, but because I speak both of them fluently, I'm writing in English but I'm thinking of the things in Spanish." The way multilingual students describe their academic language experiences indicates their astute rhetorical knowledge of how language difference functions in their academic writing experiences. Additionally, Monica also shared how she uses her knowledge of Spanish to make sense of challenging words when reading in English, and she asked if she could open one of my books to a random page to provide an example. After reading one of the paragraphs, she shared, "This word, 'methodological.' Metodología in Spanish. There isn't a negative thing knowing more than one language. It helps me in every way even at work." Even though she had not encountered the word "methodological" in the past, she immediately knew what the word meant because one of her Spanish professors had introduced and discussed it in class. Monica's use of English and Spanish as she reads and writes is an indication of her rhetorical awareness of how both languages help her academically.

To leverage challenges students may encounter in diverse communicative contexts, they often draw on their rhetorical and linguistic resources as they negotiate language expectations. Pablo's critical use of English and Spanish as a mathematics tutor provides him with opportunities to connect with his audience, predominately mathematics students who learned English as a second language. He explained, "Lo explico en español pero uso terminologia muy basica o uso analogias para explicar unos terminos que no tengo idea como se digan en español [...] because I don't have training in mathematics in Spanish." While Pablo does not have academic training in higher level mathematical concepts, he draws on analogies or definitions of concepts to communicate with his intended audience in the context of tutoring. When Pablo explained how he uses Spanish during math tutoring sessions, he found it appropriate to provide this explanation in Spanish, which indicates not only his level of comfort in using diverse languages but also his rhetorical awareness of the tutoring situation in Spanish. In a similar experience, Sofia described her rhetorical abilities when she shared, "I am impressed with the brain. I was writing an assignment in English and reading in Spanish while holding a conversation in Arabic with a friend. At one point, I lost track of what language was spoken where and everything was making sense. Once you speak a language, you just speak it and your mind adapts." If, as writing instructors, we develop activities and projects that elicit awareness of cross-linguistic moments, we can create spaces that challenge academic English monolingualism. As the experience of the participants in this study indicate, students constantly engage diverse languages and linguistic practices, and they can further develop these linguistic abilities through direct and purposeful alignment with fyw curricula.

Linguistically Inclusive Pedagogies

As fyw instructors in the current political climate, we must learn from and with multilingual writers as we explore how different languages enhance academic learning in equitable and inclusive ways. As Ofelia García argues, we must open "espacios for different people to act equitably in their worlds through their own languaging" (256). Because one of our primary objectives as fyw instructors is to teach rhetorical awareness, we can design writing assignments that invite students to consider genres and audience from varied linguistic and cultural backgrounds. Working with multilingual writers in fyw should not be perceived as significantly different from working with writers we may traditionally consider "monolingual." Informed by the rich conversations with the participants in this study, scholarship on translingual writing, and my pedagogical experiences, I offer linguistically inclusive learning objectives for fyw coursework. While I share some of these pedagogical implications and recommendations in previous publications (Cavazos, "Translingual"; Cavazos et al.), here I expand upon the implementation of these linguistically inclusive pedagogies through detailed descriptions within the fyw classroom context. I do not intend to suggest a set curriculum or portfolio of static practices because, as Min-Zhan Lu and Bruce Horner claim, translingual writing is "not to be understood as stable but as also subject to and in need of continual recreating/rewriting" (216). In an environment conducive to a translingual pedagogy and to translanguaging practices, students are:

1. encouraged to analyze their language abilities as rhetorical resources
2. exposed to language difference in multiple academic and community contexts
3. invited to compose in diverse languages and discourses for a variety of audiences

Language Abilities as Rhetorical Resources

Multilingual writers possess diverse literacy and language abilities that serve as rhetorical resources in fyw. Literacy histories or narratives are common assignments in fyw courses, and as Christina Ortmeier-Hooper suggests, they are an excellent tool for instructors to learn about their students' experiences (414-15). For multilingual writers, literacy histories can be especially empowering, as they develop a sense of agency in relation to their experiences with language and literacy. In turn, for writing instructors, students' literacy histories offer insights on how students navigate diverse linguistic contexts, which can inform pedagogical practices in writing instruction. One of the undergraduate writing courses I developed while a graduate student at Texas Christian University focused on language diversity. One of the projects asked students to reflect on and analyze their literacy and language practices in a specific community-based situation, a slightly different take on the traditional literacy narrative. Students were encouraged to think about a rhetorical experience when the language they used was significant in persuading or connecting with others. This project enabled students to become conscious of their rhetorical and linguistic choices while "repositioning" them through their writing and the rhetorical situation they experienced. One of my international students, who learned English as a second language, described her linguistic experience as a volunteer teacher at a local reformatory in her hometown in China. By integrating English and Chinese, the student learned how her use of music, poems, and a Chinese dialect facilitated her interaction with the audience through cultural and linguistic identification. Most importantly, through peer response conversations, students can teach each other about their respective languages, especially as they explain concepts that may be more effectively communicated in another language. Through this process, we engage all students in cross-linguistic exchange of ideas and knowledge, thereby recognizing the rich insights and unique perspectives all students are capable of sharing.

Language Difference in Academic and Community Contexts

A second learning outcome in my translingual writing pedagogy aims to encourage all students to develop awareness of how rhetorical situations influence language practices in English and other languages. Many scholars have argued for the benefit of a cross-language pedagogy that helps students reflect on their identities and languages (Guerra; Horner, Lu, and Matsuda; Horner and Trimbur), and pedagogical examples contribute to these scholars' call to continue developing translingual pedagogical approaches in the writing classroom. Additionally, like the writing about writing curriculum developed by Doug Downs and Elizabeth Wardle, we can expose students to conversations in the field on cross-language relations in composition studies by inviting them to contribute to these conversations as they draw on their personal experiences and research expertise in languages other than English (Cavazos, "Translingual").

When I first introduce students to rhetorical analysis, I begin with a discussion of "Toward a Writing Pedagogy of Shuttling between Languages: Learning from Multilingual Writers," in which A. Suresh Canagarajah analyzes the rhetorical practices of a multilingual academic who writes about the same topic in different languages and contexts. Canagarajah's piece is a precise example of the type of rhetorical analysis I expect students to engage in as they examine their own and other writers' language choices. Canagarajah analyzes the introductions of three articles written in two languages, English and Tamil, by professor Sivatamby. Students read Canagarajah's article for homework, and in class, we work in small groups to identify the rhetorical practices (i.e., civic ethos, humility ethos, academic ethos) Canagarajah analyzes in Sivatamby's three different articles. We focus on how Canagarajah links audience and purpose to his rhetorical choices and how he uses examples from Sivatamby's work to further support his main claims. The in-class guided discussion of Canagarajah's piece serves as a foundation for students as they write their own rhetorical analyses of course readings, which include "How to Tame a Wild Tongue" by Gloria Anzaldúa, "Mother Tongue" by Amy Tan, "English Only and U.S. College Composition" by Bruce Horner and John Trimbur, "Should Writers Use They Own English?" by Vershawn Ashanti Young, and *Students' Rights to Their Own Language*. The exposure to language difference in readings provides students with awareness of a multiplicity of rhetorical and linguistic strategies as they analyze how the authors' use of language contributes to argument and purpose.

Rhetorical analysis of language use further leads students to conduct research from multiple perspectives, including sources in languages or dialects other than Standard American English. In a translingual writing course, we can encourage students to conduct research in other languages, especially sources that will allow them to analyze an issue from multiple views. They may even consider collaborating with bilingual peers, friends, or family members to analyze the most relevant scholarship. In the second project in my fyw course, I encourage students to conduct an analysis of oral and written use of language on an issue they are interested in. One project that stands out to me is that of a student who demonstrated interest in the U.S. tariff imposed on tires imported from China. The student analyzed speeches and interviews with politicians and economists from the U.S. and China who addressed this issue. This student took advantage of her knowledge of Chinese and English to provide a detailed analysis from various perspectives and rhetorical contexts. She effectively used our initial discussion of Canagarajah's analysis of Sivatamby's use of language in different contexts to analyze how various stakeholders discuss the same topic (in this case, U.S. tariffs imposed on imported tires from China) in a variety of languages and contexts. The analysis and conclusions the student made, especially concerning the economists' arguments and sense of audience, represent knowledge and skills the student would not have developed in a course not focused on language difference. For those in class who do not know Chinese, we learned through peer response the meaning and connotations of words used in Chinese media. A translingual pedagogy requires that we trust our multilingual students and let them teach us about their languages, analyses, and strategies. Through small shifts in our pedagogy, we can encourage students to see content knowledge in English and other languages as working together.

Compose in Diverse Languages and Discourses for a Variety of Audiences

One of the goals in fyw is to help students become rhetorical users of language. When we ask students to think about their audience, purpose, and medium, we should also be open to the possibility that our students' intended audience may not consist of English-only users. Students should compose in a variety of discursive and non-discursive forms including in languages other than English. As we design writing classes, we should create espacios where students draw on their full linguistic repertoires to read, analyze, and write. In one of my fyw classes, I asked students to design a public document for a specific audience and purpose informed by their literacy narratives and their research inquiry on literacy education. I asked, "Who would benefit from knowing about your literacy experience?" One of my students asked in Spanish, "Ms., yo se a quien le importaría leer sobre mis experiencias. A mi sobrina. Pero, lo que pasa es que ella solo habla español y apenas está aprendiendo inglés. Quiero escribirle una carta. ¿Como le hago?" The student was concerned that her intended audience, her eight-year-old niece, only spoke Spanish as she was learning English as a second language. The student wanted to write a letter to her niece, but she didn't know how to approach the assignment because she was enrolled in an English composition course. I responded: "Escríbele la carta en español. She's your audience." The student wrote a heartfelt letter to her niece in Spanish in which she validated her niece's knowledge of Spanish and introduced her to specific concepts on language diversity from course readings and her own research in an eloquent and linguistically conscious approach. Students also wrote a reflective analytical piece and interpreted their choice of specific phrases, anecdotes, and examples. Through a reflective analysis, multilingual writers may articulate why they chose to use a language other than English. A reflective analysis is an ideal place for students to use all their language resources as they make sense and process their language choices.

As I learn from self-identified multilingual faculty and students how to design linguistically inclusive teaching espacios, I realize that I should model for my students how I use my language resources when I conduct research, write for academic and community audiences, and deliver presentations or speeches (Cavazos, "Multilingual Faculty"). I often share two authentic situations in which I used my knowledge of English and Spanish to reach my intended audience in my local community. The first is a speech I delivered at a Naturalization Ceremony and wrote about in the *International Journal of Bilingualism* (Cavazos, "Translingual"). Second, a keynote address I delivered to parents of students who are learning English as a second language. Students analyze these two pieces and we identify specific rhetorical strategies and language resources that proved critical in achieving my purpose and reaching my intended local audience. By sharing how linguistically diverse writers engage in translingual practices, we create rhetorically beneficial and personally meaningful writing espacios with our students (Cavazos, "Translingual").

Conclusion

To counter dominant ideologies about academic writing and challenge discriminatory rhetorics in the current political climate, we must view multilingual students as rhetors working in diverse languages, contexts, and communities. When pedagogical approaches expose students to multiple languages and the rhetorical value of diverse discourse communities, students develop a sense of identification within academia. One of the most important strategies in a translingual pedagogy is the practice of listening to and trusting students' voices, experiences, and aspirations as they engage all their languages, identities, and cultures. Multilingual writers should not feel secluded or obligated to hide their diverse language knowledge to do well in higher education. If students are not provided with opportunities to develop all their linguistic capacities, it is possible they may never see their languages as resources when they write in different contexts. By listening to our students' and our own translingual writing experiences, we can develop effective writing pedagogies and partnerships that focus on learning with rhetorically aware translingual writers, professionals, and citizens.

Acknowledgments

I want to express my gratitude to the self-identified multilingual writers who volunteered to share their perceptions and negotiations of language difference in first-year writing coursework. Muchísimas gracias por compartir sus experiencias y perspectivas ya que han sido fundamentales en mi pedagogía as I attempt to design more inclusive and equitable writing espacios. I also wish to thank editors, reviewers, and colleagues who provided invaluable feedback on this manuscript. Alyxia, siempre que escribo sobre la educación y el lenguaje pienso en ti y en tu futuro. Nunca olvides el poder de ser bilingüe. Te amo, preciosa.

Appendix

Interview Questions Protocol

1. General Background: What is your academic major and how did you choose this major? What do you hope to gain from your university experience? What do you envision as your future professional career? How many languages do you know? What do you consider to be your first/second language?
2. To what extent do you read, write, and/or speak languages and/or dialects other than English, including variations of English? In what contexts do you read, write, and speak these languages or dialects?
3. How would you describe your writing experiences in first-year composition (English 1320, 1301, and/or 1302)? What kind of projects did you compose? What challenges/successes did you encounter? What kind of feedback did the teacher/peers provide? To what extent were you encouraged to use languages other than English in your writing and/or research practices in these courses?
4. What type of writing do you engage in within the university context, across academic disciplines? What kind of feedback do you receive from your instructors? How do you respond to their feedback? To what extent have you written and/or conducted research in languages other than English in school? Outside of school?
5. How do you think teachers across academic disciplines perceive your knowledge of languages/dialects other than English or varieties of English?

6. How would you describe your experiences—successes and challenges—in balancing multiple languages and dialects in school? What do you see as an asset and/or barrier? What strategies do you enact in balancing diverse languages and/or writing contexts? Who, what classes, or institutional structures sponsored your achievements and challenges in your use of multiple languages?
7. Throughout your education, to what extent do you think you had to give up other languages or dialects in order to succeed in writing at school? Outside of school? What effect does this have on you now?
8. To what extent do you perceive your knowledge of languages other than English as a resource/strength when you write in school? Outside of school? To what extent do you perceive your knowledge of languages other than English as a barrier or challenge when you write in school? Outside of school? What specific anecdotes and/or writing assignments do you recall?
9. How do you think friends and family members perceive your knowledge of languages/dialects other than English? What specific anecdotes do you recall?
10. To what extent do you believe your knowledge (e.g., read, write, speak) of languages/dialects other than English will help you in your university experience, future professional career, and within the community?
11. **Final Comments**: My research study consists of learning how bilingual or multilingual first-year composition students perceive language difference and how their experiences with language difference help and/or hinder their writing experiences in a variety of contexts. Do you have anything else to add that would enrich this study, future research, and/or bilingual and multilingual students' personal and academic success?

Works Cited

Anzaldúa, Gloria. *Borderlands/La Frontera: The New Mestiza*. Aunt Lute Books, 1999.

Canagarajah, A. Suresh. "Toward a Writing Pedagogy of Shuttling between Languages: Learning from Multilingual Writers." *College English*, vol. 68, no. 6, 2006, 589-604.

Cavazos, Alyssa G. *Latina/os in Rhetoric and Composition: Learning from Their Experiences with Language Diversity*. 2012. Texas Christian U, PhD dissertation.

---. "Multilingual Faculty across Academic Disciplines: Language Difference in Scholarship." *Language and Education*, vol. 29, 2015, 317-31, doi:10.1080/09500782.2015.101437.

---. "Translingual Oral and Written Practices: Rhetorical Resources in Multilingual Writers' Discourses." *International Journal of Bilingualism*, vol. 21, 2017, 385-401.

Cavazos, Alyssa G., et al. "Advancing a Transnational, Transdisciplinary, and Translingual Framework: A Professional Development Series for Teaching Assistants in Writing and Spanish Programs." *Across the Disciplines: A Journal of Language, Learning, and Academic Writing*, vol. 15, no. 3, 2018, 1-10.

Charlton, Jonikka, and Colin Charlton. "The Illusion of Transparency at an HSI: A Pedagogical History of Becoming Public WPAs." *Going Public: The WPA as Advocate for Engagement*, edited by Shirley K Rose and Irwin Weiser, Utah State UP, 2010, 68-84.

Conference on College Composition and Communication. *Students' Right to Their Own Language*. CCCC, 1974, https://prod-ncte-cdn.azureedge.net/nctefiles/groups/cccc/ newsrtol.pdf.

Downs, Doug, and Elizabeth Wardle. "Teaching about Writing, Righting Misconceptions: (Re)envisioning 'First-year Composition' as 'Introduction to Writing Studies.'" *College Composition and Communication*, vol. 58, no. 4, 2007, 552-84.

Garcia, Ofelia. "Translanguaging in Schools: Subiendo y Bajando, Bajando y Subiendo as Afterword." *Journal of Language, Identity and Education*, vol. 16, 2017, 256-63, doi: 10.1080/15348458.2017.1329657.

Guerra, Juan. *Language, Culture, Identity and Citizenship in College Classrooms and Communities*. NCTE, 2016.

Horner, Bruce, and John Trimbur. "English-Only and U.S. College Composition." *College Composition and Communication*, vol. 53, no. 4, 2002, 594-630.

Horner, Bruce, Min Zhan Lu, and Paul Kei Matsuda. *Cross Language Relations in Composition*. SIUP, 2010.

Horner, Bruce, et al. "Language Difference in Writing: Toward a Translingual Approach." *College English*, vol. 73, no. 3, 2011, 303-21.

Horner, Bruce, Christine Donahue, and Samantha NeCamp. "Toward a Multilingual Composition Scholarship: From English Only to a Translingual Norm." *College Composition and Communication*, vol. 63, no. 2, 2011, 269-300.

Kells, Michelle Hall, Valerie Balester, and Victor Villanueva, editors. *Latino/a Discourses: On Language, Identity, and Literacy Education*. Boynton/Cook, 2004.

Lorimer, Rebecca. "Writing Across Languages: Developing Rhetorical Attunement." *Literacy as Translingual Practice: Between Communities and Classrooms*, edited by A. Suresh Canagarajah, Routledge, 2013, 162-170.

Lovejoy, Kim Brian, Steven Fox, and Scott Weeden. "Linguistic Diversity as Resource: A Multilevel Approach to Building Awareness in First-Year Writing Programs (and Beyond)." *Pedagogy: Critical Approaches to Teaching Literature, Language, Composition, and Culture*, vol. 18, no. 2, 2018, 317-43.

Matsuda, Paul Kei. "The Myth of Linguistic Homogeneity in U.S. College Composition." *College English*, vol. 68, no. 6, 2006, 637-51.

Ortmeier-Hooper, Christina. "'English May Be My Second Language, but I'm not ESL.'" *College Composition and Communication*, vol. 59, no. 3, 2008, 389-419.

Patton, Michael Quinn. *Qualitative Research and Evaluation Methods*. 3rd ed., Sage Publications, 2002.

Shapiro, Shawna, et al. "Teaching for Agency: From Appreciating Linguistic Diversity to Empowering Student Writers." *Composition Studies*, vol. 44, no. 1, 2016, 31-52.

Smitherman, Geneva. "The Historical Struggle for Language Rights in CCCC." *Language Diversity in the Classroom: From Intention to Practice*, edited by Geneva Smitherman and Victor Villanueva, SIUP, 2003, 7-39.

Tan, Amy. "Mother Tongue." *The Threepenny Review*, no. 43, 1990, 7-8.

Young, Vershawn Ashanti. "Should Writers Use They Own English?" *Iowa Journal of Cultural Studies*, vol. 12, 2010, 110-17.

Wojahn, Oatty, et al. "When the First Language you Use Is Not English." *Linguistically Diverse Immigrant and Resident Writers*, edited by Christina Ortemeier-Hooper and Todd Ruecker, Routledge, 2017, 173-88.

Wolfe-Quintero, Kate, and Gabriela Segade. "University Support for Second-Language Writers Across the Curriculum." *Generation 1.5 Meets College Composition: Issues in the Teaching of Writing to U.S. Educated Learners of ESL*, edited by Linda Harklau, Kay M. Losey, and Meryl Siegal, Lawrence Erlbaum Associates, Inc., 1999, 191-210.

"Nameless, Faceless People": How Other Teachers' Expectations Influence Our Pedagogy

Brooke R. Schreiber and Dorothy Worden

As second language (L2) writing teacher educators and researchers, we have seen how powerful the image of an unsympathetic future audience for students' writing is in teachers' responses to language difference. In this essay, we trace how beliefs about these future audiences influence the pedagogical decision-making of two L2 writing instructors: Amy, an experienced teacher, believes students should draw on their multiple languages as resources for writing but ultimately encourages students to be selective in the use of accented writing. In comparison, Sergei, like many novice teachers, focuses heavily on correcting surface level mechanics to prepare students for a business writing community he perceives as intolerant of grammatical errors. The result is that these teachers, struggling to work ethically within first year writing as a "service course," adopt teaching practices that do not fully align with their own beliefs or reflect best practices in the field. We discuss how teachers might articulate and reflect on their own beliefs in light of current research studies from the fields of writing across the curriculum (WAC) and business writing, and what teacher educators and WPAs can do to support such reflection.

In a scene no doubt familiar to many teacher educators, we are standing in front of a master's level class on writing pedagogy, leading a carefully prepared discussion of how to choose errors to respond to in the writing of L2 students. We draw on the best practices in our discipline to build a case for selective error correction—that is, for correcting only those errors that impede comprehension. As our explanation concludes, a student in the back of the classroom raises her hand. "I agree with all this stuff, personally," she says, "but my students will have to write for other teachers, and we can't expect *them* to be so understanding."

The above anecdote, representative of many interactions we have had as educators of writing instructors, illustrates just how powerful the image of unsympathetic future audiences can be. As writing teachers, we have often grappled with the pressure to accommodate what one of our research participants called the "nameless, faceless people" that her students would later encounter across the university. In our work as teacher educators and researchers, we have seen how this pressure can limit teachers' engagement with the best practices in the field. Like the teacher described by Paul Kei Matsuda, who worries about being too "lenient" with an L2 student's grammatical errors because "his biology teacher isn't going to be as forgiving," many writing faculty struggle with deep-seated worries about what faculty from other departments might think (142). This trope emerges in teachers' discourse with such regularity that it seemed to us valuable to investigate this set of beliefs and its effects on teachers' decision-making practices regarding language differences in the classroom.

This investigation seems particularly important given the rise of interest in practical ways to implement "linguistically inclusive approaches to writing pedagogy" that promote the agency of multilingual students (Shapiro et al. 32). As Daniel Bommarito and Emily Cooney describe, implementing a teaching approach that interrogates monolingual norms demands from teachers an "ongoing, self-reflexive attention" to their own entrenched linguistic ideologies and to ways those ideologies shape interactions with students in and outside of class (43). We suggest that one vital component of "the complex and time-consuming process of dissolving monolingual tendencies" among teachers is to interrogate teachers' beliefs about the relationship between their teaching and the expectations of their students' future audiences (40).

In this essay, we begin with a brief overview of best practices from L2 writing studies for responding to "non-standard" English in writing classrooms and describe how teachers' beliefs can impact their response to those best practices, in particular beliefs about the institutional positioning of fyw. We then examine the beliefs of two L2 writing instructors, Amy and Sergei[1], whose pedagogical choices are influenced by the imagined reactions of students' future readers in two distinct ways. Our goal in this essay is to illustrate what we see as an overlooked barrier to the implementation of linguistically inclusive teaching practices and to offer suggestions for how teachers and those who work closely with them can begin to deconstruct this barrier.

Best Practices and Teacher Beliefs

After many years of research and debate, the field of L2 writing developed a set of broadly agreed-upon best practices for responding to L2 students' writing, including selective rather than comprehensive error correction, and a tolerance for written accent where it does not impede communication (Ferris; Ferris and Hedgcock). These strategies, Matsuda suggests, can be usefully written into programmatic policy by WPAs, which alleviates part of the struggle of individual instructors to determine ethical practices. Undergirding these pedagogical methods is not only language-learning research but also a set of attitudes toward linguistic diversity which are explicitly spelled out in documents such as the Students' Right to Their Own Language (SRTOL) resolution and the "CCCC Statement of Second Language Writing and Writers." At their core, these documents promote recognition of the increasing diversity of students in higher education and appreciation for the language differences that students bring into the classroom, with the understanding that pedagogy must be adapted to the needs of a changing student population.

Particularly in the field's recent translingual turn, multilingualism and language difference are viewed not as a deficit but as the norm and as a productive resource for meaning-making. Teachers, in response, might encourage students to use their multiple languages or codes at various stages of the composing process from brainstorming and research to final drafts, provide code-meshed or dialectal models for students' writing, expose the constructed nature of language standards, take a stance of negotiation toward error, and promote learner agency around linguistic choices (cf., Canagarajah, "The Place of World Englishes," "Translingual Practice"; Horner et al.; Shapiro et al.).

When it comes to how teachers take up these best practices and principles, however, the research is somewhat less positive, showing that teachers often focus extensively on local grammatical errors over issues of content and tend to mark errors comprehensively rather than selectively (Furneaux et al.; Junquiera and Payant; Montgomery and Baker). Likewise, Christine Tardy found in a survey of the faculty in her department that more than half of the instructors never invited students to use other languages in their writing process, and that many teachers "have a limited set of strategies for supporting multilingual writers," likely due to the low level of formal training for working with multilingual students (646). As Bommarito and Cooney suggest, "dislodging monolingual norms pervading our classrooms" demands that teachers as well as students "accept an entirely new view of literacy, one that rejects the notion of a standard, abstract ideal English" (45), and this is neither a simple nor straightforward process.

More troubling is the fact that even when teachers agree with the best practices of the field, their teaching often conflicts with these beliefs (Lee; Montgomery and Baker, "Error Correction," "Ten Mismatches"). In English as a Foreign Language (EFL) settings, a commonly cited reason for these mismatches is that institutional contexts do not permit teachers to put their beliefs about language difference into practice as a result of restrictive curricula, high-stakes grammar-focused exams, and pressure from colleagues, administrators, and even students themselves (Lee, "Ten Mismatches"; Reichelt; You). In the U.S., we typically do not have standardized national curricula or (in most cases) high-stakes exams at the university level. Instead, we have the pressure of what Marjorie Roemer et al. call "the demoted status of the composition course as a service activity" (377). In this model, fyw classes for L2 students are often framed as "mere service courses, nothing more than staging areas before the real work of college literacy striving to train students primarily to accommodate themselves to the demands of others in their courses and in this country" (Leki 4).

The sense of responsibility teachers feel to prepare students for future audiences is by no means unfounded. As Daniel Cole points out, writing instructors are often held accountable in the eyes of their colleagues for the state of students' grammar, and conversations with faculty in other disciplines can be rife with "subtext concerning the 'inadequacies' . . . of first year composition" (7). This "service orientation" to the class can create considerable anxiety for writing teachers struggling to assess second language writers ethically, especially given the gate-keeping function of a writing course required for advancement or graduation. When teachers feel responsible for preparing students for other university audiences, they may well draw heavily from beliefs and practices informed by Standard English ideology. As Tardy notes,

> Perhaps the belief that poses the most significant challenge for composition scholars wanting to move toward a multilingual paradigm of FYW is that Standard English is preferred in academic and professional writing and should therefore be the focus of FYW courses. (648)

What is clear from the literature on language difference and fyw is that despite the circulation of best practices and principles, the specter of academic and other audiences who will harshly judge students' accented writing looms large in teachers' minds. In the following section, we trace how this image of the unsympathetic future audience plays out in the teaching of two in-service L2 writing instructors, affecting their thinking about their responsibilities to the students, and ultimately making them less open to best practices in the field and to WPA-mandated policies grounded in those best practices. These teachers' cases are drawn from two separate studies conducted in the same institutional context. Although the trope of the unsympathetic future audience was not the original focus of either study, it emerged strongly in the discourse of both instructors as they spoke about their pedagogical choices.

The Experienced Teacher: Amy

As a graduate teaching assistant, Amy participated in a study Brooke conducted on students' reactions to the use of texts written in World Englishes in the first-year L2 writing classroom. During the study, Amy assigned readings from two World English texts, Ken Saro-Wiwa's *Soza Boy* and Juno Diaz's *The Brief Wondrous Life of Oscar Wao*, and asked students to submit questions about the readings before class. Brooke recorded the resulting class discussions of these texts and then interviewed Amy about her pedagogical beliefs, goals for the course, and response to the class discussion.

At the time of the study, Amy was in the first year of a PhD program in Applied Linguistics. A native speaker of English, Amy had also studied Japanese, Spanish, and German. She earned her undergraduate degree in English literature and creative writing, and she held a master's degree in TESOL. Amy was already an experienced ESL instructor across multiple contexts, having taught two years in Japan, a summer in Mexico, and two years of ESL composition in the United States.

During the interview, other professors' presumed expectations of her students' writing emerged as a driving force in Amy's pedagogical decision-making. When asked to define the main goal of her course, Amy described how she felt herself to be facing a dilemma around the purpose of the class:

Brooke: What are your goals for this class? What would you like students to get out of it ideally?

Amy: Yeah (laughs) that's hard. That's something I really struggle with . . . what is the purpose of a class like this? Is it really a service class? Is it preparing students to write in the academy or university, or is it really its own standalone course to develop critical thinking skills and critical writing skills?

Ultimately, Amy decided, the most important thing for her students to gain from her course is not grammatical perfection but the ability to find resources and produce texts independently, to be "self-sufficient" writers in classes in their disciplines. She wanted to make sure students have "the tools or the skills to do what they need to do to survive and succeed in these other classes," though she notes that she has "no idea what's going on in [other classes] and…how [students] are being perceived" there. In other words, the expectations of "the academy" for her students were extremely important for Amy, yet they were also vague.

As a student of English and linguistics, like many teachers of writing, Amy reported that she had little experience writing in other disciplines, and it was through her teaching and teacher training that her understanding of what other professors might expect in writing had primarily been formed:

I feel like it's been handed down to me by other mentors or professors that I've worked with . . . saying oh, professors in the content fields, this is what they say and this is what they think and we're doing a disservice if we don't prepare [the students] in this way. So I feel this intense pressure, and I feel this influence from these nameless faceless people who have this agenda that I don't know what it is…

Amy's teaching goals have been profoundly shaped by the expectations of "these nameless faceless people," and the success or failure of her work as an instructor is directly tied to how well her students live up to those expectations once they leave her class. If students do not write in English according to those imagined expectations, she has done her students "a disservice." Aiming to make sure her students are able to "survive and succeed" in their classes in an American university means for Amy that, in addition to other rhetorical skills, students need to produce Standard Written English (SWE) because, otherwise, faculty in other disciplines will not be able to understand them. As she reported, "So many students have come to me and said my professors say they can't understand my work…they just say the grammar's too bad." Feedback from her students about their experiences writing in the disciplines has given Amy the impression that while other faculty appreciate her L2 students' ideas and input, they are unwilling to work with nonstandard grammar. Thus, she feels that the onus is on her to prepare students for this critical audience.

Amy's own ambition in her class is to promote students' sense of their linguistic differences as a resource, so that students know "they aren't less than [other students] because they're not American"—an orientation to linguistic difference as a deficit which she perceives as prominent in the academy broadly. It is the desire to counteract this deficit orientation combined with the felt need to prepare her students for an unsympathetic audience that shapes Amy's pedagogy.

As she discussed the World English texts with her students in class, she emphasized what she later called a "balancing act" between using non-standard English that expresses a cultural identity and adhering to expectations of American academic writing. She asks students to consider when and how much they can safely experiment with the types of non-standard grammar and code-mixing evident in the two readings. At the end of the class discussion, a few students commented that the way the authors "interpret their culture and views into their writing styles" could be a helpful model for the students in the class to "write in our own ways" and to "express ourselves." Amy responded by asking the students to consider the rhetorical appropriateness of this choice:

Amy: Ok, do you think you can do that for every academic article you write here at [university]?

Students: [shake heads]

Amy: No. Some of your professors might not (laughs), might not enjoy that.

While Amy concluded the discussion by reinforcing that students' cultures are "something special you bring to the table as writers," it's clear that this is held in check by other professors' potential expectations for SWE. As Amy pointed out in her interview, when she gives the two World English texts to her students in her writing class, "I'm presenting this essay to [the students] as good writing, model writing, but when [they] go write a chemistry lab report this is no longer good or model writing." In other words, because Amy believes that those other academic audiences, represented by the imagined reader of the "lab report," are unwilling to negotiate with linguistic difference, students must learn to accommodate—this is rhetorical savviness. As Amy strives to empower students to be successful in the university, she is ever mindful of that unsympathetic future audience.

The Novice Teacher: Sergei

I (Dorothy) got to know Sergei in the context of a larger study on the development of pedagogical content knowledge among first-time teachers of L2 academic writing. In terms of his language background, Sergei told me that in addition to his native language of English, he spoke some Italian and had studied elementary French in school. Additionally, he had picked up some basic German and Korean during his time serving in the U.S. military. Sergei was in his final year of a TESOL master's program, a degree he had undertaken after retiring from his career as an agricultural consultant. Though the semester of the study was Sergei's first experience teaching L2 writing, he had previous experience teaching public speaking at an academic summer camp for international high school students along with many seminars and training courses in his previous career.

I followed Sergei and three other novice teachers of L2 writing through their first semester of teaching in the same fyw program. I interviewed each teacher six times over the course of the semester, video-recorded their teaching of one of the four required assigments in the class, and conducted three teaching reflection interviews during the focus paper unit. Like Amy, Sergei was keenly aware of the expectations of his students' future readers, both potential professors and employers, and his beliefs about these audiences strongly influenced how he addressed language differences in the classroom.

As he spoke about the role of grammar instruction in the writing class, Sergei described himself as "in between" two perspectives on grammar correction, which he referred to as "descriptivists" and "prescriptivists." He associated the descriptivist view with "what linguists say" about how different "varieties of English are, you know, that have good structure." He also associated this view with the perspective of the ESL writing program and the program director in particular who, he reported, "has said we don't have to correct grammar"

(Interview 1). In contrast, Sergei described the prescriptivist view as the belief that "if you're going to learn English you learn it properly, use the grammar properly, [and] learn the pronunciation as best as you can." Sergei associated prescriptivism with his students' future teachers and employers, explaining that, "in order to get a good job there's a certain minimum level of English pronunciation and understanding that a person needs to develop" (Interview 1). For Sergei, being stuck "between" these two sets of beliefs about grammar caused him a great deal of consternation and internal debate. This struggle is most clearly articulated in Sergei's comments regarding how much he should factor grammatical accuracy into his grading:

> The thing I struggle with is they're going to have to work in an American academic community. Am I doing them an injustice if I don't show them what their problems are, and how to correct them? And if I give them a B+ or an A- [on a paper] with horrible grammar, what's that going to do to them in the future, when they're writing? (Interview 2)

Sergei frames his concern about grading grammar in terms of his obligation to prepare his students for the reality of writing for a hazy future audience who would not be so forgiving regarding grammatical errors.

Sergei's sense of obligation to prepare his students for this future intolerant audience by attending to Standard English grammar puts him into conflict with programmatic policy. The actual policy allowed for some attention to grammar, but also encouraged instructors to limit in-class grammar lessons to short, targeted activities and to use written feedback to "focus on writing problems rather than grammar problems, and encourage students to notice, identify, correct, and seek help for their individual mistakes and problems" rather than correcting every grammatical error in students' drafts (Instructor Handbook). Sergei, however, interpreted this policy to be a blanket prohibition against grammar instruction. While Sergei verbally agreed to abide by this policy, in practice he devoted significant attention to grammar in classroom teaching and while commenting on his students' drafts, during which he particularly focused on stereotypical L2 errors such as misused prepositions, subject-verb agreement, and omitted articles. In justifying these instructional practices, which he knew to be subverting the intended curriculum, Sergei referred again and again to the need to prepare his students for future, more unforgiving audiences. For example, when describing his decision to provide grammatical corrections on his students' rough drafts, Sergei again referenced the conflict between a descriptive approach to grammar and his obligation to prepare his students for future audiences:

> I understand there are different varieties of English and there are different grammar rules, different words, but I also believe there is a . . . I don't know whether I can [or] I should call it standard or not, maybe standard with quotation marks around it, that implies you have a good grasp of English language for work purposes. And when I see a journal article that has bad grammar in it I lose just a little bit of respect for that writer or for that editor. (Teaching Reflection 2)

While Sergei frames his desire to focus on grammar in terms of preparing students "for work purposes," his comment at the end about his loss of respect of published writers on the basis of their poor grammar indicates that at least some of his desire to focus on grammar is based on Sergei's own intolerance for errors, which he projects onto the supposedly prescriptive beliefs of imagined future readers to justify his error correction practices.

Throughout the semester, Sergei continued to devote significant time in class to teaching grammar and commented extensively on grammatical errors in his students' drafts, disregarding the curricular policies that encouraged him to focus primarily on content and structure. Still, at the end of the semester, Sergei noted that he had seen little improvement in his students' grammar, particularly their use of articles, explaining that he "saw improvement in parts of their papers but not [the] whole paper. There was nobody who ever had a completely perfect one with articles" (Interview 5). Because Sergei saw his role as preparing students for future intolerant readers, those errors that were most obvious received the greatest attention, and his goal became the production of grammatically "perfect" papers. Sergei was disappointed in the lack of grammatical development he saw in his students' writing, but he maintained his focus on grammar as a key element of the class and justified his decision on the basis of his students' future audiences. He explained in his final interview that his goals for his students included the following:

> I want the sentence structure to be good. I want the grammar to be good. I don't necessarily want you to enjoy writing it, but I want you to be happy with it, and your boss to be happy with it, or your supervisor, or your email companion, or your instructor. I want it to be the kind of paper that they are happy with and that will help you get along in the world. (Interview 5)

Sergei's mental image of his students' future audiences and particularly those in positions of social and economic power over the students (e.g., boss, supervisor, instructor), along with his own lingering language biases, shaped his instructional goals and lead him to continue to focus extensively on stigmatizing grammatical errors even though his pedagogical practices were not effective in achieving his goals.

The Effects of the "Nameless, Faceless People"

Amy and Sergei represent two types of teachers: Amy is an experienced language teacher who believes strongly that she has a responsibility to promote positive attitudes toward linguistic diversity, while Sergei is a novice teacher whose attitudes toward linguistic diversity were conflicted as a result of an uncomfortable tension between his own experiences in the business world and the best practices of the field. Yet for both teachers, as for many of the L2 writing teachers we have worked with, the image of their students' future readers profoundly influenced their decision-making.

For both teachers, grammatical "perfection"—defined as absence of markedly foreign language features—was not an attainable goal for a one-semester course. However, for Sergei perfection simply defined good writing, and for Amy control over SWE meant survival in the face of linguistic bias. The students' written accents, for these teachers, made the students vulnerable to future criticism, so that, for Sergei especially, what marked their writing as foreign became a potential threat teachers should help them to avoid. Preparing students to meet the expectations of these "prescriptivist" audiences came to define success or failure: If they as teachers do not adequately prepare students to meet the demands of those future audiences, they feel they have done their students a "disservice" or an "injustice." Their concern was not motivated by the effect that their students' future errors would have on their own reputations as teachers but rather sprang from their deeply held beliefs about the purpose of their course, sense of professional ethics, and feelings of responsibility toward their students.

Ultimately, for both Amy and Sergei, the trope of the unforgiving future audience shaped the way they engaged with language difference in the classroom and, in Sergei's case, limited his ability and willingness to align with best practices of the field. For Amy, the image of the "nameless, faceless" professors and their unknown "agendas" hovered over her class discussion of World English texts, and ultimately she advises students to play it safe by experimenting with nonstandard language and codemixing only in the places to which they have traditionally been relegated—creative and personal writing—precisely because other professors "may not enjoy" language difference (Canagarajah, "The Place of World Englishes"). In Sergei's case, this trope permitted him to leave unexamined his own linguistic preferences and biases, which Ilona Leki says "disturb" teachers, and ascribe them to a distant audience of others. This allowed Sergei to remain "in between" the "prescriptive" and "descriptive" views, verbally assenting to one language ideology when communicating with the program director but practicing another ideology in the classroom.

For Amy, the understanding of how those "nameless, faceless" professors will respond to her students' writing emerges from both her own experiences as a teacher and those of her mentors. For Sergei, the perception that future professors and employers would judge his students' grammar errors harshly was partially based on his own experiences in the business world and was also a reflection of his own lingering biases against such errors, biases he knew to be stigmatized in the scholarly field he was joining. These observations suggest that the origins of such beliefs, hinted at here, represent an important question that future research should address, if policies aimed at creating linguistically inclusive classrooms are to be fully implemented.

We would like to close with some recommendations for both writing instructors and those who work closely with instructors that we believe can help to combat the negative effect of this trope on teachers' practices. While linguistically inclusive policies at the programmatic level are important, both to give novice teachers a place to start and to encourage a new departmental culture (Matsuda), our experiences with Amy and Sergei show us that we must uncover and address teachers' deep-seated beliefs if these policies are to be effective.

Put a Face to the "Faceless Professors"

For Amy, the hazy, unknown nature of her students' future audiences added significantly to her own anxiety and led her to assume a conservative approach to language difference in spite of her own beliefs. One way to help teachers deal with these "nameless, faceless" professors, then, is to put names and faces to them by exposing teachers to research on the actual attitudes and beliefs of professors and employers.

Such research has not always found the intolerant beliefs and practices that Amy and Sergei seem to expect. In her longitudinal study of the literacy experiences of four English L2 undergraduates, Leki found that professors in the disciplines were not "unduly worried" about grammatical correctness in student writing (254). Even when faculty report that they highly value SWE, professors tend to be more tolerant of grammatical inconsistencies in L2 students' writing, which they see as evidence of their still-developing English proficiency, than they are toward errors in L1 students' writing (Ives et al.; Leki; Wolfe). Such varying judgements of L2 and L1 writing errors have also been found among employers (see Wolfe et al.). The faculty Terry Zawaki and Anna Habib interviewed in their study on faculty attitudes about language difference reported that they tended to be troubled by those errors which affected their ability to assess students' knowledge of course content, rather than simply wanting unaccented writing.

Moreover, the professors who took a strict stance toward language errors reported doing so not as a result of their own beliefs but out of a sense of obligation to prepare students for other "actual or perceived" stakeholders, including future professors and bosses. As one participant in Zawacki and Habib's study put it, "Personally, you know, I think that those mistakes are part of what makes the world so interesting. I don't see those as flaws. However, I worry for the students that that will prohibit them from succeeding in the [major] and the field" (197). Similar to Amy and Sergei, some instructors outside of composition are motivated by appeasing students' future (supposedly intolerant) audiences—a point that we believe merits additional future research.

We do not wish to imply here that linguistic intolerance does not exist. Anecdotal evidence from Amy's experiences, our own insights as teachers and teacher educators, and the literature tell us that intolerance is a reality in students' lives (see, for example, Cole). Students will certainly encounter audiences in gatekeeping positions, including faculty members on our own campuses, who will be unwilling to negotiate with linguistic difference, and these encounters can have profound consequences, as seen in the case of the Bulgarian student whose professor decided not to write a letter of recommendation for her graduate school application because of her accented English (Ives et al.). However, the research we have reviewed suggests that the problem is not as insurmountable as it often appears. As Cole points out, "the true grammar discrepancy between writing faculty and professors in the disciplines is more one of proportion" (18).

In addition to reading what research says about the attitudes of disciplinary faculty and employers, teachers might also conduct independent interviews with faculty across the curriculum as part of faculty development or a practicum (see Ives et al. or Zawacki and Habib for models of these sorts of interviews), exposing teachers to a wider range of actual audience expectations in their own institutional contexts. Our own experiences interacting with faculty across the disciplines through a campus center for teaching excellence (Worden et al.) enabled us to view faculty not as shadowy judges but as well-meaning partners in students' literacy education, and we encourage other teachers to seek out opportunities for this kind of sustained engagement, where possible.

Provide Ongoing Opportunities for Teacher Reflection

As Bommarito found in his own teaching, teachers need to contend with their intuitive emotional responses to nonstandard language, a process which entails "self-critique, an openness to the possibility of harboring a tacit monolingual ideology, and an openness to changing it" (49). We argue that a key part of this reflection should be ongoing opportunities to externalize and reflect on teachers' underlying beliefs about language differences as they relate to the purpose of fyw, beliefs about future readers, and responsibilities to students. One way to prompt such reflection might be to provide some of the research described above and ask teachers to respond to it, considering how it does (or does not) match their own experiences. Moreover, we would argue that such reflection should not be relegated only to the teaching practicum but should be an ongoing, iterative process that includes in-service teachers and their current teaching experiences.

Acknowledge the Reality of Standard Language Ideologies

Like Leki, we believe that fyw courses should not exist merely to serve other institutional stakeholders but are in themselves important sites for learning and thinking. Yet, we also

> take seriously the responsibility heaved on us by the institutional demand that all undergraduate students take first year writing courses. The students in these writing courses have the right to expect that their work in the writing courses will somehow contribute to their academic success. (Leki 4)

Amy and Sergei were both deeply aware of this responsibility toward their students and feared that failing to insist on SWE would be a "disservice" to their students as they moved on to the wider university. We believe that teachers should absolutely be concerned with the benefits to students in taking the course; however, in order for this concern not to become paralyzing, teachers must figure out a way to acknowledge the reality of standard language ideologies, which are real and do affect students, while simultaneously working to promote a more accepting attitude toward language difference. Instructors often feel a deep ethical responsibility to their students to provide feedback on language errors. Rather than ignoring this felt need, teachers should have tools at their disposal to give such feedback in better ways. For example, Ferris and Hedgcock provide a heuristic for selecting errors to correct when responding to student writing: These are errors that may impede successful communication, frequently repeated errors, and those associated with explainable grammatical rules. In other words, teachers might look for patterns of grammatical errors which interfere with reader understanding, such as incorrect word use, rather than correcting errors which mark writing as non-native, such as making mistakes with articles and prepositions (for more details see Ferris; Ferris and Hedgcock; Matsuda). We would add that we should make every attempt to rely on research to identify which errors actually trouble students' future audiences, rather than focusing on the errors that are easiest to identify or the ones most often marked as "foreign." For example, Wolfe et al. found that pragmatic errors such as an informal address or an overly direct request in emails to business people were generally more bothersome than marked L2 errors such as omitted articles.

In addition, we recommend including curricular activities and assignments that teach students how to recognize situations of linguistic tension or discrimination they are likely to face, such as being essentialized or overlooked because of accented speech or writing and feeling afraid to take the floor in class discussion. Students could then investigate strategies for overcoming these challenges, including how to access institutional anti-discrimination resources and how to advocate for themselves with authority figures. As Leki writes,

> Using [students'] developing literacy skills as tools to work toward analyzing such situations, including their hidden ideological dimensions, and developing possible solutions communally not only honors their intellect and experience but also might make L2 writing classes be remembered for more than only the use of the comma. (285)

By teaching such strategies, we help students take a more active role in shaping their readers' attitudes, rather than just being accommodating to them. This is one more way to promote student agency (Shapiro et al.) and work toward a more linguistically inclusive academic culture generally.

Conclusion

For teachers, the "nameless, faceless people" that they imagine reading their students' future work can have a significant impact on their responses to language differences in the classroom. In responding to their vague conceptions of these potentially narrow-minded unknown readers, writing instructors may adopt teaching practices that do not reflect best practices in the field or even their own beliefs. It's important to acknowledge that teachers are responding to a deeply felt sense of responsibility toward their students. These beliefs seem to be so resistant to change because they are grounded in a sense of social justice, a desire to give students access to the codes of power that will make them successful in the university and beyond. Our goal as teachers and teacher educators is to improve writing education for L2 students by promoting inclusive language policies and practices. In order for these practices to take root, it is essential to grapple directly with our underlying beliefs about the purposes of our classes and our role in the larger university. Only then can we begin to make lasting change.

Notes

1. Pseudonyms chosen by the participants.

Works Cited

Bommarito, Daniel V., and Emily Cooney. "Cultivating a Reflective Approach to Language Difference in Composition Pedagogy." *Composition Studies*, vol. 44, no. 2, 2016, pp. 39-57.

Canagarajah, A. Suresh. "The Place of World Englishes in Composition: Pluralization Continued." *CCC*, vol. 57, no. 4, 2006, pp. 586-619.

---. *Translingual Practice: Global Englishes and Cosmopolitan Relations*. Routledge, 2012.

Cole, Daniel. "What if the Earth is Flat? Working with, not against, Faculty Concerns about Grammar in Student Writing." *The WAC Journal*, vol. 25, 2014, pp.7-35.

"CCCC Statement on Second Language Writing and Writers." Conference on College Composition and Communication, 2014. Accessed 10 June 2017.

Ferris, Dana. *Treatment of Error in Second Language Student Writing*. U of Michigan P, 2011.

---, and John Hedgcock. *Teaching L2 Composition: Purpose, Process, and Practice*. Routledge, 2013.

Furneaux, Clare, et. al. "Teacher Stance as Reflected in Feedback on Student Writing: An Empirical Study of Secondary School Teachers in Five Countries." *International Review of Applied Linguistics*, vol. 45, 2007, pp. 69-94.

Horner, Bruce, et al. "Language Difference in Writing: Toward a Translingual Approach." *College English*, vol. 73, no. 3, 2011, pp. 299-317.

Ives, Lindsey et al. "'I Don't Know if That Was the Right Thing To Do': Cross-Disciplinary/Cross-Institutional Faculty Respond to L2 Writing." *WAC and Second Language Writers: Research Toward Linguistically and Culturally Inclusive Programs and Practices*, edited by Terry Myers Zawacki and Michelle Cox, WAC Clearinghouse and Parlor Press, 2014, pp. 211-32.

Junqueira, Luciana, and Caroline Payant. "'I Just Want to Do it Right, but It's So Hard': A Novice Teacher's Written Feedback Beliefs and Practices." *Journal of Second Language Writing*, vol. 27, 2015, pp. 19-36.

Lee, Icy. "Error Correction in L2 Secondary Writing Classrooms: The Case of Hong Kong." *Journal of Second Language Writing*, vol. 13, 2004, pp. 285-312.

--- "Ten Mismatches Between Teachers' Beliefs and Written Feedback Practice." *ELT Journal*, vol. 63, no. 1, 2009, pp. 13-23.

Leki, Ilona. *Undergraduates in a Second Language: Challenges and Complexities of Academic Literacy Development*. Routledge, 2012.

Matsuda, Paul Kei. "Let's Face It: Language Issues and the Writing Program Administrator." *WPA: Writing Program Administration*, vol. 36, no. 1, 2012, pp. 141-63.

Montgomery, Julie L., and Wendy Baker. "Teacher-Written Feedback: Student Perceptions, Teacher Self-Assessment, and Actual Teacher Performance." *Journal of Second Language Writing* vol. 16, no. 2, 2007, pp. 82-99.

Reichelt, Melinda. "A Critical Evaluation of Writing Teaching Programmes in Different Foreign Language Settings." *Writing in Foreign Language Contexts: Learning, Teaching, and Research*, edited by Rosa M. Manchon, Multilingual Matters, 2009, pp. 183-206.
Roemer, Marjorie, et al. "Reframing the Great Debate on First-Year Writing." *CCC*, vol. 50, no. 3, 1999, pp. 377-92.
Shapiro, Shawna, et al. "Teaching for Agency: From Appreciating Linguistic Diversity to Empowering Student Writers." *Composition Studies*, vol. 44, no. 1, 2016, pp. 31-52.
"Students' Right to Their Own Language." Conference on College Composition and Communication, National Council of Teachers of English, 1974. Accessed 12 June 2017.
Tardy, Christine M. "Enacting and Transforming Local Language Policies." *CCC* (2011): 634-61.
Wolfe, Joanna. "Disciplining Grammar: A Response to Daniel Cole." *The WAC Journal*, vol. 25, 2014, pp. 36-41.
---, et al.. "Grammatical Versus Pragmatic Error: Employer Perceptions of Nonnative and Native English Speakers." *Business and Professional Communication Quarterly*, vol. 79, no. 4, 2016, pp. 397-415.
Worden, Dorothy, et al. "Collaborative Power: Graduate Students Creating and Implementing Faculty Development Workshops on Multilingual Writing Pedagogy." *Teaching/Writing: The Journal of Writing Teacher Education*, vol. 4, no. 1, 2015, pp. 28-46.
You, Xiaoye. *Cosmopolitan English and Transliteracy*. SIUP, 2016.
Zawacki, Terry Myers, and Anna Sophia Habib. "Negotiating 'Errors' in L2 Writing: Faculty Dispositions and Language Difference." *WAC and Second Language Writers: Research Toward Linguistically and Culturally Inclusive Programs and Practices*, edited by Terry Myers Zawacki and Michelle Cox, WAC Clearinghouse and Parlor Press, 2014, pp. 183-210.

Decolonial Potential in a Multilingual FYC

Cruz Medina

Scholars in rhetoric and composition have questioned to what extent the field can be decolonial because of the gatekeeping role that writing plays in the university. This article examines the decolonial potential of implementing multilingual practices in first-year composition (fyc), enacting what Walter Mignolo calls "epistemic disobedience" by complicating the primacy of English as the language of knowledge-building. I describe a Spanish-English "bilingual" fyc course offered at a private university with a Jesuit Catholic heritage. The course is characterized by a translanguaging approach in which Spanish is presented as a valid language for academic writing. The students' writing highlights the enduring influence of colonialism in the form of monolingual ideology within the linguistically diverse geographical context of Silicon Valley, where the potential of decolonial practices are tempered by the economic power of the tech industry and its hiring practices, which have resulted in a low number of employed women and minorities in comparison to both national employment levels and diversity within the region.

Multilingual students experience monolingual ideology in their education, which undermines their abilities to communicate, make meaning, and be effective writers. A multilingual student, Selena[1], describes in her literacy narrative the feeling of vulnerability she experienced in elementary school when she moved from Mexico City, Mexico, to Toronto, Canada:

> I would rather be in a tank full of hungry sharks than once again be vulnerable to a language barrier that had barely been trespassed months before. I was determined to master the English language as to avoid another encounter where nobody could understand me and I couldn't understand them. . . . After having lived my entire seven-year-old life in Mexico City, my father received a job offer in Toronto, Canada. This resulted in my small four-member family to move two countries north into an unknown culture, weather, people, and more importantly language (at least by me).

Selena communicates the vulnerability of starting a new school as a young student who is unable to speak English and is an emerging multilingual learner in an academic institution that imposes assimilation. This article examines the literacy narratives of multilingual speakers in a fyc course themed as "bilingual," the first course in a two-course sequence, which was taught in Spanish. After examining these literacy narratives, I recognized students had used translingual theories we discussed in class to conceptualize their multilingual struggles not as obstacles they had to overcome but as advantages they could use to create new meanings and discover new knowledge. The negative experiences that students related to assimilation, isolation, and insecurity reveal the need for decolonial practices that redress the damage of assimilation and monolingual ideology.

Before moving on, I want to clarify how I'm using key terms in this article. By multilingual, I refer to someone who speaks or writes in more than one language, with linguistic abilities ranging from emerging skills to more complex rhetorical awareness of linguistic practices in a language other than what was spoken at home. The term bilingual describes the specific Spanish fyc course that I co-taught with my colleague Juan Velasco, which was followed by a second course in English. The term bilingual falls under the larger umbrella of multilingual; however, the application of bilingual is limited because it reduces multilingualism to two languages, whereas many of the student writers in this piece speak or write in more than two languages. The term translingual refers to the dispositions, theories, and frameworks that propose inclusive approaches to the use of multiple languages, or translanguaging, for communication, in spite of monolingual efforts to invalidate non-Standard Academic English (SAE). By translanguaging, I refer to "both the complex language practices of multilingual individuals and communities, as well as the pedagogical approaches that draw on those complex practices to build those desired in formal school settings" (Garcia, Johnson, and Seltzer 2). The writing examined in this piece is by multilingual students in a bilingual fyc taught with a translingual approach that was incorporated through readings, discussions, and writing assignments.

Within rhetoric and composition, African American, American Indian, and Latinx scholars have questioned the extent to which the field can, across university contexts, operate within higher education and against colonial paradigms undergirded by racism, sexism, classism, and other systems of oppression that impact whose voices or English(es) are valued (Gilyard; Powell; Villanueva, "On the Rhetoric"). Indigenous scholar Angela Haas explains that decolonial theory informs practices, methodologies, and pedagogies that examine

> (1) how we have individually and collectively been affected by and complicit in the legacy of colonialism; (2) how these effects and complicities of historical and contemporary colonialism influence research and educational institutions, theories, methodologies, methods, and scholarship; and (3) how the effects and complicities of co-

lonialism play out in our everyday embodied practices. ("Decolonial Digital" 191)

Indigenous scholars such as Ellen Cushman focus on the coexistence of language and digital spaces in her call for decolonizing digital archives for the purpose of sharing the Cherokee language ("Wampum"), and Qwo-Li Driskill advocates for decolonial skillshares and exposure to indigenous language to counter colonial perceptions of indigenous knowledge and communities ("Decolonial Skillshares"). The issues of language and intellectual production that are central to the rhetorical sovereignty of Indigenous scholars in writing studies provide generative support for considering how translingual practices in fyc have the potential to disrupt colonial practices. By incorporating languages other than SAE into classrooms, students create knowledge and become familiar with translingual practices that frame their linguistic differences as resources and embodied practices and that disrupt colonial monolingual narratives.

To that end, I assigned a literacy narrative in the required fyc class that I taught in English, which students took after completing the first course in Spanish with my colleague Juan Velasco. When I examined the student narratives, I recognized students had used the translingual theories we discussed in class to reconceptualize their multilingual struggles not as obstacles they had to overcome but as advantages they could use to create new narratives about their linguistic differences. This analysis does not posit that literacy narrative assignments on translingualism will be effective for teaching all English language learners across all institutional contexts; instead, this student writing reveals how reconceptualizing multilingual practices through the introduction of translingualism in a fyc course highlights the potential for redressing perceptions of language, people, and communities based on the colonial influence of monolingual ideology. Additionally, both multilingual writing and writing in different forms of English provide a heuristic for recognizing how composing always requires a rhetorical awareness of translating a writer's message and how competing ideologies affect audience reception, which highlights ideological factors.

The Bilingual Fyc Course

From 2013-2017, my institution offered four sections of an fyc two-course sequence that enacted a translanguaging approach. Serving approximately 80 students over four years, each class of approximately twenty students began the fyc course titled Critical Thinking and Writing 1 Bilingual in Spanish (CTW1) with my colleague Juan Velasco, which focused on analytical skills, before continuing the sequence with me in CTW2 Bilingual in English, which focused on argumentation, information literacy, and research. In this sequence, Spanish was presented as a valid linguistic mode of academic writing, and identities and experiences of multilingual students were validated through critical examination of monolingual ideology in course readings and discussion. The course theme of "bilingual" would have been better titled "multilingual" because multiple enrolled students grew up with languages other than English and Spanish.[2]

The bilingual fyc course was developed by English faculty[3] based on the understanding that multilingual students possessed linguistic resources that informed their rhetorical awareness and discursive skills, in part answering Ellen Cushman's language-based decolonial question, "How can teachers and scholars move beyond the presumption that English is the only language of knowledge making and learning?" ("Translingual" 234). Students opted into the bilingual course based on questionnaires they completed during orientation[4]. The students' levels of Spanish proficiency ranged from native speakers, those who have spoken Spanish as a first language, to native English speakers, who felt their Spanish speaking skills were still emerging, even though they passed Advanced Placement (AP) Spanish classes and tests in high school. Some AP students were the children of educators who spoke some Spanish with a care-giver growing up, while others learned English as a second language during their elementary education[5]. The students who learned Spanish in school tended to come from privileged backgrounds while the first-generation students spoke of immigrant parents, commuting to school and holding jobs[6]. With a student body of approximately 5,500 undergraduates, the twenty or so students who took part in the bilingual fyc courses each year were hardly a significant representation of the entire university; however, the percentage of Latinx students in each course exceeds 50% even though Latinx students make up only 15% of the overall student population.

In the first quarter of bilingual fyc (CTW1), my colleague Juan Velasco[7] conducted the course in Spanish, providing space for students to discuss the spectrum of their languaging abilities, including positive and negative experiences associated with their multilingual identities. Velasco introduced Gloria Anzaldúa's *Borderlands/La Frontera* as a central text to provide a model for thinking about writing as an expression of multiple linguistic identities and translanguaging with English, Spanish and Nahuatl. Steven Alvarez suggests that translingual literacy studies could undergird a decolonial definition of literacy that "contribute[s] to a necessary shift in literacy studies by treating heterogeneity in contact zones as the norm rather than the exception" (19). He continues, the "rhetorical dimension of translingual literacies allows it to consider communicative competence as not restricted to predefined meanings within individual languages" (19). The diverse population of students in the bilingual fyc, which included white, Latinx, African American, Asian American, and Middle Eastern American students, understood linguistic heterogeneity because it was a part of their lived experiences as multilinguals. By addressing the negative impact of monolingual ideology on the linguistic abilities of multilinguals, the translingual readings, discussion, and analysis contribute to the decolonial potential of this framework, which decentralizes a singular, authoritative version of language.

During the second fyc course in the two-course sequence (CTW2), which focused on argumentation and research, I assigned readings that theorized multilingual experiences within monolingual university writing classrooms, articulating important arguments about diversity within a single language. The students read Paul Kei Matsuda's "Myth of Linguistic Homogeneity," which problematizes teaching SAE as a primary goal of writing instruction and describes how the myth of linguistic homogeneity privileges monolingual English speakers. Students agreed with Matsuda's claim that "the dominant discourse of U.S. college composition not only has accepted English Only as an ideal but it already assumes the state of English-only, in which students are native English speakers by default" (637). Additionally, many agreed with Matsuda's explanation that "resident second-language writers" and "native speakers of unprivileged varieties of English" are harmed when educators assume English homogeneity (648). The class next read Bruce Horner et al.'s "Language Difference in Writing: Toward a Translingual Approach" and discussed how translingualism speaks to the myth of a singular English and frames linguistic difference as a resource. Students appreciated learning that a translingual approach "acknowledges that deviation from dominant expectations need not be errors; that conformity need not be automatically advisable; and that writers' purposes and readers' conventional expectations are neither fixed nor unified" (Horner et al. 304). These articles not only helped establish a shared vocabulary for discussing how audiences base responses to linguistic differences on monolingual ideology but also proposed a framework for advocating using languages other than English in the writing classroom.

Following the Matsuda and Horner et al. pieces, I assigned a literacy narrative assignment that asked students to discuss their experiences with reading and writing while reflecting specifically on language and identity. These narratives generated inquiry about language and multilingualism that often resulted in preliminary research topics. For the literacy narrative assignment, the purpose was to "write a literacy narrative that draws on your experiences with reading and writing, identifying how these experiences have contributed to how you see yourself negotiating the different ways that people think about language" (see appendix). Students were asked to treat their experiences with language, whether positive or negative, as generative sites of analysis that should be supported or complicated by quotations from the course readings. In the assignment, I emphasized "negotiating" the different ways that audiences think about language because a translingual approach benefits from the understanding "that English is always a language in translation" (Pennycook 34) and "recognize[es] all language use as acts of translation" (Horner, NeCamp and Donahue 287), thereby framing linguistic "difference as the norm of all utterances" (Lu and Horner, "Introduction" 208). Literacy narratives allowed students to focus on their diverse uses of language, creating a space where they could describe tangible instances of how audiences' respond to language difference and what those responses reveal about their ideology. These moments of translation and negotiation provide generative experiences for writing literacy narratives because students are keenly aware of the moments when they have been made to feel inferior for their language use. Through writing, multilingual students express how they experience frustration, rejection, and feelings of not belonging that motivate the work of translingual scholars, providing more critical perspectives on monolingual ideology's colonizing effect.

Isolation

One of the reasons that introducing translingual theory into writing classes supports decolonial practices has to do with its ability to create more inclusive spaces for knowledge creation, counteracting the isolation that marks multilingual speakers as "others." Below I return to the quote by Selena in which she describes her feeling of vulnerability after having moved from Mexico City to Toronto, Canada, without knowing English:

> I would rather be in a tank full of hungry sharks than once again be vulnerable to a language barrier that had barely been trespassed months before. I was determined to master the English language as to avoid another encounter where nobody could understand me and I couldn't understand them…After having lived my entire seven-year-old life in Mexico City, my father received a job offer in Toronto, Canada. This resulted in my small four-member family to move two countries north into an unknown culture, weather, people, and more importantly language (at least by me).

Because she would prefer to be in "a tank full of hungry sharks," her experience as an English language learner arriving in an unfamiliar linguistic space is characterized as worse than living in constant fear due to her inability to communicate. Selena's response underscores the fear associated with the experience of forced assimilation to dominant linguistic practices through the linguistic containment she faced in school. Assimilation remains a topic of concern in literacy studies, because as Gregorio Hernandez-Zamora explains in *Decolonizing Literacy: Mexican Lives in the Era of Global Capitalism*, literacy learning is "not just a psycholinguistic process, but centrally… a cultural, political and ideological experience of *adopting and assimilating to the language, culture and ideologies of the dominant other*" (32). Fortunately, Selena describes her teacher in Canada as dedicating extra time to help her and another student who spoke only French, as well as "other classmates who not only tolerated us but also made a warm welcoming environment." The multilingual context of Canada no doubt informed the teacher's approach to language; however, Selena's experience speaks to the necessity of professional development opportunities to prepare educators to work with multilingual student populations (Canagarajah, "Translingual Writing"; Ferris and Hedgcock; Matsuda).

Selena's experience with the English language became further complicated when her family moved from Toronto to Corpus Christi, Texas, where she describes being exposed to Spanglish as a form of translanguaging that challenged her experiences with languages as being distinctly separate. She felt uncomfortable with the translingual practices of multilinguals in Corpus Christi because Selena's educational experiences in both Mexico and Canada had reinforced monolingual beliefs about the homogeneity of languages. Moving again from Texas to a small town in Montana, Selena references Matsuda's "Myth of Linguistic Homogeneity" to address the lack of diversity she faced when her English teachers focused primarily on grammar in her writing, a salient feature of her writing as a non-native English writer. Selena's teacher imagined that she had had the same experiences as the other students, so her teacher paid less attention to the content of her writing:

> [W]henever I was returned a red ink drenched homework assignment, I never connected that failure to the fact that English was indeed my second language but simply to the fact that I hadn't worked hard enough or hadn't invested enough time into it. I had fallen victim to the idea that "'writing well' is the ability to produce English that is unmarked in the eyes of teachers who are custodians of privileged varieties of English." (Matsuda 640)

Although Selena makes no claims about discrimination because English was her second language, her experience demonstrates how the overemphasis of certain grammar rules enacts a form of linguistic discrimination that reinforces the exclusionary and punitive aspects of monolingual ideology. Even though Selena's writing teachers may have intended to contribute to Selena's transferable writing skills for future classes, the overemphasis of grammar and syntax correction served to demoralize Selena. "Drenching" an assignment with red ink overwhelms students and detracts from higher-level writing goals; it serves only to reinforce the gatekeeping role of colonial institutions that mark non-white multilingual students as inferior.

Selena's negative experience with writing, based on a teacher's overemphasis on a specific variety of English, highlights the need for translingual practices. These practices refer to the pedagogical "disposition of openness and inquiry the people take toward language and language differences" and the advocacy "to be more humble about what constitutes a mistake (and about what constitutes correctness) in writing" (Horner et al. 310-11). Enacting translingual practices reframes linguistic difference as a skill in the semiotic toolkit, following Suresh Canagarajah's assertion that "[t]he term translingual conceives of language relationships in more dynamic terms" (*Literacy as Translingual Practice* 8). Translingualism and translanguaging offer a dynamic paradigm for students to understand their multilingual identities and linguistic differences within monolingual universities where students like Selena have often been inculcated to think of multilingual abilities as a deficit.

In his literacy narrative, Julian describes the difficulty of growing up with parents who were emerging multilinguals, speaking primarily a non-privileged dialect of Spanish. After immigrating from Zacatecas, Mexico, to Aspen, Colorado, Julian describes the confusion that results from moving between two languages dominated by monolingual ideology:

> Before starting school, my parents had taught me their imperfect versions of Spanish; dialects coming from a rural area of Zacatecas, México. Both of them had received very little education and thus had little experience with the more academic forms of Spanish. I was raised very monolingual, to the extent that I wasn't even aware of all the other languages that existed in our surrounding community and around the world. Thus when I was taught to read and write in English at school in Colorado, my mind was blown away and I felt very confused and frustrated.

Julian's experience highlights the clash of colonial influence. Spanish and English monolingual ideology negatively impacted his move between Mexico and the U.S. Julian's frustration follows what Anzaldúa argues in "How to Tame a Wild Tongue" about academic rules oppressing English and Spanish speakers: "Even our own people, other Spanish speakers *nos quieren poner candados en la boca* [they want to put padlocks in our mouths]. They would hold us back with their bag of *reglas de academia* [academic rules]" (76; my translations). The student's experience of moving between locations dominated by monolingual ideology highlights how the enforcement of *"reglas de academia,"* in both English and Spanish, exert the worldview's power through standardization.

Anzaldúa's *Borderlands/La Frontera* articulates many of the frustrations multilinguals experience because of the standardization that monolingual ideology imposes, which is part of the reason why my colleague Velasco taught the first quarter in Spanish using *Borderlands/La Frontera* as the primary text in the course. Anzaldúa's translanguaging with English, Spanish, and Nahuatl provides students with arguments and experiences they can relate to about language and identity. For students like Julian, writing in a language other than English offers decolonial potential since their English abilities have been called into question due to their multilingual identity. The high percentage of Latinx students in the class provided an exigence for the incorporation of the Spanish language, which Anzaldúa describes as embodying a "tolerance for contradictions, a tolerance for ambiguity," with the mestiza who learns "to be an Indian in Mexican culture" (101). Native scholar Driskill also introduces Anzaldúa's *Borderlands/La Frontera* into courses where the indigenous Cherokee language is incorporated because the book supports the claim that "[l]anguage revitalization and continuance is one of the central struggles of Native people in the United States and Canada" (Driskill 65). Language provides a generative heuristic for helping students to arrive at a nuanced understanding of the deeply rooted and intermingled cultures and people who live on colonized indigenous lands in the U.S.

Maria, a first-year Latina in my class who was actually a junior because of dual-enrollment credits, describes having felt, or having been made to feel, as though her first language of Spanish was inferior for creating knowledge. In her literacy narrative, she interprets her experience through the myth of linguistic homogeneity and translingualism**,** revealing how monolingual ideology is internalized and used to subjugate speakers of non-dominant varieties of English. She advocates for translingualism:

> Throughout my education, I always viewed English as a superior language to my native Spanish language due to the constant separation of students into classrooms of different English levels. . . . Enacting a translingual approach to learning institutions is essential to break the borders that are built between several languages and their variations.

Maria's advocacy for a translingual approach follows Cushman's view, expressed in "Translingual and Decolonial Approaches to Meaning Making," that translingualism offers potential for decolonial practice because of its premise that knowledge can be made in languages other than English. Maria's literacy narrative also underscores Juan Guerra's reasons for using of translingual theory in writing classrooms. Guerra argues that translingualism "introduces more of our students in the first-year and advanced writing courses to the competing ideologies that inform their current writing" ("Cultivating" 232). Using multiple languages in the writing classroom, Maria appreciates how a writing course creates a space where multilingual students can reclaim agency over their linguistic practices while addressing competing ideologies in those practices. For multilingual speakers like Maria, monolingual ideology manifests in a colonial rhetoric of assimilation urging students to should hide their abilities and identities as people who are able to speak more than standard U.S. English. When instructors teach languages other than English as contributing to knowledge in academic institutions, they create a space where decolonial practices serve to reveal how colonialism has benefited from erasing alternative epistemologies, cultures, and communities in order to justify expansion and "discovery" of occupied territories.

What makes Maria's experience further indicative of how colonial ideology discriminates against multilingual students is that she entered the university with junior-level status as a result of dual-enrollment courses, and yet she was still indoctrinated to believe her linguistic heritage made her academically inferior. Maria's heightened awareness about the impact of monolingual ideology demonstrates why students should be taught "communicative practices as not neutral or innocent but informed by and informing economic, geopolitical, social-historical, cultural relations of asymmetrical power" (Lu and Horner 208). Despite Maria's academic success, she was still left feeling that her linguistic heritage was framed as inferior by the pervasive monolingual ideology. Maria's experience is atypical for the many Latinx students who internalize myths of monolingual superiority because hers remains a relative success story. Many times, Latinx students with Spanish as their first language or heritage language are less academically successful because they are segregated in public and charter schools through implicit and explicit linguistic and socioeconomic containment (Blume; "Choice Without Equity").

Insecurity

The feeling of insecurity that Maria describes demonstrates the impact of monolingual ideology, although the continued use of the term "broken English" by the multilingual students in their literacy narratives shows how these beliefs are internalized and then manifested, often to describe the linguistic differences of family members. One student, Kerry, defines the Korean English she spoke when she was young as a kind of "broken English." She writes, "As a child, I was raised by my grandparents who spoke broken English yet primarily spoke Korean. Thus, I spent most of my youth speaking to them in what I called 'Ko-nglish,' a mixture of grammatically incorrect Korean and English." Kerry's description of her family's English echoes Matsuda's point about the implied connection between grammar and intelligence and his critique of educators "who judge the writer's credibility or even intelligence on the basis of grammaticality" (640). That Kerry was made to feel shame or embarrassment about her family members' way of communicating with the world demonstrates why decolonial and anti-racist scholars continue to critique the colonial imperative of assimilation (Baca, *Mestiz@*; Martinez; Villanueva, *Bootstraps*). When arguing for integration rather than assimilation, these scholars seek to recognize and increase the epistemological work recognized, as well as "the breadth of meanings available within a language," such as variations across Chicanx English, African American English, and Hawaiian English (Pennycook 43). In addition, the continued use of concepts such as "broken English" undermines the dynamic nature of language and of how language changes across genres, in different contexts, for different audiences.

However, Kerry also comments on how Anzaldúa's *Borderlands/La Frontera* re-conceptualizes effective writing by emphasizing the content of what is being communicated, rather than focusing primarily on grammar. Kerry writes,

> Our [fyc in Spanish] professor showed us a variety of writing pieces with mixes of Spanish and English or grammatically incorrect Spanish, emphasizing that the message and content were more important than just the grammatical contents. He similarly encouraged us to not focus as much on the grammar in our Spanish, but more about our content as well as expressing our writing in creative manners. This was a complete change from all the previous standard language classes that I had taken . . . languages could intermingle, mix, and vary in an artistic manner, rather than be something that needed to be corrected.

Kerry's appreciation of the "artistic" intermingling of languages and the attention to writing content demonstrates how translingual practices can create decolonial disruptions, positively impacting how students perceive their own language use. By drawing attention to how and what Anzaldúa writes, the course reveals "decolonial potential, [where] translingual approaches need to avoid simply changing the content of what is studied and taught and work toward dwelling in the borders to revise the paradigmatic tenets of thought structuring everyday practices" (Cushman, "Translingual" 236). When Kerry writes about Anzaldúa's writing and the fyc's approach to language, she alludes to how the course impacts the tenets of thought regarding her everyday practices with language and writing. As Cushman notes, the decolonial potential of translingual practices is rooted in unsettling what students have been taught about the possibilities of writing. The "creative manners" that Kerry mentions also speak to a broadened definition of writing that includes multiple modes and semiotic resources for knowledge-making available to students.

While discussing the potential for constructing knowledge in the Cherokee language, Ellen Cushman calls for decolonizing digital spaces, a result of which might be multimodal composing. Both translingual and multimodal digital writing draw on a wide range of composing resources in non-alphabetic, multimodal, digital, and multiple linguistic modes of communication (Baca, *Mestiz@*; Banks; Canagarajah, *Translingual*; Cushman, "Wampum"; Haas; Palmeri; Selfe; Shipka). Cushman supports a translingual approach though remains critical of its application in much the same way she calls on composers to remain critical of the media they use. Cushman explains that "a translingual approach to meaning making evokes a decolonial lens with its focus on the ideologies implicit in any tool chosen for meaning making (be it mode, media, or genre), as these are always laden with cultural, historical, and instrumental import for the people who use them" ("Translingual" 236). I would add that the responses digital texts generate can reveal an audience's ideology and conceptualization of writing. Like the additional affordances that digital, visual, and non-alphabetic modes offer students for communicating, translingualism offers another approach for understanding how linguistic diversity is regarded as a resource for intended audiences.

Similar to Kerry's experience with "broken English" and "Ko-nglish," a student named Jennifer highlights how translingual practices can teach multilingual students to view their linguistic differences as something to leverage rather than hide. In the following, Jennifer presents her Filipino mother's English as having a negative impact on Jennifer's idiomatic phrasing and pronunciation. Jennifer relays the feeling related to the use of "broken English" when she describes her mother's variations as grammatical errors:

> Many of the grammatical and pronunciation errors that my Filipino family regularly make when speaking or writing in English have been passed down onto my own use of language. Although English is my first language, I have still managed to adopt the same nuances as my mom as a result of primarily learning how to speak and write from her. Sometimes I catch myself mistakenly saying to "open" and "close" the light instead of "turn the light on and off," pronouncing the word "alumni" as "a-loom-ni", and interchangeably using the pronouns she and he.

Contextualized language practices such as the use of "open" instead of "turn on" are misidentified as grammatical errors within the dominant monolingual ideology. In reality, the language use by Jennifer's mother represents "the normal transactions of daily communicative practice of ordinary people" (Lu and Horner 212). These "normal transactions" of "ordinary people" like Jennifer and her mother demonstrate how overemphasizing privileged forms of English in the classroom can serve to uphold colonial standards that stigmatize linguistic variances, especially within the families of multilingual students.

Jennifer's response to her mother's English is an internalization of monolingual ideology, which manifests in the English Only movement, rebranded as "English Official." Through a decolonial lens, English Official demonstrates an enduring colonial project that privileges nativism and excludes non-white multilinguals from institutional power due to linguistic difference that mark multilinguals as "other." Here in California, monolingual ideology was concretized in the passage of Proposition 63 in 1982, making English the "official" language (Dyste). Opponents of English Official/English Only policy, Bruce Horner and John Trimbur explain that English Official policy "continues to exert a powerful influence on our teaching, our writing programs, and our impact on U.S. culture" (595). Students like Jennifer fear replicating the linguistic patterns of their parents because of the systematic remediation and poor assessment of multilingual students' writing, supported by state policy authorizing discriminatory practices at the programmatic and classroom levels. Tensions over which language can be used for knowledge production continue to be an issue at the state level, where legislation such as West Virginia's English official House Bill 3019 passed as recently as 2016 ("U.S. English"). These policies exert colonial power by delegitimizing the linguistic practices of anyone other than monolingual English speakers. With the majority of states having English as the official language, colonial paradigms operate through the establishment of a standard, against which the subjugated population always falls short (Bhaba).

Decolonial Implications for Multilingual Practices in Composition Studies

The literacy narratives by students like Jennifer highlight the enduring influence that colonialism maintains through monolingual ideology, even in a geographical context as diverse as the Bay Area in northern California. The tech industry in Silicon Valley contributes to the colonial influence that flattens differences in the name of innovation and economic growth. The writing by the students in the bilingual fyc course brings to light how isolation and insecurity continue to impact multilingual speakers in composition classrooms. Even as my colleague Juan encouraged students to use both Spanish and English in their writing assignments to demonstrate how their multilingualism provided an additional semiotic resource, Juan noted how the students often self-censored their use of English when writing predominantly in Spanish. By adhering to monolingual practices in this multilingual writing class, students allude to how the prestige of SAE supersedes students' multilingual abilities. When students accommodate to the dominant language, they follow the logic of Western modernity that "is still at work assimilating and consuming" (Ruiz and Sánchez xvi). Students' desires to perform an educated version of English no doubt contributes to the discomfort that students described when speaking Spanish in a writing course. This is particularly poignant in Silicon Valley because diversity is often celebrated publicly as aligned with innovation (Massaro and Najera). The institutional context and its adherence to monolingualism support the belief that universities should be viewed as sites for job preparation exclusively, where learning rules translates into future employment.

My institution's geographical context of Silicon Valley also provides a useful metonymy for the juggernaut tech industry[8] to consider in the analysis of student literacy narratives because of the economic ethos of the area; that is, arguments for colonialism often use economic development as evidence of a positive net benefit. In "The Case for Colonialism," Bruce Gilley claims there is "evidence for significant social, economic, and political gain under colonialism: expanded education, improved public health, the abolition of slavery, widened employment opportunities, improved administration, the creation of basic infrastructure...access to capital, the generation of historical and cultural knowledge, and national identity formation" (4).[9] Gilley's claims that colonialism helped generate cultural knowledge contradicts accounts by native populations, such as the Nahua in what is now Mexico, where colonial forces destroyed literacy artifacts following contact with indigenous populations (León-Portilla). Similarly, Gilley's claims about abolishing slavery ring false given the forced conversion, labor and enslavement of native populations; colonial forces, ultimately, are those that benefit from inequitable economies and employment possibilities.

Within writing studies, decolonial theory continues to gain attention because it reveals and resists enduring colonial legacies that subjugate those marked by linguistic or racial difference. In *Decolonizing Rhetoric and Composition Studies*, Raúl Sánchez points to Walter Mignolo's influence on decolonial theory in writing studies: "Mignolo's decoloniality is of interest to scholars in our field who wish to continue expanding the concept of writing, especially as we continue to consider the rich varieties of Latin American and Latinx written experience past, present, and future" (87). Mignolo's influence in writing studies can be traced back to his work on breaking from colonial knowledge that standardizes and enforces beliefs about language ("Delinking"), his advocacy for epistemic disobedience ("Epistemic"), and his arguments for recognizing parallel sites of knowledge making (*Darker*). Mignolo's work is important for writing theory, methodology, and pedagogy seeking to break from colonial narratives about what is authorized as writing for knowledge-making and what knowledge is valued. Decolonial theory enriches the analysis of multilingual student writing because colonial ideology imposes itself through the control of indigenous knowledge and knowledge by people of color. In previous work, I drew on decolonial theory in the examination of texts by predominantly Latinx students in Tucson responding to culturally relevant assignments in the context of anti-ethnic studies legislation that targeted a program scaffolded around indigenous and Latinx ways of knowing. In the context of Arizona HB 2281, which sought to outlaw a program that increased graduation rates and state test scores for a predominantly Latinx student population, I argued for the application of "decolonial theory, writing, and practices [such] as those which work against hegemonic institutions and policies that support colonial assumptions of white supremacy" (Medina 61) because district administrators sought to discredit the work of the ethnic studies program. Through the analysis of student writing in these contexts, we can observe the decolonial potential through the benefits students describe from having experienced a decentering of colonial knowledge and monolingual practices in the classroom. A decolonial framework provides a critical method for analyzing student texts because experiences with language cannot be separated from the social and cultural ecologies of student knowledge.

Decolonizing "Good Writing"

For decolonial practices to be effective, they need to be iterative and reconstituted by taking local institutional contexts into account. Indigenous scholars such as Driskill incorporate decolonial practices through Native American language usage in the classroom relating to the demographics of a particular geographic location ("Decolonial Skillshares"). By standardizing the use of language other than English, Driskill argues that "Indigenous languages not only carry cultural memory, because language is so central to rhetoric, they also change the way we think about rhetoric and how rhetoric works" (67). Unfortunately, my students' literacy narratives suggest that writing instruction and assessment continue to overly emphasize grammar and syntax. Decolonial scholars might argue that over-enforcing syntax and grammar is rooted in colonial belief systems dating to at least 1492, when "one writing system was so brutally and quickly imposed upon others" (Baca, "Rethinking" 232).

Multilingual students have been discouraged from using their linguistic resources because of how their language practices have been policed by assessment practices based on colonial standards that emphasize mimicry (cf. Bhabha) through assimilation. In both the students' literacy narratives and class discussions, their perceptions of themselves as writers reveal the negative impact grammar rules have had on them and their writing. In writing studies, the discussion of grammar can be traced back to the 1966 Dartmouth Seminar, where scholars in composition and writing studies fought for the recognition of writing as entailing more than grammar and syntax. However, recent critiques of Vershawn Young's use of African American English (AAE) in the 2019 College Composition and Communication Conference call for papers demonstrate the need for more inclusive understandings of linguistic diversity within the U.S. Responding to Young's language use, such as his assertion that "We gon show up, show out, practice, and theorize performance-rhetoric and performance-composition," contributors on the Writing Program Administration listserv (WPA-L) echoed colonial appeals to standards, arguing that Young's writing should reflect the English taught in first-year classes (Young). These national conversations about the centrality of SAE reflect what students described in their literacy narratives regarding the enforcement of monolingual ideology. Nationally and locally, the reduction of writing to little more than grammar stands in for monolingual ideology because of how English and writing become narrowly defined as homogeneous. Canagarajah points out that these responses demonstrate how "[m]onolingual ideologies have relied on form, grammar, and system for meaning-making, motivating teachers and scholars to either ignore strategies and practices or give them secondary importance" (*Literacy as Translingual Practice* 4). Students' focus on writing for content, not simply for correctness, supports advocacy for translingual practices. These practices can help make writing more relevant and can "push composition from its parochial status as a U.S.-centric, English monolingual enterprise to a discipline directly confronting, investigating, and experimenting with, rather than simply correcting, language practices on the ground" (Horner, NeCamp and Donahue 291). Presenting translingualism in the classroom increases student awareness of the evolving nature of language and disrupts monolingual arguments that negatively impact how multilingual students view the validity of their writing.

Translingual theories and practices contribute to decolonial practice when curricular materials and assignments call attention to monolingual ideology and provoke students' critical reflection on the discriminatory institutional practices that affect how multilingual speakers negotiate language use. This work—beyond making writing about more than error correction—counters deficit-model terminology embedded in phrases like "broken English" and proactively responds to naming the enduring legacies of colonialism and having *la facultad* to see beneath the surface of these structures (Anzaldúa 60). At this moment when xenophobia functions as a strategy in mainstream political campaigns[10], language remains a tangible curricular avenue through which to discuss the unequal distribution of power and the importance of critical communication for civil discourse. Instead of continually fortifying walls that separate and authorize language use, educators have the opportunity to engage students in critical discussion about language difference and multiple literacies and to continue the work of decolonizing the borders of what writing is and how it can be composed. The literacy narratives discussed here reveal the decolonial potential of providing students with an alternative paradigm through which to understand language differences. Translingual practices provide a pedagogical intervention for reframing discussion of linguistic difference within the classroom and for redressing how colonial legacies affect multilingual students' perceptions of themselves as writers.

Acknowledgments

Thanks to Juan Velasco and Sharon Merritt for making the bilingual writing class possible. Thanks to Bob Mayberry for the support with revisions, to Laura Micciche for editorial guidance, and to reviewers for generous feedback.

Notes

1. Student names have been changed.

2. This diversity of language is similarly reflected in U.S. Census data cited in a 2014 *Silicon Valley Index* report that the percentage of Spanish speakers is smaller in Silicon Valley compared to California and the rest of the U.S., with Chinese, Vietnamese, other Indo-European, and Tagalog spoken at higher rates by those who are five years and older (*Silicon Valley Index* 13).

3. Juan Velasco and Sharon Merritt worked together to develop the course in 2011. Velasco and I piloted it in its second year when I began at Santa Clara University in 2013.

4. The mechanism for identifying students for this class has been an issue since the inception of the bilingual fyc. Students are often uncertain about why they were placed in the course.

5. At this small liberal arts private institution, a student commuting can be indicative of a working class background, especially in the context of the visibly privileged student population.

6. Anecdotally, the division in cultural and economic capital between students who could have benefited from bilingual education and those students whose parents exposed them to immersion education highlights how outlawing bilingual education disproportionately negatively impacts students of color from lower socioeconomic backgrounds.

7. Juan Velasco earned a PhD in his home country of Spain and an additional PhD in Chicano Studies from UCLA.

8. When most students were asked why they chose to attend this institution, proximity to the Silicon Valley tech industry ranked highest.

9. Since the publication of this article, the journal has withdrawn this essay after it "received serious and credible threats of personal violence," according to the Taylor & Francis webpage.

10. The xenophobia evidenced in Donald Trump's remarks about Mexico as a country sending drug dealers and rapists to the U.S. is echoed by lesser-known political candidates such as Mike Pape (see Pape's campaign ad on YouTube).

Appendix

First Year Writing |
Session Year | **Literacy Narrative**

> A literacy narrative tells the story of a particular incident or a series of vignettes that contributed to the awareness of becoming literate. It is a meaningful narrative constructed with scenes, events, dialogue and detail that communicate experiences.

During this unit, we're engaging with writers whose writing addresses issues related to language, a writer's identity, and myths of a singular English. Some of these issues are described by Gloria Anzaldúa as literacy moments, and we will think of literacy "as a set of socially organized practices which make use of a symbol system and a technology for producing and disseminating it" and "apply this knowledge for a specific purpose in specific contexts of use" (Scribner and Cole 236). Because the theme of this class is education and identity, this writing assignment will ask you to reflect on aspects of literacy as they relate to your identity and your use of knowledge about language in specific situations.

Assignment: Write a literacy narrative that draws on your experiences with reading and writing, identifying how these experiences have contributed to how you see yourself negotiating the different ways that people think about language. For example, you might consider specific instances when you made conscious decisions about language that either achieved a desired outcome or perhaps when your choice of language led to an unexpected response from someone who thought differently about language than you. You will incorporate quotes from the course readings that support, refute or complicate your point and experience with language and literacy.

Required Texts: Paul Kei Matsuda, "Myth of Monolingualism" and Bruce Horner et al., "Toward a Translingual Approach"

Audience: For this assignment, you will be writing for an academic discourse community in a non-fiction style of writing that uses Standard Academic English as well as non-English to demonstrate your claim about language.

Should Include:

- A central claim/thesis about yourself as a reader/writer and how it reveals an aspect of your educated identity
- Clear scenes with description and explanation of significance of this scene
- Evidence in the form of quotes from Matsuda or Horner et al.
- Analytical explanation about how and why this experience impacted your identity as a reader, writer and educated person
- Paragraphs organized by content rather than focused on length

Remember that you are working to:

- Demonstrate how experiences from your life contributed to how you are critically aware of language
- Demonstrate critical thinking, which includes the whole process of selecting complex enough claims, appropriate evidence (and the appropriate amount of analysis)
- Demonstrate insights about experiences through analytical explanations
- Demonstrate the strategic use of details to communicate the tone and emotion of the experience

Format: MLA format, 12 pt font, Times New Roman, double spaced, 1-inch margins, page numbers (see MLA example on OWL Purdue on d2l), 3-4 pages, works cited page

Grading Rubric Criteria

Analysis: How effectively are experiences explained and their impact on literacy/education communicated?

Clarity: Did the scenes/experiences provide details, description or dialogue that communicated the feeling of the experience?

Organization: Did the sequence of events or the choice of included events contribute to an effective communication of experiences with education?

Academic Convention and Style: Did the style match the content of the scenes and analysis? Did the quotes effectively contribute to analysis of the experiences?

Process: Did you engage in the drafting activities with your group? Work across drafts to make the best summary possible?

Works Cited

Alvarez, Steven. "Literacy." *Decolonizing Rhetoric and Composition Studies: New Latinx Keywords for Theory and Pedagogy*, edited by Iris Ruiz and Raúl Sánchez, Palgrave MacMillan, 2016, pp. 17-30.

Anzaldúa, Gloria. *Borderlands/ La Frontera*. Aunt Lute, 1987.

Baca, Damian. *Mestiz@ Scripts, Digital Migrations, and the Territories of Writing*. Palgrave MacMillan, 2008.

---. "Rethinking Composition, Five Hundred Years Later." *JAC*, vol. 29, no. 1/2, 2009, pp. 229-42.

Banks, Adam J. *Digital Griots: African American Rhetoric in a Multimedia Age*. SIUP, 2011.

Bhabha, Homi. "Of Mimicry and Man: The Ambivalence of Colonial Discourse." *October*, vol. 28, 1984, pp. 125-33.

Blume, Howard. "Charter Schools' Growth Promoting Segregation, Studies Say." *Los Angeles Times*, 4 Feb. 2010, articles.latimes.com/2010/feb/04/local/la-me-charters5-2010feb05.

Canagarajah, Suresh, editor. *Literacy as Translingual Practice: Between Communities and Classrooms*. Routledge, 2013.

---. *Translingual Practice: Global Englishes and Cosmopolitan Relations*. Routledge, 2012.

---. "Translingual Writing and Teacher Development in Composition." *College English*, vol. 78, no. 3, 2016, pp. 265-73.

"Choice Without Equity: Charter School Segregation and the Need for Civil Rights Standards." *The Civil Rights Project: Proyecto Derechos Civiles*, 6 March 2012, www.civilrightsproject.ucla.edu/research/k-12-education/integration-and-diversity/choice-without-equity-2009-report.

"*College English* Call for Submissions: 'And Gladly Teach.'" NCTE, www2.ncte.org/resources/journals/college-english/write-for-us/#AGT.

Cushman, Ellen. "Translingual and Decolonial Approaches to Meaning Making." *College English*, vol. 78, no. 3, 2016, pp. 234-42.

---. "Wampum, Sequoyan, and Story: Decolonizing the Digital Archive." *College English* vol. 76, no. 2, 2013, pp. 115-35.

Driskill, Qwo-Li. "Decolonial Skillshares: Indigenous Rhetorics as Radical Practice." *Survivance, Sovereignty, and Story: Teaching American Indian Rhetorics*, edited by Lisa King, Rose Gubele, and Joyce Rain Anderson, Utah State UP, 2015, pp. 57-78.

Dyste, Connie. "Proposition 63: The California English Language Amendment." *Applied Linguistics*, vol. 10, no. 3, 1989, pp. 313-30.

Ferris, Dana R., and John Hedgcock. *Teaching ESL Composition: Purpose, Process, and Practice*. Routledge, 2004.

García, Ofelia, Susana Ibarra Johnson, and Kate Seltzer. *The Translanguaging Classroom: Leveraging Student Bilingualism for Learning*. Caslon, 2017.

Gilley, Bruce. "The Case for Colonialism." *Third World Quarterly*, 2017, pp. 1-17.

Gilyard, Keith. "The Rhetoric of Translingualism." *College English*, vol. 78, no. 3, 2016, pp. 284-89.

Guerra, Juan C. "Cultivating a Rhetorical Sensibility in the Translingual Writing Classroom." *College English*, vol. 78, no. 3, 2016, pp. 228-33.

Haas, Angela. "Toward a Decolonial Digital and Visual American Indian Rhetorics Pedagogy." *Survivance, Sovereignty, and Story: Teaching American Indian Rhetorics*, edited by Lisa King, Rose Gubele, and Joyce Rain Anderson, 2015, pp. 188-208.

Hernandez-Zamora, Gregorio. *Decolonizing Literacy: Mexican Lives in the Era of Global Capitalism*, 2010.

Horner, Bruce, Min-Zhan Lu, Jacqueline Jones Royster, and John Trimbur. "Language Difference in Writing: Toward a Translingual Approach." *College English*, vol. 73, no. 3, 2011, pp. 303-21.

Horner, Bruce, Samantha NeCamp, and Christiane Donahue. "Toward a Multilingual Composition Scholarship: From English Only to a Translingual Norm." *CCC*, vol. 63, no. 2, 2011, pp. 269-300.

Horner, Bruce, and John Trimbur. "English Only and U.S. College Composition." *CCC*, vol. 53, no. 4, 2002, pp. 594-630.

León-Portilla, Miguel. *The Broken Spears: The Aztec Account of the Conquest of Mexico*. Trans. Lysander Kemp, Beacon, 1992.

Lu, Min-Zahn, and Bruce Horner. "Introduction: Translingual Work." *College English* vol. 78, no. 3, 2016, pp. 207-18.

Martinez, Aja Y. "'The American Way': Resisting the Empire of Force and Color-Blind Racism." *College English*, vol. 71, no. 6, 2009, pp. 584-95.

Martinez, Aja Y, Cruz Medina, and Gloria Howerton. "Comment and Response: A Response to Kim Hensley Owens's 'In Lak'ech, the Chicano Clap, and Fear: A Partial Rhetorical Autopsy of Tucson's Now-Illegal Ethnic Studies Classes.'" *College English*, vol. 80, no. 6, 2018, pp. 539-45.

Massaro, Rachel, and Alesandro Najera. *Silicon Valley Index*. Joint Venture: Silicon Valley Institute for Regional Studies, 2014.

Matsuda, Paul Kei. "The Myth of Linguistic Homogeneity in US College Composition." *College English*, vol. 68 vol. 6, 2006, pp. 637-51.

Medina, Cruz. "Nuestros Refranes: Culturally Relevant Writing in Tucson High Schools." *Reflections: A Journal of Public Rhetoric, Civic Writing, and Service Learning*, vol. 12, no. 3, 2013, pp. 52-79.

Mignolo, Walter. *The Darker Side of the Renaissance: Literacy, Territoriality, and Colonization*. U of Michigan P, 1995.

---. "Delinking." *Cultural Studies*, vol. 21, no. 2, 2007, pp. 449-514.

---. "Epistemic Disobedience, Independent Thought and Decolonial Freedom." *Theory, Culture and Society*, vol. 26, no. 7-8, 2009, pp. 159-81.

Palmeri, Jason. *Remixing Composition: A History of Multimodal Writing Pedagogy*. SIUP, 2012.

Pennycook, Alastair. "English as a Language always in Translation." *European Journal of English Studies*, vol. 12, no. 1, 2008, pp. 33-47.

Powell, Malea. "2012 CCCC Chair's Address: Stories Take Place: A Performance in One Act." *CCC*, vol. 64, no. 2, 2012, pp. 383-406.

Ruiz, Iris, and Raúl Sánchez. "Introduction." *Decolonizing Rhetoric and Composition Studies: New Latinx Keywords for Theory and Pedagogy*, edited by Iris Ruiz and Raúl Sánchez, Palgrave MacMillan, 2016, pp. xiii-xx.

Selfe, Cynthia L. "The Movement of Air, the Breath of Meaning: Aurality and Multimodal Composing." *CCC*, vol. 60, no. 4, 2009, pp. 616-63.

Shipka, Jody. "Transmodality in/and Processes of Making: Changing Dispositions and Practice." *College English*, vol. 78, no. 3, 2016, pp. 250-57.

"U.S. English Efforts Lead West Virginia to Become 32nd State to Recognize English as Official Language." U.S. English, Inc., 5 March 2016, www.usenglish.org/u-s-english-efforts-lead-west-virginia-to-become-32nd-state-to-recognize-english-as-official-language/.

Villanueva Jr, Victor. *Bootstraps: From an American Academic of Color*, NCTE, 1993.

---. "On the Rhetoric and Precedents of Racism." *CCC*, vol. 50, no. 4, 1999, pp. 645-61.

Young, Vershawn. "Call for Program Proposals: Performance-Rhetoric, Performance-Composition." NCTE CCCC, cccc.ncte.org/cccc/conv/call-2019.

The Reader in the Textbook: Embodied Materiality and Reading in the Writing Classroom

Carolyne M. King

While composition research recognizes the importance of the body and bodily knowledge, literacy instruction, especially as relayed in writing textbooks, often disembodies the material practice of reading. This move, in turn, contributes to normative assumptions about students' corporeal reading experiences. Drawing together scholarship on embodiment, disability, and reading pedagogies in an analysis of popular composition textbooks, this article showcases common methods that cast reading and the reader as disembodied in instructional materials. I argue that by ignoring the materiality of reading and its instruction, we ignore the body's role in meaning making and thus limit our students' understanding of their own corporeal and situated responses to texts. This article calls attention to reading as always material and embodied and encourages composition instructors to seek out teaching methods that will help students to investigate their bodily knowledge of a text.

I don't play music when I am reading or writing anymore and have to find a silent area to do my work.

—Jesse

Some strategies I have found to help me when reading digital texts is to print them off. I have found out that the best way I can read is highlighting.

—Maria

I have begun to highlight as I read as well as turning off my phone.

—Owen

I turn to embodied rhetoric because one body cannot stand in for another, constructed or not, as lived experiences in a specific body help shape the ways in which that body, that person, make sense of the world.

—Abby Knoblauch (2012)

As teachers, it is easy for us to look at statements like those of Jesse, Maria, and Owen[1] and see an acknowledgment of the reading practices we already encourage: highlighting, annotating, creating conditions for good attention and focusing upon what is to be learned. Yet in their seemingly simple descriptions of reading practices, these first-year students also articulate the impact of materiality, showing that reading practices cannot be separated from corporeal aspects of interacting with texts. In the students' reflections, reading is thus a material activity, not merely a cognitive one, because they express meaning making as a bodily experience, understood in the process of using physical activities like highlighting or sitting in silence. As such, their bodies both act and are acted upon by the tools and objects in their environment and which may mediate or participate in their literate activities. By emphasizing the materiality of the practices that enhance meaning making, the students' reflections contribute to what Abby Knoblauch describes as "embodied rhetoric." These students articulate the "lived experiences in [their] specific bod[ies]" (Knoblauch 60) through which they make sense of the world, or at least of a text they have read.

Drawing together Knoblauch's description of embodied rhetoric with these students' emphasis on the corporeality of their textual interactions calls attention to the need for an embodied, material approach to reading instruction. Yet, attentiveness to corporeal practice, especially within composition textbooks, remains limited. While our instructional texts often reference the conditions that the epigraphs touch upon, they rarely address reading embodiment in a sustained fashion. In fact, reading instruction in textbooks largely continues a tradition of treating students as disembodied heads—focusing upon critical thinking without attending to the corporeal experiences of the students who are to replicate specified interpretive practices. Exhortations like "pa[y] attention to what you read" (Lunsford et al. 25) are common, yet students are rarely asked to think about what their bodies feel like when they "pay attention" to a text; rather, they are given a list of focal points to "pay attention to" and descriptions of activities that may (or may not) demonstrate attention—things like highlighting, underlining, and looking up key terms. Moreover, such practices are positioned separately from the body's influence and experience of reading—for example, textbooks do not ask students to notice what it feels like when they made the decision to underline, or what the physical movement required to highlight adds to their reading experience. Problematically, then, the textbooks that populate our composition classrooms often promote a narrow and distorted perspective on the physical experience of reading and thus of

---

1. The names of students are pseudonyms. The excerpted student comments were collected from an IRB-approved study of classroom materials, including this written reflection on their reading practices, during spring 2016.

the body's influence on reading practices. If students are to better understand the ways in which they create meaning when they read, then we must create conditions in our classrooms for students to investigate the manner in which their embodied, corporeal presence participates in meaning making.

While neglected in instructional texts, we have long known that the body plays an important role in meaning making. It was more than twenty years ago, for example, that Christina Haas emphasized how tools and technologies create new ways of bodily knowing that impact writing. A few years later in 1999, Kristie Fleckenstein used the idea of "somatic minds" to describe the way that "mind and body [are] a permeable, intertextual territory that is continually made and remade" (281), and in 2004 Sondra Perl described bodily knowledge as a kind of "felt sense," arguing that "meaning emerges not only from cognition but also from intuition" and that "the body itself is implicated in knowing and in the construction of knowledge" (xvi). Also during the last twenty years, feminist and disability studies scholarship has continued to emphasize the body as a way of knowing (Alaimo and Hekman; Conboy et al.; Dolmage; Lewiecki-Wilson and Brueggemann; Wilson and Lewiecki-Wilson). As reading instructors, we can draw upon these theories in order to help our students recognize the embodied materiality of their reading practices. Much as Jesse, Owen, and Maria note the impact of physical aspects of their reading experiences, we must guide students in reflecting upon their "felt-senses," their intuitive understandings that are part of engaging with a text.

Contrasting with this theoretical emphasis on the body, composition textbooks continue a tradition of cursory attention to corporeal experience, reproducing the neglect of students' embodied experiences. While a few recent publications, like Elizabeth Losh et al.'s *Understanding Rhetoric*—which uses a graphic medium rather than alphabetic text to engage students—have begun to challenge disembodied approaches to reading, composition textbooks largely continue to overlook materiality and its influence upon the composing processes of students. This inattention is doubly troublesome for reading instruction, often relegated to a single chapter in a writing textbook and thus already the subject of limited attention. Even when consideration is given to reading's materiality, as in Lisa Ede's *The Academic Writer: A Brief Guide*, in which Chapter Two, "Reading Rhetorically," draws attention to "Understanding How Medium and Device Affect Your Reading," the influence of this consideration is undercut because reading instruction remains ancillary to the focus on writing. The various textbooks that populate our composition classrooms—from rhetorics to readers to writing guides—consistently overlook the importance and impact of our students' bodies to the experience of reading. Yet Losh et al.'s and Ede's recent publications suggest that the time is ripe for us to attend more thoroughly to the body's role in meaning making. We can no longer ignore the "lived experience of a specific body," to reference Knoblauch (60).

Many composition textbooks give only cursory attention to the materiality of the reading experience. For example, Lester Faigley's *Writing: A Guide for College and Beyond*, Sidney Dobrin's *Writing Situations*, and John Ramage et al.'s *The Allyn and Bacon Guide to Writing* all mention notetaking, annotation, and highlighting texts as necessary reading practices for students. Even though the advice they offer references material practices of reading, the bodily involvement of notetaking and the sensory aspects of highlighting receive no attention. For example, Ramage et al. advise students to "[m]ake extensive marginal notes as you read. Expert readers seldom use highlighters, which encourage passive, inefficient reading" (96), and Faigley directs them to "read with a pencil in hand" because "pens and highlighters don't erase" (21). Despite pointing towards the bodily experience of reading as mediated by distinct tools, both texts fail to engage readers' lived experiences or invite reflection upon these practices. Moreover, such admonishments ignore a wide variety of readers and practices, including those who use audiobooks or record verbal comments for annotation, for example. Furthermore, neither do they draw attention to how print versus digital texts create different bodily knowledge of a text through technologies and visual design. A robust discussion of corporeality and its influence is necessary if we are to help students deepen their understanding of literacy and of the embodied materiality of their own reading processes.

While reading pedagogy may avoid explicit discussion of corporeal experience, reading itself is always material. Just as the reader's bodily experience matters, so, too, does the text's physical structure and substance as it impacts the reader's encounter. The corporeality of the text effects its use, as when a book's narrow margins make it difficult for a reader to annotate paragraphs. Corporeality, however, does not apply to print texts exclusively. The importance of attending to the text's structure and physical experience appears most often alongside attention to the proliferation of new media and the impact of digitization (Baron; Wysocki et al.). While electronic texts offer new strategies for interaction—using the search function to selectively read passages around key terms, for instance—much of the attention to new media continues to emphasize cognitive, rather than embodied, engagement. For example, scholars interested in the internet's impact on cognition have even used neurological imaging to better understand what the brain looks like as reading occurs (Small and Vorgan). Yet this perspective largely focuses upon changing technologies, an emphasis that subtly gives agency to literacy tools as they act upon the body, and which overlooks how the bodily experience of reading is rather an interaction between the reader and their literacy tools. Therefore, much of the attention to digitization continues the trend of overlooking how the reader's material, embodied experience of reading is actually a complex interaction between their body and the use of various literacy tools. Although such research offers new perspectives on reading, it has not facilitated greater attention in composition textbooks to the physical experience of reading, nor a pedagogy that emphasizes reading as an embodied practice.

Moving towards remedying this neglect, this essay foregrounds the treatment of reading in two reading-focused textbooks. While many composition textbooks include instruction in reading, David Bartholomae and Anthony Petrosky's *Ways of Reading* (*Ways*) and Mariolina Salvatori and Patricia Donahue's *The Elements (and Pleasures) of Difficulty* (*Elements*) center reading and have been widely recognized for their rigorous approaches (Carillo "Reading"; Harris; Hutchings and Huber; Lockhart and Soliday; Salvatori "Conversations"; Sweeney and McBride). These texts contribute to classroom norms about the interaction between reader and text because they offer authoritative instruction in how students *should* read. As such, they are evocative sites of study.

In arguing that reading instruction overlooks an embodied and material understanding of reading, I first draw on disability studies scholarship to focus on the way pedagogical design can create or hinder access. Disability scholarship calls attention to embodiment by continually emphasizing how our experiences are always bodily; in doing so, it demonstrates the manner in which normed expectations enforce bodily conformity and divide bodies into normal or deviant categories. Because reading is always material and embodied, this lens calls attention to the limited ways that the instructional texts we use help students investigate and learn about reading as a physical, as well as cognitive, knowledge process. The second section of this essay applies this theoretical discussion to concrete classroom materials. I identify three problematic patterns shared across *Ways* and *Elements*: first, in the form and structure—the materiality—of these texts, each promotes an assumption of an able-bodied reader; second, each describes reading in a disembodied manner, failing to attend to the corporeality of the reading experience; and third, student success narratives in these textbooks construct a limited performance of reading that enacts a normative identity position for student users.

Ultimately, I suggest that when textbooks ignore the materiality of reading and its instruction, teachers are encouraged to ignore the body's role in meaning making and thus limit students' understanding of their own corporeal and situated responses to texts. The essay concludes by suggesting ways in which teachers can highlight embodiment and the materiality of reading through various classroom exercises and deliberate classroom attention to textbooks. It thus promotes an understanding of reading as rooted in the corporeal materiality of the reader reading. Doing so, it pushes back against a longstanding academic tradition—reproduced by instructional materials and the practices recommended by these guides—of failing to treat students and their meaning-making processes as shaped by specific material experiences.

When We Disembody Reading: Learning from Disability Studies

Trends in reading scholarship increasingly stress that reading instruction should emphasize "how" students read. For example, Linda Adler-Kassner and Heidi Estrem remind teachers of the importance of "considering what we ask students to read, how we ask them to read it and why" (35), and they ultimately argue for greater attention to "practice-based reading" where students examine the context of the reading and the activity itself (42-45). Ellen Carillo's suggestion of the passage-based paper ("Making") and Meghan Sweeney and Maureen McBride's recent study of difficulty papers echoes this attention, as each closely analyzes students' responses to texts and offers teachers insight into student practice. Reflecting these values more broadly, even traditional approaches like close reading and rhetorical reading have been re-appraised, with scholars arguing for renewed attention to the multiple practices that make up each of these oft-referenced activities (Bialotsky; Brent; Bunn). As such, recent reading scholarship pushes back against "an impoverished and reductive understanding of reading" (xiii), instead situating reading as a network of "human activities" (xiv) that is epistemic and explorative (Sullivan et al.). Ellen Carillo's "mindful framework" certainly illustrates this understanding as she argues that students' ability to transfer reading knowledge from one activity or environment to another requires them to "become knowledgeable, deliberate, and reflective about how they read and the demands that contexts place on their reading" ("Creating" 11). Collectively, this attention to the manner in which students read is poised to welcome a material, embodied approach to reading instruction that is rooted in students' particular experiences.

While the new responsiveness to how students read invites attention to their individual practices, instructors' expectations of students' abilities to engage in reading practices remain largely unarticulated and unexamined. Disability studies, which emphasizes the way unexamined values often limit access, draws attention to such oversights and can help to unpack unarticulated expectations of the student reader. For, as Cynthia Leweicki-Wilson and Brenda Brueggeman powerfully remind teachers, differently abled bodies and minds highlight embodiment as always present because bodies that move and perform differently showcase the tendency to "ignore embodied aspects of learning and treat students as detached minds" (6). Because disability often disrupts the "'normal ways of doing things'" (6), it throws into relief those unspoken expectations about embodied learning experiences.

Disability scholar Rosemarie Garland-Thomson, investigating the impact of assumptions about how bodies and minds work, famously defines our collective expectation as a "normate"(8)—or what she describes as the physical manifestation of the collective, un-stigmatized characteristics of a culture. Normates create an unexamined "everyman" which simultaneously suggests that all students should be able to do X or to understand Y without providing any attention to dominant discourses and how such expectations are produced. For example, a normate-oriented perspective equates a textbook with an object that all students can hold, carry, and read regardless of tight lines of text or other physical obstacles. In other words, such textbooks assume an able-bodied student. Only by being centered in students' embodied sense of meaning making can reading instruction instead bring attention to the evolving state of literate practices, practices that themselves flex and change in response to alterations in the materials of reading and the corporeality of the reader. While it is important to recognize how normates shape instructors' and students' expectations of literate activities, merely critiquing activities and practices as founded upon normate assumptions is largely ineffective. Rather, as Garland-Thomson explains, analyses that point out the normate should not stop at simple dichotomies but should work to reveal the interrelational aspects of social life that rely upon the normate. Responding to this charge, incorporating materiality into reading instruction not only reveals the normate, but also emphasizes that all practices occur in and through the bodies of students—bodies that differ and use texts in varied ways.

Textbooks make visible our expectations regarding students' literate practices because they describe what students should do when reading. Long recognized as sources of authority and guidance, textbooks represent and enforce ideological and identity positions upon their consumers (Connors; Gale; Jordan; Marinara et al.). While instructors may not proscriptively follow a textbook, these manuals do guide curriculum development and classroom activities. As such, while textbooks may not give us perfect insight into classroom practices or even how real, embodied teachers utilize these manuals with their equally embodied students, textbooks do reflect dominant disciplinary norms and assumptions. Indeed, the authoritative standing of textbooks, particularly within composition programs, shapes the views and practices of instructors and students (Miller; Welch). Because of their authority and the constancy of their use, textbooks can help us to understand the way that theories of reading permeate college writing classrooms and normate constructions of readers.

No Bodies: Normative Assumptions and the Restriction of Reading Practice

Although few fyw textbooks focus explicitly on reading, *Ways* and *Elements* direct their attention to helping students gain critical reading practices through specific ways of interacting with texts. Reading is, of course, addressed in many composition textbooks, but these two maintain an intentional emphasis upon how students should learn to interact with texts. In particular, they promote an understanding of reading as meaning making (not merely an activity requiring comprehension) and thus of students' powers as readers. While more recent textbooks like Ellen Carillo's 2017 publication, *A Writer's Guide to Mindful Reading*, may also focus upon reading instruction explicitly, *Ways* and *Elements* have garnered scholarly accolades and have served as the focus of classroom study (Carillo "Reading"; Harris; Hutchings and Huber; Lockhart and Soliday; Salvatori "Conversations"; Sweeney and McBride). The recognition of their approaches in composition scholarship—suggesting both widespread appeal and use—implies that these texts have changed the way we think about instructing students in reading. As my study proposes to investigate the predominant manner in which textbooks prescribe reading practices, *Ways* and *Elements* are paradigmatic sites. Carefully examining normative assumptions about reading—be they in the textbooks of our discipline or in our classrooms—can help us to make our classrooms more accessible and more useful to our students as they decide upon what it means to read.

Form and Structure: Guiding Material Reading Practices

To approach these textbooks as would student readers, we must first confront the materiality of the books themselves. Physically, *Ways* is an imposing textbook, weighing in at almost 1.5 pounds. *Ways* has a shiny, flexible cover and thin, slippery, white pages printed with black text. *Elements* shares some of these qualities, as it also has a shiny, flexible cover and uses paragraphs with full justification as the default reading form. As the figure below shows, both texts use long, fully justified block paragraphs—a presentation that assumes a reader whose eyes can easily maintain focus upon a single line of text.

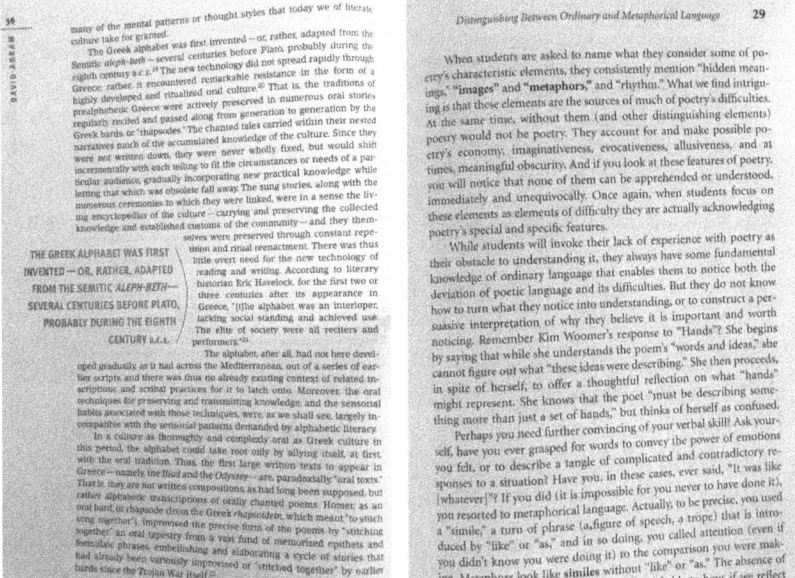

Fig. 1. On the left, a page from *Ways*; on the right, a page from *Elements*. These images show *Ways*' preferred use of callouts to draw attention to important passages, whereas *Elements* often uses bolded text, as shown.

Font size further implies a reader whose eyes easily focus upon small text, as both books use a typical point size for a written text, between 10-12 points for body text. While all of *Elements* is written in a serif font, parts of *Ways*, including the introductory chapter and the framing comments and the questions for readings, are written in a sans-serif font. Although *Ways* uses callouts and *Elements* incorporates bullet points and bolded text, there is little in the way of typographical features that help call attention to the end of a sentence or paragraph. Moreover, choosing to use minimal margins and spacing between paragraphs means that only a small amount of white space breaks up the reading experience and that the text does not provide places for the eye to rest. In sum, the design of both texts limits readers' abilities to do more than underline or highlight; any form of notetaking or annotation must occur outside of the printed page.

These textbooks reinforce a traditional formatting through their materiality and do not encourage students to notice physical aspects of page design or spacing and its impact on their reading experience. As Stephen Bernhardt argues, texts "display their structures through white space, graphic patterning, enumerative sequences, and so on" (67) and taking note of these details benefits students in both reading and writing. While the design of these textbooks emphasizes their authority and the seriousness of their academic work via the formal organization schema and limited ability of the reader to mark up the text, such features do not help readers to develop insight into the materiality of the reading experience. Rather, these textbooks conform to norms as readers must be able to physically hold and turn pages and be able to see relatively small and tightly spaced text. Readers also must be able to read a page holistically which allows easier noting of paragraph breaks rather than having to use, for instance, a magnifying glass or other tool that often limits the reader's ability to experience the full scope of the page peripherally. In short, the design of these textbooks does not encourage the reader to reflect upon their bodily relationship to the text.

While printed textbooks do not allow readers to manipulate text size themselves, using various fonts or typeface sizes throughout the text, for example, could build student awareness of the constraints of materiality and could help them to consider the impact of typographical features on the reading experience. Emphasizing the importance of such considerations, a study by Aries Arditi, for example, describes the way typographical features impact a reader's relationship to the text. Because *Ways* and *Elements* do not emphasize the impact of materiality on the reader, their designs stand at odds with the reflective reading practices explicitly encouraged by both reading scholars and the textbook authors themselves. Currently, the materiality of these books structures the student's textual experience without ever encouraging the reader to question these designs and to examine their impact. Admittedly, these design choices are very typical of textbooks and reflect a normate construction of readers and reading materials in the classroom, but it is this very ubiquity that makes creating such awareness in our students necessary. For when they contribute to constructing a normate, our materials do not reflect the implicit invitation to consider corporeality and embodiment that lies within so much of the extant reading scholarship. For example, how might textbook materials limit students' approaches to reading as a mindful "way of being" as recommended by Carillo? If teachers and textbooks reinforce a specific construction of reading, then the prescriptive materiality of such texts also narrows the ways that students may be able to reflect upon their reading experiences, despite teachers' best intentions.

Disembodied Reading Practices

It is not only the physical presence of the volumes that winnows to a normate reader, but also the reading pedagogy that implicitly hails a specific, able-bodied reader. Both Salvatori and Donahue and Bartholomae and Petrosky emphasize reading as a process of interpretation, inviting students to go beyond merely memorizing content. In emphasizing the process of interpretation, they use embodied language—drawing upon evocative, body-centric description to portray reading as a process of understanding in which both text and reader contribute to meaning making. Yet, embodied language, as Knoblauch reminds us, "echoes bodily functions and bodily motives" (52). Because bodies function and experience differently, such language can mean different things to different people. "The multiplicity of potential response," Knoblauch warns, "is one of the things that makes embodied language so tricky" (54) as it is as likely to forge a connection with the reader through shared experience as it is to drive them further away by highlighting a different way of being.

Ironically, perhaps, *Ways* and *Elements* disembody the reading experience even as they use embodied language. Each text ultimately focuses on reading and writing as solely cognitive work rather than investigating the body's contribution to the process of meaning making. The focus upon reading as a cognitive, imaginative activity appears most strongly in *Ways*' use of the metaphor of conversation to describe reading. Bartholomae and Petrosky describe the roles and elements of "speaking," "listening," "talk[ing] back to," "hearing" (1-5) and even turn-taking to describe the back and forth "social interaction" that is reading. While numerous bodily markers appear as part of their metaphorical description, including, for example, "when you read, you hear an author's voice"; "you believe a person ... is talking to you"; writing occurs when "the author is silent" (1-2), the authors fail to fully commit to this metaphor by discussing the way that conversations are embodied. While Bartholomae and Petrosky invite students to utilize what they know of conversation to understand reading, their description does not engage how conversation is embodied: Bodies move differently in conversation based upon race, gender, class, and dis/ability; yet these differences, and thus how the body impacts conversation, are never addressed.

Whereas *Ways* describes reading as a conversation, *Elements* introduces reading as a transaction. Salvatori and Donahue ask readers to think about the nature of transaction as "something that occurs between living beings, how getting and keeping a transaction going is determined by the participants" (6). They then detail things like "voice" and the responsibility of the reader "[t]o hear this voice" (7). Much like the failure to embody conversation in *Ways*, Salvatori and Donahue rely upon embodied language to describe the relationship between reader and text without considering the specific experience of the body that they call upon. Their approach to reading as a form of mental activity thus prominently invokes embodied language while simultaneously disembodying reading. Salvatori and Donahue write: "insofar as reading involves thinking—thinking the thoughts of another, inhabiting someone else's mind, temporarily adapting somebody else's argument—learning to read in ways that nurture this flexibility of mind can be good preparation for encountering and working through difficult life situations" (3). To those of us versed in academic discourse, these descriptions may appear as merely being that of a generous, engaged reader. However, these descriptions call attention to the need to approach reading by engaging embodied readers and their reading experiences. As scholars focusing upon materiality and embodiment constantly remind, discourse circulates through an actual body. We cannot simply "inhabi[t] someone else's mind" (3) as if their perspective took shape outside of their lived experience and identity—communicated in and through the body. Similarly, describing reading as conversation requires attending to the corporeal aspects, the body language, that is always present in such interactions as well. Although using embodied language seems to invite attention to reading as a corporeal and material process, ultimately the descriptions in *Ways* and *Elements* fail to engage the reader in reflecting upon the manner in which the body is involved in reading.

Much as the physical presence of the textbooks work against the individualized reading experience that each exhorts, students are also surprisingly limited in the ways that they can make use of these descriptions of the reading process. While the embodied language in *Ways* and *Elements* suggests that the body is always present and indeed, is even necessary to help describe to students how reading occurs, this language falls short of encouraging students to reflect upon the ways their own experiences echo, or disconnect from, the manner in which bodies are described in the textbooks. In practice, the refutation of the bodies' importance in meaning making creates what Susan Bordo criticizes as a "dis-embodied view from nowhere" (4) which supports the belief that the body can be transcended. This view, especially within academic discourse, is synonymous with an unspoken acceptance of all positions implicitly reflecting that of the dominant body in the discourse: white, heteronormative, and male (Knoblauch 58-59). Thus, by ignoring the embodied experience of student-readers, the model interpretive practices easily slip back into promoting normative, hegemonic discourse. This discourse further elides the lived identity of the reader and the personal, social and historical contexts that impact the way they make meaning. In the section that follows, the stories about reading that the authors tell show exactly why it is vital to always consider the real people that these textbooks are instructing in desired reading practices.

Stories About Reading: A Disembodied Student Performance

Ways and *Elements* each use the story of a real—not hypothetical—student to exemplify their ideal reading process and outcome. These stories "embody" students in an effort to connect with the equally embodied reader of the textbook. However, the presentation of these model students lacks particular details necessary to promote a corporeal understanding of the physical and material reading practices these model stories are intended to describe. In this way, these anecdotes serve to concretize a normate reader, rather than to create circumstances that would help the textbook's reader to reflect upon their own embodied meaning-making process. Doing so, these idealized narratives narrow and limit the possible, successful student reader and their reading practices.

Although they may appear innocuous, these stories inevitably inscribe a normate of expected student performance. In *Ways*, readers are introduced to an unnamed student who goes from writing a "not wrong" essay to creating a text that is "not nearly so confident and skillful" but where "thought is taken seriously" (13-14). Responding to a difficult reading by Paulo Freire, the student describes his process, saying "'I read through the Freire essay, and I worked with what I understood and I ignored the rest" (13). Of course, "ignor[ing] the rest" is not a desirable practice as Bartholomae and Petrosky explain, and the student ultimately finds success after copious revision and focusing upon what he did not understand in his first reading. The narrative is intended to describe the embodied experience of the common student. To this end, the student is deliberately unnamed: no picture of the student is given; no description of the student—his race, class, dis/ability, appears; indeed, the story elides any particular characteristics of him or of his reading practices. Yet by omitting these details about the student and his actual practices, it also fails to describe the physicality of the reading process itself. Neither the student essay that accompanies the story nor Bartholomae and Petrosky's own comments explicitly reference how the student might use re-reading, or how his eyes moved, or how he took notes or used a dictionary to look up unfamiliar terms. In fact, his actual experience and process of reading remains mysterious and invisible to the reader of the textbook. Despite the fact that Bartholomae and Petrosky emphasize that the point of the story is "what has happened to the writer's understanding of what it means to *work* on reading" (11, emphasis original), they do not create a context that allows the textbook's reader to actually understand the way in which this work takes place, work that is grounded in the tools and bodily experiences of the unnamed student.

The student story in *Elements* functions similarly. Salvatori and Donahue introduce the example student, Kim Woomer, as part of an explanation for why students should pay attention to difficulty and to work on reading difficult texts despite common beliefs in natural ability. Paralleling learning to read with difficulty to the work of "genuinely talented artists" or peak "tennis players" who can "effortlessly" (3) perform—because of the hours of hidden practice that lead to this performance—Salvatori and Donahue use Woomer's essay where she explains the "difficulty of thinking about difficulty" (3) to encourage students to try out this approach. However, Woomer is not embodied in the presentation of her story. Once again, the reader receives no details about who she is as a student in the class; as a woman in the academy; her age; her race; in short, her presence in the world and its influence on her meaning-making processes remain obscured. Instead, the closing lines of the excerpt from Woomer's reflection are emphasized: "[T]he difficulties I have in understanding poetry can be overcome with some extra work. Through this extra work I personally have discovered certain strategies that help me overcome my obstacles" (4). A reader mindful of the materiality of practice might ask: what "certain strategies" were discovered? How might these strategies be accessible to another reader? Why aren't these strategies described? Woomer's actual practices are noticeably lacking yet Salvatori and Donahue's commentary only reinforces this: "As Woomer tells us, by *reframing* her understanding of difficulty and doing extra work, she made an important discovery" (4). No attention to the actual embodied process of understanding difficulty or reading is given. For the narrative to model what student readers of the textbook should do, it needs to be specific as to the embodied meaning that Woomer experienced. Such description might encourage other student readers to engage their own embodiment—at least in how their experiences and practices are similar to or different from Woomer's.

While these stories thus offer a pseudo-embodiment of reading, the narratives continue to cloak reading practice in invisibility and to deny reading as an embodied experience. In doing so, the stories enact a moralizing and normative identity position as necessary for successful student performances as readers. Joseph Janangelo has argued that narratives about student experiences are used to endorse those practices sanctioned by the discipline (94). Accordingly, the stories in these textbooks model the reader position that students are expected to take up. Although useful for illustrating the desired student performance, these stories are not "position-neutral pedagogical improvisation" (Rex et al. 769). As Lesley Rex and colleagues point out, classroom stories attempt to motivate students to "enac[t] . . . acquired schemas of thought and expression" (769) by imitating the "successful" student performance. Thus, even stories that ostensibly celebrate student success can elide the complexity of the learning experience and ignore the potential violence enacted upon the student's identity. This is perhaps easiest to see in Salvatori and Donahue's commentary about Woomer's reflection: "She got there when she learned to ask . . . *the kind of questions that her teacher had asked*" (4, emphasis added). Salvatori and Donahue's final description about the narrative ultimately constructs achievement for user-readers as "predicated on following instructions and listening to teachers" (Janangelo 101). Ultimately, both narratives construct these students as disembodied models that easily and fluidly perform in the teacher-sanctioned practices of the classroom.

In positioning stories of exemplary students without details as to the social and material ways in which they create meaning, textbooks cut off these model students from the specific aspects of embodiment that contribute to success. Research on literacy practices in various communities has long reminded educators that the expected process of reading and interpreting a text within the educational curriculum is best approximated in the home literacies of white, middle-class households (Edwards and Turner). Thus, the model students in *Ways* and *Elements* may be exemplary performers because the material conditions of their prior existence most closely align with the classroom. Because there is no attention to the identities of these students, we lack the context necessary to understand the way they responded to the material practices of reading in that specific classroom. If we do not position model stories with attention to embodied materiality, then, much as Janangelo suggests, stories will continue to "control" user-readers by "show[ing] the discernible progress that a good student makes by obediently following the rules" (95).

As textbook readers who were not present in the originating classroom context, we read incomplete narratives, cut off from important experiential information that might allow us to embody and to better understand the students' narratives. By obscuring the reality from which these stories emerge, textbooks replicate the dominant normative constructions in which only certain bodies and speakers matter in society. Doing so, they enact barriers to gaining literacy for students whose social and material realities do not match an assumed norm. When considering the guided instructions a textbook offers, teachers must be critical of the specific habitus they seek to enforce and the way this may structure access for the students in our classrooms. In contrast to the normative reading descriptions in textbooks, approaching reading through embodiment requires attention to the particulars of reading processes and thus encourages students to recognize the ways in which materiality impacts meaning making, and how their prior experiences inflect each engagement with a text.

"Looking Deeper into Reading": Creating Material and Embodied Practices

Textbooks—in their materiality, in their use of common metaphors like that of conversation, and in the presentation of success narratives—create a normate reader and thus limit the potential for teachers and students to create meaning relevant to their actual, embodied situations. As teachers, we must call attention to the process of meaning making that these texts outline, ultimately requiring this process to be situated in the social and material aspects of students' literacies. In this way, we can push back against normative conceptions of reading that pervade our classrooms and instructional practices.

Teaching reading as an embodied and material approach requires recognizing that while reading is of course a cognitive activity, it is also and equally a physical, social, and emotional one. It particularly promotes understanding the body's impact on meaning making and requires us to take seriously how students' bodies create their experience of a text. When reading, the material conditions of the text act upon the body; for example, eye movement differs for a digital versus printed text (Mangen et al.). However, the body also enacts the reading experience: It retains and produces practices that reflect students' various communities because the body houses their sociocultural identity. As such, instructing students in reading following an embodied and material approach requires us to:

- Recognize that the materiality of the text acts on the reader and participates in meaning making (as it contributes to and even shapes the reading experience, and the reader's bodily perception of that experience).
- Emphasize individual meaning-making even as we seek to help students recognize and situate their responses within larger discourse communities, both academically and socially.
- Include multiple ways of knowing, especially because our students may gravitate to modes other than text-based ones, and thus their reading experiences may be more or less informed by spatial, visual, and environmental markers.
- Embrace students' ownership of their reading experience and encourage them to investigate and understand it, particularly by examining the efficacies for reading practices in specific contexts. Doing so may require students to challenge normative assumptions about how their bodies and minds work, especially when those assumptions foreclose multiple ways of knowing.

We can begin this practice by helping students to more deeply engage with the textbooks we already use—whether by changing the mediums in which they experience the textbook, or by drawing attention to typographic features and how they influence attention to the text itself. Emphasizing how their reading experience is constructed through textual features can begin a discussion with students about the manner in which these constructions impact their meaning-making processes.

Attention to reading as a material practice can start by inviting students to attend to their use of texts and devices in the classroom. Activities and assignments around this principle vary, although each emphasizes the constraints different tools create and thus the differing experiences produced by these tools. For example, recently Kathleen Yancey and colleagues describe three activities—a syllabus redesign, a reading practice inventory reflection, and an assignment on annotating in three different mediums (print, computer, and phone)—that encourage students "to consider how the technologies involved in these practices are beneficial or detrimental" to their meaning-making process (52). Yancey et al. conclude that "our best opportunity to help students make good choices as they read and research is to engage them in considering" (54) how they make meaning, and how the materiality of the reading experience impacts that meaning.

Forwarding these types of activities, we can apply the principles of an embodied and material approach to reading by calling attention to students' experiences of texts and of different ways of knowing. Patricia Dunn, in *Talking, Sketching, Moving*, argues that "all writers would benefit from multiple intellectual pathways to generate knowledge" (1) and describes how to draw upon different modalities in designing our classrooms, specifically by decreasing our reliance on one way of knowing—writing. For reading, we can engage our students in making their engagement with a text perceivable in multiple ways. Utilizing aspects of DIY crafts, we might ask students to cut apart and re-arrange readings in order to create texts that mirror their own process of engagement: What do students select, ignore, reorder, or remove? When composing their reading experience, students can utilize different typefaces and fonts, physically directing reader attention to relevant passages; they can even disrupt a linear progression through the text to model what occurs experientially for them while reading. Construction-oriented activities offer opportunities for examining source use in more depth as well. Students can create conversations between sources to illustrate the constituent voices that make up academic texts. These conversations can take various corporeal forms, from a dramatic dialogue to a hand-drawn map.

Working with students to construct a digital reading experience can engage students in recognizing the materiality of reading, and of thinking about visual design and the impact of new media on reading. By translating the reading experience from that of a print-based typical academic text to the style of a *Buzzfeed* or *Huffington Post* article, students can learn about how the rhetorical and visual design of texts impact comprehension. Other versions of such tasks might have students construct texts to be read on phones versus laptops, furthering their recognition of how technology impacts materiality as well. Alternately, quick reading activities and collaborative annotation software can be utilized to encourage students' perceptions of reading as embodied and material. For example, students could use emojis to chart their reading experience as a form of annotation, noting how they feel while moving through the text. Such activities ultimately offer purposeful strategies for helping students to recognize and theorize reading as an embodied and material activity. We want our students—as Maria, Jesse, and Owen illustrate in the epigraphs that began this article—to choose purposefully the reading practices that best help them to create meaning. By emphasizing the material and embodied aspects of reading, we help students to recognize a wide-range of factors that contribute to that meaning making. Having students engage in activities that demonstrate reading as an active construction of meaning can help them to recognize the way in which reading is an embodied and material experience.

In concluding this essay, I turn once again to student reflections that manifest the importance of an embodied and material approach to reading. Summarizing how her reading practices have changed over the course of the semester, Student Priya writes:

> Before taking this class, I would simply read an article, try to grab the 'jist' of it, and sit at my computer to type up a small summary of the article's main point. This course asks us to look deeper into a piece of reading though … I am a nursing major and thus mostly read scientific textbooks, highlighting and annotating [help me to] turn a 5 chapter memorizing nightmare into a much more manageable couple of pages of bullet points to learn.

Priya's description of what she does and why reveals her embodied knowledge that *this* is how she best navigates academic reading tasks. She makes connections across classes, and across types of learning by comparing the need to "look deeper into a piece of reading" in her composition class to the concise list of bullet-points for studying that is more "manageable" than lengthy chapters of scientific textbooks. While she focuses upon common activities—highlighting and annotation—these practices are the important corporeal tasks that allow her to pull out meaning during reading and she uses them in different but appropriate ways for the contexts in which she engages texts.

Priya, Jesse, Maria, and Owen all offer glimpses into their individual embodied, material approaches to reading. However, as we have seen in my critique of *Ways* and *Elements*, textbooks may fail to situate reading practices in the specific, embodied experiences of student readers. As such, students asked to follow these practices may not develop the rhetorical agency that Priya, Jesse, Maria, and Owen show, because they act without reflection upon their embodied presence during reading. When our textbooks privilege a version of reading that is not embodied and which does not emphasize the materiality of reading, our classrooms actively construct barriers for students whose embodied, material realities do not reflect an assumed norm. Rather than replicating common uses of embodied language as we encourage students to try out new interpretive practices and to engage with difficult texts, we need to engage them in reflecting on their own bodily knowledge. We must not continue instructional practices that concretize reading and the reader in normative ways. Rather, teaching reading must include an embodied and material focus that supports students in becoming aware of and responsive to the physical, emotional, and sociocultural factors that create their reading experience.

Works Cited

Adler-Kassner, Linda, and Heidi Estrem. "Reading Practices in the Writing Classroom." *WPA*, vol. 31, no. 2, 2007, pp. 35-47.

Alaimo, Stacie, and Susan Hekman. *Material Feminisms*. Indiana UP, 2008.

Arditi, Aries. "Adjustable Typography: An Approach to Enhancing Low Vision Text Accessibility." *Ergonomics*, vol. 47, no. 5, 2004, pp. 469-82.

Baron, Naomi. "Redefining Reading: The Impact of Digital Communication Media." *PMLA*, vol. 128, no. 1, 2013, pp. 193-200.

Bartholomae, David, and Tony Petrosky. *Ways of Reading: An Anthology for Writers*. 9th ed., Bedford/St. Martin, 2011.

Bernhardt, Stephen A. "Seeing the Text." *CCC*, vol. 37, no. 1, 1986, pp. 66-78.

Bialotsky, Don. "Should College English be Close Reading?" *College English*, vol. 69, 2006, pp. 111-16.

Bordo, Susan. *Unbearable Weight: Feminism, Western Culture, and the Body*. U of California P, 1993.

Brent, Doug. *Reading as Rhetorical Invention*. NCTE, 1992.

Bunn, Michael. "Reading Visual Rhetoric in Composition Courses: Adopting an Approach That Helps Students Produce their Own Visual Discourse." *Reader*, vol. 61, 2011, pp. 87-103.

Carillo, Ellen. "Creating Mindful Readers in First-Year Composition Courses: A Strategy to Facilitate Transfer." *Pedagogy*, vol. 16, no. 1, 2016, pp. 9-22.

---. "Making Reading Visible in the Classroom." *Currents in Teaching and Learning*, vol. 1, no. 2, 2009, pp. 37-41.

---. "Reading and Writing Centers: A Primer for Writing Center Professionals." *Writing Center Journal*, vol. 36, no. 2, 2017, pp. 117-45.

---. *A Writer's Guide to Mindful Reading*. WAC Clearinghouse, 2017.

Conboy, Katie, et al. *Writing on the Body: Female Embodiment and Feminist Theory*. Columbia UP, 1997.

Connors, Robert J. "Textbooks and the Evolution of the Discipline." *CCC*, vol. 37, no. 2, 1986, pp. 178-94.

Dobrin, Sidney. *Writing Situations*. Pearson, 2015.

Dolmage, Jay. *Disability Rhetoric*. U of Syracuse P, 2014.

Dunn, Patricia. *Talking, Sketching, Moving: Multiple Literacies in the Teaching of Writing*. Boynton/Cook, 2001.

Ede, Lisa. *The Academic Writer: A Brief Rhetoric*. 4th ed., Bedford/St. Martin, 2016.

Edwards, Patricia A., and Jennifer D. Turner. "Family Literacy and Reading Comprehension." *Handbook of Research on Reading Comprehension*, Routledge, 2009.

Faigley, Lester. *Writing: A Guide for College and Beyond.* 4th ed., Pearson, 2016.

Fleckenstein, Kristie. "Writing Bodies: Somatic Minds in Composition Studies." *College English*, vol. 61, no. 3, 1999, pp. 281-306.

Gale, Xin Liu, and Fredric G. Gale, editors. *(Re)Visioning Composition Textbooks: Conflicts of Culture, Ideology, and Pedagogy.* SUNY Press, 1999.

Gale, Xin Liu. "The 'Full Toolbox' and Critical Thinking: Conflicts and Contradictions in *The St. Martin's Guide to Writing*." Gale and Gale, pp. 185-216.

Garland-Thomson, Rosemarie. *Extraordinary Bodies: Figuring Physical Disability in American Culture and Life.* Colombia UP, 1996.

Haas, Christina. *Writing Technology: Studies on the Materiality of Literacy.* Lawrence Erlbaum Publishers, 1996.

Harris, Joseph. *A Teaching Subject: Composition Since 1966.* Utah State P, 2012.

Hutchings, Pat, and Mary Taylor Huber. "Placing Theory in the Scholarship of Teaching and Learning." *Arts and Humanities in Higher Education*, vol. 7, no. 3, 2008, pp. 229-44.

Janangelo, Joseph. "Appreciating Narratives of Containment and Contentment: Reading the Writing Handbook as Public Discourse." Gale and Gale, pp. 93-112.

Jordan, Jay. "Rereading the Multicultural Reader: Towards More 'Infectious' Practices in Multicultural Composition." *College English*, vol. 68, no. 2, 2005, pp. 168-85.

Knoblauch, Abby. "Bodies of Knowledge: Definitions, Delineations, and Implications of Embodied Writing in the Academy." *Composition Studies*, vol. 40, no. 2, 2012, pp. 50-65.

Lewiecki-Wilson, Cynthia, and Brenda Jo Brueggeman. *Disability and the Teaching of Writing: A Critical Sourcebook.* Bedford/St. Martin's, 2008.

Lockhart, Tara, and Mary Soliday. "The Critical Place of Reading in Writing Transfer (and Beyond): A Report of Student Experiences." *Pedagogy*, vol. 16, no. 1, Jan. 2016, pp 23-37.

Losh, Elizabeth, et al. *Understanding Rhetoric: A Graphic Guide to Writing.* Bedford/St. Martin's, 2013.

Lunsford, Andrea, Michael Brody, Lisa Ede, Beverly J. Moss, Carole Clark Papper, and Keith Walters. *Everyone's An Author.* 2nd ed., Norton, 2016.

Mangan, Anne, et al. "Reading Linear Texts on Paper versus Computer Screen: Effects on Reading Comprehension." *International Journal of Educational Research*, vol. 58, 2013, pp. 61-68.

Marinara, Martha, et al. "Cruising Composition Texts: Negotiating Sexual Difference in First-Year Readers." *CCC*, vol. 61, no. 2, 2009, pp. 269-96.

Miller, Susan. "Is There a Text in this Class?" *Freshmen English News*, vol. 11, no. 1, 1982, pp. 2-4.

Perl, Sondra. *Felt Sense: Writing With the Body.* Boynton/Cook, 2004.

Ramage, John D., et al. *The Allyn and Bacon Guide to Writing.* 6th concise ed., Pearson, 2012.

Rex, Lesley A., et al. "Teachers' Pedagogical Stories and the Shaping of Classroom Participation: 'The Dancer' and 'Graveyard Shift at the 7-11.'" *American Educational Research Journal*, vol. 39, no. 3, 2002, pp. 765-96.

Salvatori, Mariolina. "Conversations with Texts: Reading in the Teaching of Composition." *College English*, vol. 58, no. 4, 1996, pp. 330-54.

Salvatori, Mariolina, and Patricia Donahue. *The Elements (and Pleasures) of Difficulty*. Pearson Longman, 2005.

Small, Gary W., and Gigi Vorgan. *iBrain: Surviving the Technological Alteration of the Modern Mind*. Harper, 2008.

Sullivan, Patrick, et al. "Introduction." *Deep Reading: Teaching Reading in the Writing Classroom*, NCTE, 2017, pp. xiii-xxvii.

Sweeney, Meghan A., and Maureen McBride. "*Difficulty Paper* (Dis)Connections: Understanding the Threads Students Weave between Their Reading and Writing." *CCC*, vol. 66, no. 4, 2015, pp. 591-614.

Welch, Kathleen E. "Ideology and Freshman Textbook Production: The Place of Theory in Writing Pedagogy." *CCC*, vol. 38, no. 3, 1987, pp. 269-82.

Wilson, James C., and Cynthia Lewiecki-Wilson. *Embodied Rhetorics: Disability in Language and Culture*. SIUP, 2001, pp. 1-26.

Wysocki, Anne Frances, et al. *Writing New Media: Theory and Applications for Expanding the Teaching of Composition*. Utah State UP, 2004.

Yancey, Kathleen Blake, et al. "Device. Display. Read: The Design of Reading and Writing and the Difference Display Makes." *Deep Reading: Teaching Reading in the Writing Classroom*, edited by Patrick Sullivan, Howard Tinberg, Sheridan Blau, NCTE, 2017, pp. 33-56.

To Ensure Warfighting Function: Writing Inside a U.S. Army Brigade Headquarters

J. Michael Rifenburg

A chief aim of the U.S. Army is ensuring warfighting function. Army doctrinal publications dictate that soldiers achieve this aim through integration and synchronization, both of which point to ensuring that the necessary people and things arrive on time. This article takes up circulation as an analytical lens to trace how a U.S. Army major coordinates writing tasks across people and places to ensure the warfighting function of 4,500 soldiers at Fort Wainwright in Fairbanks, Alaska. Data include in-person observations, semistructured interviews, and textual analysis of unclassified documents.

Reveille

It's 0545 hours. I'm less than two hundred miles from the Arctic Circle, sitting in the passenger seat of a creaky Subaru Outback driven by U.S. Army Major Brian Forester. Forester, a graduate of West Point and Ranger school and veteran of three deployments, pulls into the parking lot of the Brigade headquarters at Fort Wainwright in Fairbanks, Alaska. I step out of the car into the bright morning; the sun is smiling during this season of twenty-two hours of daylight. We stretch, chat, wait for another army officer to show up, and then take off on a four-mile run, across bridges, along sidewalks, beside the rolling Chena River. We talk admissions processes at West Point, the recent death of a soldier in Iraq who graduated from my university, and merits of a local golf course. I keep up during the run, though I suspect they lessened their pace for me.

It's 0830 hours. I'm sitting in Forester's large office. Forester, an Assistant Chief of Staff, Operations Officer (abbreviated S-3), coordinates all operations for the Brigade, the highest echelon at Fort Wainwright.[1] He is behind his standing desk, emailing via the encrypted army network, thumbing through his iPhone, swigging coffee from his steel gray thermos. He is immersed in a project of dizzying logistical complexity: sending seven hundred soldiers—including himself—to three different countries over the course of ninety days for an international training exercise. The exercise, which I retitle Tidal Trek at the Army's request, will be a ninety-day joint and combined training exercise. *Joint* means it will include various services of the U.S. Armed Forces; *combined* means it will involve different countries. Forester's conference table is covered in printer paper; his dry erase board displays timelines drawn in five different colored markers; a green notepad, full of Forester's handwritten, work-related miscellany, sits on his desk next to his iPhone. Through many literate practices resulting in clear written deliverables, Forester will plan and execute this three-month long international training exercise with the singular goal of ensuring the Brigade's warfighting function.

It's 0840 hours. The encrypted network goes down. Shaking his head, Forester leaves his office.

*

With IRB approval, I observed Forester over the course of two days as he worked on Tidal Trek. I collected unclassified documents and conducted a semistructured audio-recorded interview with Forester at the end of day two. My IRB application requested permission to talk with Forester. I do not directly quote any other voices and do not directly identify the many people moving through Forester's office. Though Forester did allow me into a sensitive military space and granted me access to all unclassified information, he asked that I not mention dates, times, specific locations, or titles connected to current and future Brigade training exercises. Forester read my initial draft and ran it through the Army's Public Affairs office. He asked me to redact a PowerPoint slide from one of his presentations and assign a pseudonym to the international training exercise. Both of which I did. At times, passive voice slides into this essay because I have been asked not to directly mention the subject of a sentence—the who or what that drives the action. My observations, interview, textual analysis, and overall thinking about the two days I spent within the Brigade headquarters center on one research question: How do written deliverables circulating through the headquarters ensure integration and synchronization, which, in turn, ensure the warfighting function of the Brigade?

Within my research question, I draw attention to integration, synchronization, and warfighting function. I define these terms according to army doctrinal publications available as free pdf downloads. These publications cover a wide range of details, from coordinating with different services of the armed forces, to developing critical thinking, creativity, and imagination in officers. The Army's use of doctrinal language (i.e., terms with stated definitions) throughout these publications is of most relevance to my purpose. According to U.S. Department of the Army Field Manual (FM) 5-0, *The Operations Process*, "Doctrine provides a military organization with a unity of effort and a common philosophy, language, and purpose." Integration, synchronization, and warfighting function are specific army doctrinal terms. I reference them according to FM

6-0, *Commander and Staff Organization and Operations*, which uses these terms in the job description of an Assistant Chief of Staff, Operations Officer (S-3), a role Forester fills. In the abbreviation S-3, "s" stands for staff; the "3" stands for his "operations." Chapter two, section 46 of FM 6-0 defines the work of an Assistant Chief of Staff, G-3 (S-3), Operations:

> The operations officer is the primary staff officer for integrating and synchronizing the operation as a whole for the commander . . . the operations officer ensures warfighting function integration and synchronization across the planning horizons in current operations integration, future operations, and plans integrating cells . . . Additionally, the operations officer authenticates all plans and orders for the commander to ensure the warfighting functions are synchronized in time, space, and purpose in accordance with the commander's intent and planning guidance.

In brief, Forester ensures the necessary people and things arrive on time to an event—no matter if this event is a maneuver during an armed conflict or training exercise in a garrison environment. As an S-3, Forester is one of ten people on a post of 4,500 soldiers who report directly to one of the three colonels (the commander specified in Forester's job description above) stationed at Fort Wainwright.

After introducing in more detail the setting and subject of this essay, I pull from my interview with Forester to hear how he understands integration and synchronization. I then turn to the research question and trace the circulation of texts Forester uses to accomplish one specific component of Tidal Trek: how to plan and execute the unloading and inspection of gear on friendly soil at the beginning of the international training exercise. I draw from circulation studies when undertaking this tracing. Scholars working in this sub-discipline of composition studies enlarge the ancient western five canons of rhetoric by positioning circulation, not delivery, as the final canon. Describing previous scholarship in circulation studies, Laurie E. Gries writes that such work "investigate[s] not only how discourse is produced and distributed, but also how once delivered, it circulates, transforms, and affects change through its material encounters" ("Iconographic" 333). Such an investigatory approach enlarges the ancient western canon. In Gries's conception, production encompasses the first four canons (invention, arrangement, style, and memory) and distribution stands in for the final canon (delivery). Gries's model, and the work of circulation studies, hangs on the conjunction *but*. Circulation follows delivery and attends to how discourse transforms through time and space and bodies. Broadly, then, Gries's articulation of circulation invites us to follow text as it moves through the world, colliding with various animate and inanimate actors that shape and reshape the text. More specifically, drawing on new materialism, circulation studies grants agency in rhetorical production to a wide range of actors, mudding the waters of original authorship. As Laura Micciche argues in her explication of new materialism, writing is a "codependent interaction with a host of others—materials, power grids, people, animals, rituals, feelings, stuff, and much else" (498). These others collectively give rise to text. Such a position runs counter to common and erroneous conceptions of writing that, in the words of Paul Prior, "freeze writing . . . to see writing as a noun, rather than a verb" (22). Circulation studies, then, connects with larger interdisciplinary efforts to see text as always unfurling and locates rhetorical production in the spatiotemporal flows of the public sphere, while examining how circulation propels community building (Sackey, Ridolfo, and DeVoss). If writing is "discourse in motion" (Gries, "Iconographic" 333) and, following Micciche, if writing is "a practice of coexistence" (498), then an avenue for exploration is how text, broadly defined, facilitates—maybe even constitutes—community. I am particularly taken by Micciche's selection of the noun *coexistence* as it implies harmonious comingling; the noun implies community.

I turn to circulation studies because it captures how people and things across time and space co-produce and co-facilitate rhetorical production toward the communal goal of ensuring warfighting function. Like Gries and previous scholars working in circulation studies, I see production as encompassing the first four canons of ancient western rhetoric. The production of army writing accounts for doctrinal publications that facilitate the invention, arrangement, and style of texts soldiers produce. In warfighting action, soldiers embody and enact deeply embedded memories of training and doctrine. After production, army texts are delivered horizontally or vertically. Texts then circulate and "transfor[m] and affect[t] change" through encounters with spaces and people (Gries, "Iconographic" 333). The effective circulation of discourse within a controlled army workspace constitutes integration and synchronization—the two terms central to warfighting function. My larger goal in this article is to further our collective understanding of circulation studies, particularly in the wake of Gries's argument that it is a "core concept . . . [and] an emergent threshold concept" of "rhetoric and writing studies" ("Introduction" 4-5). As an emergent threshold concept, circulation studies has potential to illuminate the complex flow of workplace writing practices. It does so, my study of army workplace writing reveals, by making visible how collective goals are sustained, space constrains writing's production, and deadlines drive execution.

My interest in the circulation of army writing comes at a kairotic moment. Because of the U.S.'s long-running wars and because of a now decidedly hawkish Donald Trump administration, our classrooms are witnessing and will continue to witness a growing student-veteran population. The current presidential administration is raising troop levels (Myers) and overseeing a return to conventional, force-on-force warfare driven by an interventionist foreign policy, as exhibited in the 2018 Department of Defense National Defense Strategy and the National Defense Authorization Act for Fiscal Year 2018, which allocated $626 billion for the U.S. Department of Defense's base budget and an additional $66 billion for operations.

Many of these soldiers will wisely use government grants to find their way into our classrooms. The field of composition studies is responsive to this population. For instance, Sue Doe and Lisa Langstraat's 2014 edited collection *Generation Vet: Composition, Student-Veterans, and the Post 9/11 University* helped drive the 2015 CCCC position statement, "Student Veterans in the College Composition Classroom: Realizing Their Strengths and Assessing Their Needs." The recently launched *Journal of Veteran Studies*, an interdisciplinary journal largely facilitated by composition studies scholars, offers a dedicated digital platform for veteran studies. In 2016, D. Alexis Hart and Roger Thompson continued their solo and collaborative work on student-veterans with their award-winning article on writing programs designed to support student veterans and, that same year, guest edited a roundtable titled "Veterans' Voices" in *Pedagogy*. Most recently, Mark Blaauw-Hara painted a rich picture of the academic lives of our student-veterans. Though not directly focused on student-veterans, Chris Anson and Shawn Neely's 2010 webtext challenged us to understand important rhetorical differences between military writing and academic writing. These differences add to the challenges faced by soldiers re-entering civilian society through the classroom.

I interrupt this tidy chronology to end with Anson and Neely because their work aligns most closely to the rich portrait of in-the-moment army writing I offer in these pages. I add an additional element to our nascent study of army writing. I enter an army brigade headquarters with the goal of illustrating how writing helps Forester accomplish the collective brigade goals, and I respond to Bronwyn T. Williams's exhortation to expand "composition and rhetoric research beyond college writing" in hopes of "enrich[ing] our understanding of the interconnected nature of literacy practices" (133). I trace the rich kaleidoscope of written deliverables coloring the daily interactions of a specific workspace and how writing, coordinated across time and space with other rhetors, ensures the warfighting functions of an army brigade.

An Arctic Outpost and an Army Major

Fort Wainwright sits on the eastern edge of Fairbanks, Alaska, a town of roughly 32,000 in Interior Alaska. Roughly a six-hour drive north of coastal Anchorage, Fairbanks is home to the aurora borealis, twenty-two hours of daylight in the summer, and twenty-two hours of darkness in the winter. Unlike Anchorage's Instagram-worthy vistas, Fairbanks is dry, flat, and harsh land. The Alaska Range faintly dots the horizon, hundreds of miles away.

The U.S. Army established Fort Wainwright in 1941, about fifteen years before President Eisenhower granted Alaska statehood. And Alaska still maintains a strong military presence, particularly in a political climate where North Korea commonly tests ballistic missiles, and Russia maintains capricious relations with the United States. Fort Wainwright still sits confidently in Fairbanks, Alaska, from which soldiers watch for threats from across the Pacific and people and stuff are ready for deployment thanks to the work of Major Forester and his subordinates.

Forester cuts a tall, well-proportioned figure. His shaved brown hair is receding from his forehead into a widow's peak. His round, welcoming face reveals his engaging personality. He gained early admittance to the United States Military Academy at West Point, where he rowed crew and graduated ninth in his class of 930. After graduation, he completed Ranger School, then Air Assault School, then Airborne School. In the wake of 9/11, Forester and his fellow graduates were caught up in the wargaming plans of a jingoistic George W. Bush administration. Shortly after proposing to his now wife, he found himself on a flight to Iraq for a four-month deployment. Another deployment to Afghanistan for fifteen months. Another to Iraq for twelve months. He was gone for thirty-one of the first sixty months of marriage. Kids came along between deployments, and so did multiple relocations. He started at Fort Bragg in North Carolina, then onto Fort Benning in Georgia. He moved to Fort Lewis just outside Seattle and then negotiated a gig following his three deployments and three moves: heading back to school to receive a Master of Arts in Political Science from Duke University with the promise to teach for three years at West Point. He moved to Durham, completed graduate school, and relocated to West Point as a teaching instructor. After West Point came Fort Wainwright.

Integrating and Synchronizing to Ensure Warfighting Function

Forester and I are in the brigade headquarters, a three-floor building in the center of post. Inside Forester's office, four small rectangular windows line the wall opposite the door. His view looks out over a small parking lot, a field, and a large hangar. I see a birch tree dancing in the wind. He has a wooden right-angled standing desk with dual monitors and his laptop off to the side. Data critical to the operations of the brigade covers two walls of his office. Three large military installation maps of the area (essentially topography maps with impact and bombing areas marked in red) hang on one wall; a dry erase board hangs on the opposite wall. Information covers the board.

A color-coded timeline takes up most of the board. He plugs his common access card into the laptop and enters the encrypted network (see fig. 1).

Fig. 1. Forester at desk.

As FM 6-0 specifies, Forester's job hinges on effective integration and synchronization. He ensures that during training exercises or operations all 4,500 soldiers at Fort Wainwright are coordinated around a collective goal and that the necessary warfighting functions (the guns, ammo, vehicles) are present to accomplish the collective goal. Put more simply, he brings these two terms down to time and stuff. In our interview, Forester started with integration:

> I think integration and I think in terms of function, warfighting functions. The operations officer is kinda at the center of that and builds the base plan for whatever it might be but integrates the war fighting functions to support that plan. For example, if there were a Brigade attack, we would first start with the baseline maneuver plan—you know, this unit is going to go that way; this unit is going to go this way—and kinda get that solidified and then we would integrate the fire—the warfighting support—to provide the fire support and, you know, indirect fires, assets to support that maneuver plan. That's integration.

He then described the *how* of integration:

> That occurs in a variety of ways. In the tactical sense, everyone is kinda sitting in a central area, communicating face-to-face. There's a lot of product sharing and creation on a centralized network. You have what we call a common operating picture that can be digital or it can be an actual physical, which is what we often used in my most recent training center rotation—a map on the table in the center of a central planning tent. That's where integration occurs.

Synchronization works alongside integration. As Forester told me,

> I think of synchronization, I think in terms of time, in particular synchronizing, in the tactical sense, effects so that you are massing effects at a specific time and place on the battlefield to achieve some effect you are wanting to achieve. So that's when a tool, a particularly useful communicative tool, is the synchronization matrix. That is like you saw on the table there [in my office]. Kinda shows over time what each function or unit is executing.

Integration and synchronization form his duties. He accomplishes both through written deliverable: PowerPoint presentations, Excel spreadsheets, handwritten notes, timelines, and a synchronization matrix, which Forester mentions, and I detail later.

Written Deliverables Support Integration and Synchronization

By way of example and to avoid generalities, I will trace the circulation of written deliverables guiding a specific activity the brigade was planning when I visited. The brigade was planning an international training exercise held in three countries over ninety days. Forester is the logistics point-person for this training exercise which I call Tidal Trek. One of the countries the soldiers will enter has a protocol designed to stop the entry of foreign seed or soil contaminants. When seven hundred U.S. soldiers and gear from Fort Wainwright land in this country, all need to be processed and inspected under this country's strict biosecurity protocol. How does one ensure the efficient inspection of seven hundred soldiers and their gear? That falls to the operations officer Major Brian Forester. In this section, I trace the circulation of the written deliverables leading to a planned and efficient inspection.

Before Forester can synch and integrate operations, he needed to establish policy for conducting internal communication with his subordinates. Forester's brigade nickname—the one given to a person in his position and not to Forester individually—is Wolf 3, a riff on the arctic climate; the nickname for operations is "shop." During his first weeks in his new position as operations officer, Forester created a document titled "Wolf 3 Shop Business Rules." (see fig. 2). At the top of the landscape page layout document, Forester spells out three values (discipline, humility, courage) and three doctrines (over-communication, no surprises, golden rule). At the bottom of the document, Forester states the two goals of the shop: "Enable the Battalions" and "Inform the Commander." The verbs *enable* and *inform* are the actions of the nouns *integration* and *synchronization*. An image of eight people rowing a boat with a coxswain shouting encouragement anchors the bottom middle of the document. "I use a lot of crew metaphors," he tells me, harkening back to his days rowing and coaching crew at West Point.

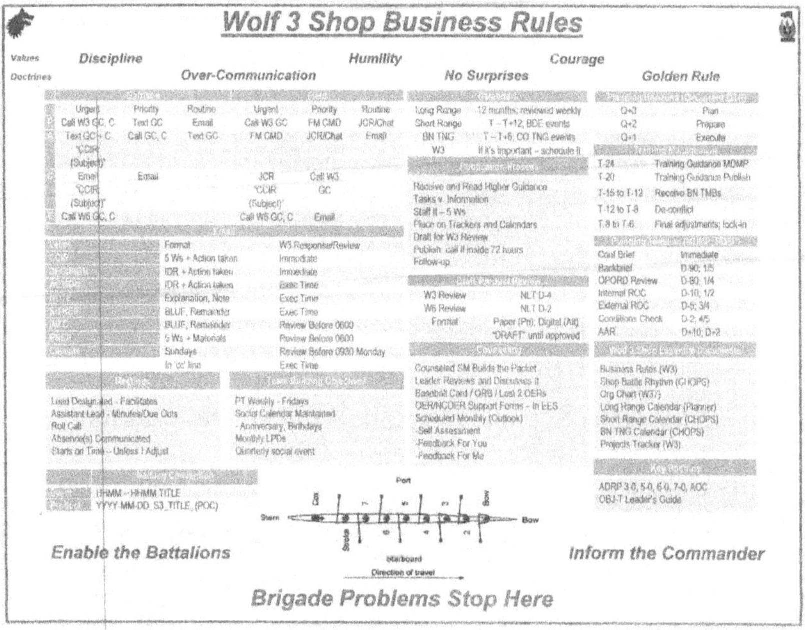

Fig. 2. Image of "Wolf 3 Shop Business Rules."

With this document guiding communication, Forster and his subordinates turn to their planning horizon. Army Doctrinal Reference Publication (ADRP) 5-0, *The Operations Process*, defines the planning horizon as "a point in time commanders use to focus the organization's planning efforts to shape future events." The Brigade's planning horizon is twelve to eighteen months out. Forester captures his planning horizon on the dry erase board in his office. It's a basic timeline—just the year, date, and action briefly inscribed in Forester's all-cap handwriting. Forester color-codes the planning horizon according to a key in the upper-left hand corner of his board. He migrates the easy-to-erase notes to a more durable text, which the Army refers to as a synchronization matrix, defined in FM 5-0 as "a format . . . to synchronize a course of action across time, space, and purpose." Forester creates his synchronization matrix as an Excel landscape document. After printing all the pages off in color, he tapes them together to form one long scroll running the length of his conference table. The synch matrix's running title signifies its use for the upcoming training exercise: Tidal Trek [redacted dates] Day-by-Day Timeline. In columns, each day of the training is listed—all ninety days. "Event" is organized into rows and broken into three categories (MSN CMD [mission command], Movement & Maneuver, and Sustainment) and each of these categories is further broken down. For example, Sustainment includes TRANS, MED, and MAINT; the category Movement & Maneuver includes Flights. In total, the sheet contains twenty-five columns. Most of the document is in black and white, except for periodic segments of purple, one long segment of red, and one brief box of blue.

The activities included on the dry erase board and replicated on the synch matrix are assigned by Forester to his subordinates. Forester uses a project tracker to track whom he assigns each task. He often called this document a fighting document in our interviews. It's titled "Wolf S3 Projects Tracker." Forester makes use of Excel to design this portrait spreadsheet. Under the title, he typed, "How does the event create readiness?" Running on the rows are thirty-five different tasks. Eleven different subordinates are working on these thirty-five tasks. Ten items run along the columns (I added parenthetical content for clarification):

- event
- lead
- team
- execution date
- higher order
- warno (warning order)
- conop (concept of the operation)
- opord (operation order)
- ipr (in-process review)
- rxl (rehearsal)

The unloading and inspection project (nested under event) is delegated to a captain who reports directly to Forester.

At this point in the circulation of text, four different deliverables support the collective goal of unloading and inspecting gear: shop business rules, planning horizon timeline, synchronization matrix, and project tracker.

These deliverables connect bodies and texts for geographically and physically constrained activities. Circulation studies helps us attend to how texts change and flow through time and space as they encounter material objects. Through a daily 1700-hour synch meeting Forester holds with his subordinates, these deliverables will undergo fundamental transformation based on material, physical, geographical, temporal, and economic constraints. But these deliverables will still adhere to the central broad goal of ensuring warfighting function and the specific goal of unloading and inspecting gear.

*

It's 1700 hours. Forester looks over the project tracker while sitting at his conference table, surrounded by subordinates. He is waiting for two additional subordinates to arrive. Forester breaks the silence and spins a yarn about his time at cadet troop leader training (CTLT). Leaning back in his chair, his hands folded behind his head, Forester recalls sitting around bored. "This is before iPhones," he reminds his audience of five. "And this older guy comes and tells us, 'You always gotta have a piece of paper, and you always gotta look busy. If you do that, no one will mess with you.'" A few chuckles greet the narrative. "That is all I learned in CTLT," Forester admits. The additional men arrive. The meeting begins. All present have a lime-green notepad, about the size of a two-hundred-page paperback novel, a three-ring white binder, and something to drink: a Red Bull, some bottles of water, an Odwalla juice (see fig. 3).

Forester makes his way down the project tracker, and the subordinate responsible for the given task provides a brief update. For the unloading and inspection task, a captain suggests purchasing large heavy-duty plastic bags at The Home Depot. By stuffing gear into a transparent plastic bag and then placing these plastic bags into the standard-issue army travel bag, the captain suggests, soldiers will not scatter their clothes and gear when preparing for inspection. Forester nods along and asks the captain to get a price quote on seven hundred bags. Later, Forster tells me he expects an email within 48 hours from his captain with this price quote. When he receives the information, he will need to decide. As he told me, "I prefer face-to-face [communication] to ensure it is clearly understood, the message is received." But even face-to-face conversations result in the production of text: "So if I communicated something face-to-face, there is going to be some sort of written deliverable. And an acknowledgment of receipt from them to me so we can ensure we are moving in the direction we want to go." Forester saves both the project tracker and synchronization matrix on a shared internal network drive.

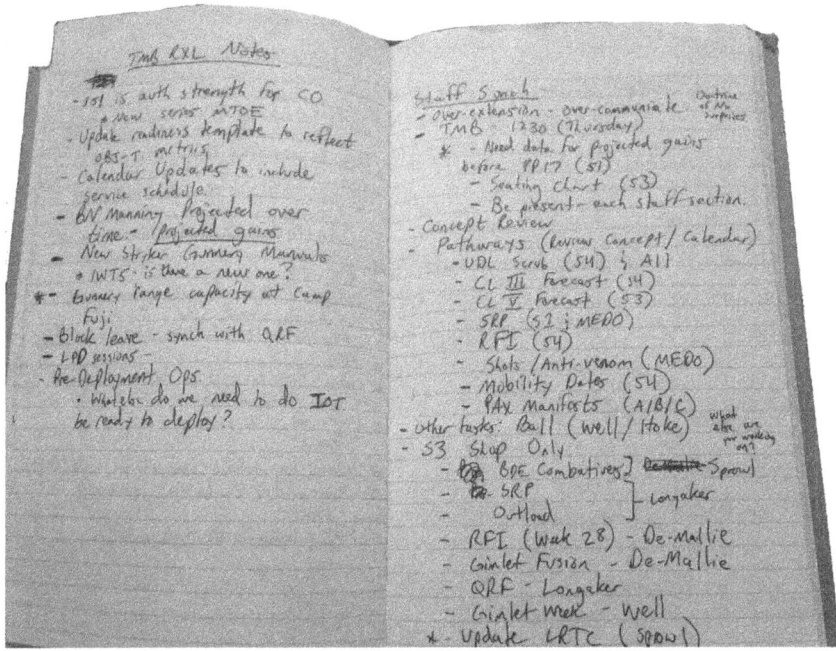

Fig. 3. Forester's lime-green notepad.

Moving up the chain of command, Forester briefs his immediate boss (the colonel) and higher headquarters during a weekly Brigade staff synch. For these meetings, Forester prepares and delivers what he calls "PowerPoint quad charts," which display "priorities last week, priorities this week, tasks, and friction points." As the training exercise Tidal Trek is a few short weeks away, most of Forester's presentation will speak to the Brigade preparation. Forester granted me access to his synch meeting with his staff but not the synch meeting with higher headquarters. Just like the synch meeting with his staff, Forester's synch meeting with his immediate boss and higher headquarters ensures synchronization across all echelons. Army doctrine refers to this sort of synchronization as battle rhythm: "A deliberate daily cycle of command, staff, and unit activities intended to synchronize current and future operations" (FM 6-0). During my interview with Forester, he alternated between the term *synch meeting* and *battle rhythm meeting* when describing daily or weekly scheduled face-to-face or video teleconferenced meetings.

Depending on the activity, the circulation of written deliverables continues from verbal modes present at synch meetings to, again, written text. At this point, the two most common written deliverables are warning orders (WARNOs) and operation orders (OPORDs). These genres are defined in army doctrinal publications, illustrated by way of templates, and used in the garrison and field environment for the rapid transmission of information according to typified textual arrangement. Armed Forces of the United States' Joint Publication 5-0, Joint Operation Planning, defines a WARNO as a "preliminary notice of an order or action that is to follow." A WARNO prepares the recipient for an OPORD, defined in JP 5-0 as a "directive issued by a commander to subordinate commanders for the purpose of effecting the coordinated execution of an operation." As variables of an operation change (e.g., weather, enemy forces, civilian presence), a fragmentary order (FRAGO) may be authored. A FRAGO modifies portions of the standing operation order. In the case of unloading and inspecting gear in a foreign country, for example, say more soldiers needed to make the trip; a FRAGO would then modify portions of the OPORD reflecting this change. To borrow composition terms, with the authoring of orders (be it a WARNO, OPORD, or FRAGO), the trajectory of text has moved from brainstorming and planning to the first round of drafting and possible revision.

Before the order is executed, it is visualized through a terrain model, a construction more commonly used for tactical operations. ADRP 5-0 defines commander's visualization and even provides a figure illustrating how commanders are trained to visualize the end-state of a given operation.[2] Built on satellite imagery or reconnaissance intelligence, a terrain model is a small-scale model in which soldiers use yarn, rocks, sand, figurines, and other everyday objects to represent visually the topography and people presence of an upcoming operation. Soldiers use the terrain model to prepare for the topography and friendly, enemy, and civilian forces. As Forester told me, "It's like a map but better. It allows you to—and we used them all the time in the national training center in a tactical environment—to rehearse the training." Forester reflects on his time as a battalion S-3, a position one notch below his current position of being an S-3 for a brigade:

> So when I was a battalion S-3, I was issuing orders that the companies would take, digest, and come up with their own plans to support the larger battalion plan. We would then, you know, prior to execution, would gather round a constructed terrain model and go through a rehearsal of sorts. Talking through over *time and space where units are going to be on the battlefield*, what tasks they are going to be conducting, at what time. So, the S-3 job is to kinda orchestrate that rehearsal. (emphasis added)

I draw attention to one of Forester's phrases that reflects the importance of synchronization and integration. A physical representation of the upcoming action supports the mission of aligning all parts of an operation across time and space and ensuring the necessary warfighting elements are present. A terrain model is another method of ensuring the who, where, when, and what of an operation—no matter if the operation is designed to enter hostile territory and secure a high-value target or inspect the gear of seven hundred soldiers who just got off a sixteen-hour flight. Designing this model is very much a DIY project. Forester told me, "Typically, you would have some props, like yarn and stuff like that, to build out roads, rivers, and use rocks and dirt to construct relief in the terrain so you can see 3D effects. We construct them quite frequently. My shop has a terrain model kit. An actual kit that is in a tough box that, you know, we pull out whenever we are getting close to an operation. This is a task I give to a captain to oversee the construction of the terrain model prior to the rehearsal." The terrain and visualization lead to execution.

The mission's execution does not conclude with the circulation of written deliverables. The Army follows a text's trajectory beyond execution. ADRP 7-0 *Training Units and Developing Leaders* defines the after-action review (AAR) as a "facilitated self-analysis of an organization's performance, with the objective of improving future performance." ADRP 7-0 ties AARs to developing leaders and critical thinking. ADRP 7-0 stresses that AARs are "not critiques . . . [but designed to] identify unit strengths to be sustained and weaknesses that need to improve." And here is where the cyclical nature of writing is highlighted. Much like the metacognitive and reflective assignments we offer in our writing classes, the AAR as text reflects on previous action and looks to future action. The AAR at once states what went well and what didn't with an operation. But it also ignites brainstorming for a future operation. AARs facilitate a new or modified synchronization matrix, a new or modified WARNO, OPORD, PowerPoint slide, terrain model. One operation leads to another. One text leads to another and another and another—a continual cycle of text undergirding and facilitating warfighting function.

Retreat

Based on this single bounded case study, how do various written deliverables ensure integration and synchronization, which, in turn, ensure the warfighting function of the brigade? Tracing brigade-level activity through circulation studies calls attention to how meaning making moves across various semiotic resources during organizational planning and highlights the accompanying role text and talk play in a mission's execution. When the training exercise Tidal Trek came down the chain of command and landed on Forester's desk, he scribbled the dates on the planning horizon he keeps on his dry erase board. Shifting the verbal confirmation of Tidal Trek to a more durable materiality like a hand-drawn timeline helps Forester visually conceptualize where the training exercise falls within the many other activities floating through his office. The inscription on the planning horizon provided a cognitive anchor for Forester, an anchor that does not often come with ephemeral talk. To provide an additional anchor, Forester utilized a synchronization matrix and a project tracker. Both texts necessitated the involvement of others; Forester synched Tidal Trek with other training exercises and then assigned a point person specific details pertinent to the training exercise. Before moving into verbal kinds of meaning making, Forester dropped three cognitive anchors (i.e., three written deliverables) to support the future execution of this international training. Verbal meaning making helped Forester refine the tasks accompanying Tidal Trek; he gained a stronger sense of how to move forward with the unloading and inspection of gear through the feedback of his subordinates. The synch meeting led back to written deliverables as he developed PowerPoint slides to update his colonel and higher headquarters. Though I was not privy to this meeting, Forester did tell me that feedback led to his revising written deliverables; verbal meaning making again led to durable meaning making. Through a WARNO and terrain model, Forester used various written deliverables to push closer to the collective goal of the brigade.

As Gries reminds us, the Western rhetorical tradition has long been undergirded by the concept of circulation. Socrates's and Phaedrus's oral recitations in *Phaedrus* are, at their core, the recitation and circulation of speeches by the sophist Lysias and an example of how text undergoes transformation when circulating through different bodies. Yet in the past two decades, scholars in composition studies have turned to circulation studies as a prominent lens for understanding how text and people operate together because, for one, digital advancements have opened doors for large scale mapping projects that captures the dynamics of people working with text across time and space (see Mueller). Though I do not engage in these kinds of mapping projects, my close reading of the circulation of text within an army brigade headquarters offers important takeaways. This article offers three implications for circulation studies, which I hope will spur continued work on circulation studies. I suggest we engage with these takeaways while we consider if circulation is, indeed, a threshold concept of our field.

First, all text circulating through the brigade headquarters adheres to a collective goal articulated by the brigade headquarters. The Army generally, and the brigade headquarters in Alaska specifically, operate from a communally agreed-upon goal. In *Still Life with Rhetoric*, Gries reports data from her five-year case study on the digital circulation of the iconic image Obama Hope used by then-senator Obama in his successful 2008 presidential campaign, and which has since been re-appropriated by a wide-range of global actors for a wide-range of rhetorical pursuits. This image circulated through a dizzying array of spaces, which Gries visually captures in a map (see her figure 10.1,

282). The various actors are not coming to this image with the goal the original artist, Shepard Fairey, brought to the design or the goal Obama and his team brought to the image. Circulation studies allows for the varied motivations of the various actors and agents within rhetorical production. For the Army, a text is repurposed and circulated through various people and spaces but still adheres to a single communal goal. My research helps us ask and begin to answer how texts traverse multiple spaces and collide with multiple bodies but still adhere to a communally agreed-upon goal.

Second, all text circulating through the brigade headquarters is grounded in the logistical constraints of spaces. These texts are constrained by the when and where of a task. A dry climate allows certain operations; a cold climate allows different operations. Our armed forces underwent growing pains when adjusting to warfare in the humid jungles of Vietnam and the arid streets of Fallujah. The tactical approach changed, the camouflage changed, the communication methods changed. Military history offers a productive lens for analyzing the ineluctable relationship between writing and physical space. Broadly, then, physical spaces are agents in rhetorical production (Pigg; Pink; Rule). For Forester, how text circulated through the space—up and down the chain of command, across the various semiotic resources of talk, gesture, alphabetic text—changed per the logistical possibilities of the space. Currently, circulation studies pushes us to see how the circulation of text helps constitute a public sphere, a community (Sackey, Ridolfo, and DeVoss). But pulling from research on the situatedness of writing, I suggest we consider how the logistical capabilities of a space, like a community or organization, help constitute the circulation of text.

Third, all text circulating through the brigade headquarters is driven by dates of execution. Time is central to the brigade's operation. Forester follows time with a project tracker and a twelve- to eighteen-month planning horizon. Military operations are executed at prescheduled moments—or revised or scrubbed if unable to meet that prescheduled time. Army doctrinal publications offer sections on the importance of planning and scheduling and sections reading the unique form in which army publications illustrate time. Just as the unloading and inspection of gear hinged on certain bodies and certain locations, this course of action also hinged on a specific time so that, if unanticipated actions forestalled the soldiers from arriving at the designated time, the course of action would shift. Circulation studies attends to the spatiotemporal flow of rhetorical production, but we might account for time—in the form of deadlines and execution dates—as a constraining factor in how a text traverses processes of production, dissemination, and implementation.

Goals, bodies, spaces, and time figure prominently into how text circulates through Fort Wainwright. The circulation of army writing is predicated on communal goals, constrained by bodies and spaces, and driven by clear dates of execution. These texts support integration, synchronization, and warfighting function by involving a host of material objects in a never-ending cascade of meaning making processes. Inside this Alaskan brigade, writing is integration, writing is synchronization. Writing is the tool through which Forester and the 4,500 other soldiers ensure their warfighting function. As our field continues to mine the pedagogical and theoretical possibilities of threshold concepts, writing within a workspace like a brigade headquarters in Interior Alaska has much to teach us about how text and people flow together.

Notes

1. The Army organizes itself into echelons. Moving from smallest to largest, the Army organizes as squad, platoon, company, battalion, brigade, division, corps, and field army. Forester helps oversees the first four echelons.

2. ADRP 5-0 defines commander's visualization as "the mental process of developing situational understanding, determining a desired end state, and envisioning an operational approach by which the force will achieve that end state" (3).

Works Cited

Anson, Chris, and Shawn Neely. "The Army and Academy as Textual Communities: Exploring Mismatches in the Concepts of Attribution, Appropriation, and Shared Goals." *Kairos*, vol. 14, no. 3, 2010, kairos.technorhetoric.net/14.3/topoi/anson-neely/index.html.

Armed Forces of the United States. Joint Publication 5-0: *Joint Operation Planning*. August 2011, www.dtic.mil/doctrine/new_pubs/jp5_0.pdf.

Blaauw-Hara, Mark. "'Learning Shock' and Student-Veterans: Bridging the Learning Environments of the Military and the Academy." *Composition Forum*, vol. 35, 2017, http://compositionforum.com/issue/35/learning-shock.php.

Conference on College Composition and Communication. *Student Veterans in the College Composition Classroom: Realizing Their Strengths and Assessing Their Needs*. CCCC, 2015, www.ncte.org/cccc/resources/positions/student-veterans.

Doe, Sue, and Lisa Langstraat, editors. *Generation Vet: Composition, Student-Veterans, and the Post-9/11 University*. Utah State UP, 2014.

Gries, Laurie E. "Iconographic Tracking: A Digital Research Method for Visual Rhetoric and Circulation Studies." *Computers and Composition*, vol. 30, 2013, pp. 332-48.

----. "Introduction: Circulation as an Emerging Threshold Concept." Gries and Brooke, pp. 3-27.

---. *Still Life with Rhetoric. A New Materialist Approach to Visual Rhetorics*. Utah State UP, 2015.

Gries, Laurie E., and Collin Gifford Brooke, editors. *Circulation, Writing, and Rhetoric*. Utah State UP, 2018.

Hart, D. Alexis, and Roger Thompson. "Veterans in the Writing Classroom: Three Programmatic Approaches to Facilitate the Transition from the Military to Higher Education." *CCC*, vol. 68, no. 2, 2016, pp. 345-71.

Hart, D. Alexis, and Roger Thompson, editors. "Roundtable: Veterans' Voices." *Pedagogy: Critical Approaches to Teaching Literature, Language, Composition, and Culture*, vol. 13, no. 3, 2016, pp. 511-49.

Micciche, Laura. "Writing Material." *College English*, vol. 76, no. 6, 2014, 488-506.

Mueller, Derek. "Grasping Rhetoric and Composition by Its Long Tail: What Graphs Can Tell Us about the Field's Changing Shape." *CCC*, vol. 64, no. 1, 2012, pp. 195-223.

Myers, Meghann. "Army Looking to Recruit 80,000 New Soldiers in 2018." *Army Times*. 27 Nov. 2017. https://www.armytimes.com/news/your-army/2017/11/27/sma-army-looking-to-recruit-80000-new-soldiers-in-2018/.

Pigg, Stacey. "Emplacing Mobile Composing Habits: A Study of Academic Writing in Networked Social Spaces." *CCC*, vol. 66, no. 2, 2014, pp. 250-75.

Pink, Sarah. "From Embodiment to Emplacement: Re-thinking Competing Bodies, Senses, and Spatialities." *Sport, Education, and Society*, vol. 16, no. 3, 2011, pp. 343-55.

Plato. *Phaedrus*. Translated by W.C. Helmbold and W.G. Rabinowitz, Bobbs-Merrill, 1956.

Prior, Paul. "From Speech Genres to Mediated Multimodal Genre Systems: Bakhtin, Voloshinov, and the Question of Writing." *Genres in a Changing World*, edited by Charles Bazerman, Adair Bonini, and Débora Figueiredo, WAC Clearinghouse, 2009, pp. 17-34.

Rule, Hannah J. "Writing's Rooms." *CCC*, vol. 69, no. 3, 2018, pp. 402-32.

Sackey, Donnie Johnson, Jim Ridolfo, and Dànielle Nicole DeVoss. "Making Space in Lansing, Michigan: Communities and/in Circulation." Gries and Brooke, pp. 27-43.

U.S. Congress. "National Defense Authorization Act for Fiscal Year 2018." 2018. https://www.congress.gov/bill/115th-congress/house-bill/2810.

U.S. Department of the Army. Army Doctrinal Reference Publication 5-0: *The Operations Process*. May 2012, http://www.apd.army.mil/epubs/DR_pubs/DR_a/pdf/web/adrp5_0.pdf.

---. Army Doctrinal Reference Publication 7-0: *Training Units and Developing Leaders*. August 2012, https://armypubs.army.mil/epubs/DR_pubs/DR_a/pdf/web/adp7_0.pdf

---. Field Manual 5-0: *Army Planning and Orders Production*. January 2005, ww1.udel.edu/armyrotc/current_cadets/cadet_resources/manuals_regulations_files/FM%205-0%20-%20Army%20Planning%20&%20Orders%20Production.pdf.

---. Field Manual 6-0: *Commander and Staff Organization and Operations*. May 2014, www.milsci.ucsb.edu/sites/secure.lsit.ucsb.edu.mili.d7/files/sitefiles/fm6_0.pdf.

U.S. Department of Defense. "Summary of the National Defense Strategy of the United States of America: Sharpening the American Military's Competitive

Edge." 2018. https://www.defense.gov/Portals/1/Documents/pubs/2018-National-Defense-Strategy-Summary.pdf. Accessed 11 June 2018.

Williams, Bronwyn T. "Seeking New Worlds: The Study of Writing Beyond Our Classrooms." *CCC*, vol. 62, no. 1, 2010, pp. 127-46.

Beginning at the End: Reimagining the Dissertation Committee, Reimagining Careers

Amy J. Lueck and Beth Boehm

> In this article, we forward a perspective on interdisciplinarity and diversity that reconsiders the notion of expertise in order to unstick discussions of graduate education reform that have been at an impasse for some forty-five years. As research problems have become increasingly complex so has demand for scholars who specialize narrowly within a discipline and who understand the importance of contributions from other disciplines. In light of this, we reimagine the dissertation committee as a group of diverse participants from within and beyond the academy who contribute their knowledge and skills to train the next generation of scholars and researchers to be members of interdisciplinary teams. Graduate students, then, are not expected to be interdisciplinary themselves, but to work in interdisciplinary and diverse teams to discover new insights on their research areas and to prepare for careers interacting with a range of academic and non-academic stakeholders.

In May 2014 the Modern Language Association (MLA) Task Force on Doctoral Study in Modern Language and Literature released a report of their findings on and recommendations for improving doctoral education. Responding primarily to the realities of a constrained academic job market, the task force recommended changes to doctoral education that centered around "recognizing the wide range of intellectual paths through which we produce new knowledge" and "the wide range of career possibilities that students can pursue" (MLA 1). The authors argued for increased opportunities for doctoral students to work interdisciplinarily, collaboratively, and with a range of individuals across and beyond the university community, in part to prepare students for work outside the academy. Additionally, the report suggested that while "an extended research project . . . should remain the defining feature of doctoral education," programs should "expand the spectrum of forms the dissertation may take and ensure that students receive mentoring from professionals beyond the department as appropriate" (14). The MLA report garnered a great deal of attention among English faculty, of course, but the concerns about doctoral education raised in it are not new. Indeed, studies supported by the Carnegie Foundation, the Pew Charitable Trust, the Council of Graduate Schools, and the National Endowment for the Humanities have addressed similar concerns for years.

As early as 1973 a report from a Panel on Alternative Approaches to Graduate Education commissioned by the Council of Graduate Schools identified academic job market constriction as one serious threat to doctoral studies and proposed reforms to graduate education that would entail preparation for an expanded array of careers beyond the tenure track. The report urged that in every discipline, "graduate training should include, for all candidates who do not already possess such experience, a deliberate and significant component of discipline-related work outside the university walls" (40). Part of the impetus for this recommendation, of course, is the belief that "work outside the university walls" will provide graduate students with professional skills and networking opportunities useful for careers outside academe. But skills training is not the primary reason for the panel's imperative. From its title, *Scholarship for Society*, through its final recommendations, the report advances the argument that doctoral study should not exclusively aim to create more faculty in the mold of students' mentors in research universities, but rather, graduate education should also support socially oriented research in order to close the gap between knowledge and society and to create a well-educated citizenry with strong training in problem-solving and analysis who will make valuable contributions to "society as a whole" (28).

Since that publication in 1973, we have heard similar refrains across academe and within our own field. Rhetoric and composition scholars have been particularly sympathetic to the emphasis on public engagement, as suggested by articles in this journal, several recent monographs, edited collections, and conferences focused on public engagement and public work from organizations such as NCTE, CCCC, and WPA. The emergence of the Conference on Community Writing at Boulder similarly signals this turn. But while the "public turn" in composition is widely acknowledged and aligned with an interest in community-based learning and civic engagement, we have less often discussed these trends in terms of how they might shape our approaches to graduate education and training. More specifically, as a discipline we have done very little to encourage the idea that the public turn—the focus on scholarship for society—can develop dispositions and skills in graduate students that will prepare them for careers outside of academe.

Though one may not need a doctoral degree for the majority of positions outside of academia, surely humanistic training and specialization is valuable to a wide range of careers and social questions. As MLA director of research David Laurence points out: "The discussion becomes muddled when it fails to distinguish occupational destinations that directly depend on the advanced forms of humanistic expertise acquired in the course of doctoral study [from] the much broader array of occupations that programs need to make it possible for students to be open to considering, and to consider openly, without fearing that they are placing their chances for an academic career in jeopardy" (5).

The publication of collections from within and outside of our field has laid important groundwork for this discussion of how the public turn can help us begin to imagine changes to graduate education and careers. For example, the edited collection *Collaborative Futures* (Gilvin, Roberts, Martin) discusses publicly engaged graduate education across disciplines, and work by composition scholars is included. Also, Cindy Moore and Hildy Miller's *A Guide to Professional Development for Graduate Students in English* provides practical considerations for graduate students to prepare for jobs on and off the tenure track, considering issues of dissertation reform along the way. Most notably, perhaps, *Rewriting Success in Rhetoric and Composition Careers* (Goodburn and Leverenz) focuses on increasing the visibility of non-traditional or "alt-ac" careers and pathways into them. A kindred project to ours, that volume "concentrates attention on the interrelation of three points—career training, knowledge-making, and disciplinarity—to examine both how rhetoric and composition literally 'disciplines' itself via its assumptions about what constitutes its work (materially and intellectually) and how such assumptions manifest themselves in our graduate training and career advice" (x). Bringing together personal accounts from individuals across academic appointment types and those beyond the university, the collection is a valuable addition to the conversation about graduate education and alternative careers for rhetoric and composition degree holders.

Featured as the subject of such edited collections and addressed in professional venues like *Inside Higher Education* and *The Chronicle of Higher Education*, alt-ac jobs are increasingly a part of our local programmatic considerations. Still, the alt-ac movement remains under-addressed in our discipline's major journals. Little has changed in terms of cultures, structures, or metaphors for imagining or enacting doctoral education differently.

This is, of course, understandable: Those of us comfortably tenured or in tenure-track positions within the academy may find it difficult to conceive of how our skills can be deployed outside of the academy. As the "10 humanities scholars" who responded to the MLA report note (all but one of whom seem to be tenured associate professors), the recommendation for "new career training places increased burdens on graduate program directors." They criticize the report because it "somehow expects faculty to provide training for students in areas where faculty themselves may not be adequately trained" (2).

While we recognize that, like most who hold English PhDs, we have not ourselves been trained explicitly for work outside the academy, we see the public turn and non-academic job preparation as an opportunity. To this end, we follow Sylvia Gale and Evan Carton in their call toward "reorienting—if not dissolving entirely—the expert's stance" in public scholarship, producing a shift in how we think about expertise, specialization, and training that might move us forward ever so slightly towards addressing the needs of students in our programs (42). We draw on the work of economist Scott Page, who theorizes the benefits of diversity, to demonstrate how disciplinary and career diversity (including an expanded understanding of expertise) might be harnessed as a productive force on dissertation committees.

In short, we are exploring how to reconfigure the dissertation committee as a structure capable of supporting a wide range of future careers both inside and outside of the academy for degree recipients.[1] As the "pivot point for change in doctoral education," the dissertation is a productive place to begin reimagining both the means and the ends of doctoral education (MLA 14). MLA past president Sidonie Smith claims that we "redefine the mission of the humanities doctoral degree by reimagining the dissertation" ("Beyond"). The Dissertation Consortium group that drafted contributions for a 2001 Interchanges section of *CCC* used the same language of "reimagining" in their own title, "Challenging Tradition: A Conversation about Reimagining the Dissertation in Rhetoric and Composition," while the edited collection *The Dissertation and the Discipline* identifies its own transformational purpose in the subtitle, *Reinventing Composition Studies*. Many others have likewise suggested expanding the form of the dissertation over the past several decades, to include digital and multimodal dissertations as well as a suite of essays, as alternatives to the proto-monograph (see Cassuto and Jay; The Dissertation Consortium; Lang; Olson and Drew).

Building on these contributions, we focus on mentorship provided by a diverse dissertation committee rather than on the product or form the dissertation takes. Our logic is as follows: Models of expertise and mentorship are not compatible with current understandings of interdisciplinarity, public work, and alternative career preparation for graduate students. As we will demonstrate, current models of dissertation supervision in composition and rhetoric—and in the humanities generally—underemphasize the power and importance of groups and collaboration and perpetuate myths about individual expertise. Patricia Sullivan argued twenty years ago that the idea of the independent scholar is an outdated myth, and the notion of apprenticeship that undergirds it is similarly outdated.

So perhaps we are not encouraging innovative, tradition-challenging dissertations because we have not developed the theoretical and material structures to support that work on dissertation committees. Sullivan argues that dissertation committees already offer a space for collaborative work, even as we obscure this group knowledge construction and continue to promote the notion of the individual scholar. To address this issue, we are imagining a committee that insists on collaboration, diversity, and interdisciplinarity—one that has members with different kinds of expertise, including different academic and practical/professional expertise, and one where all members are fully involved in the project from its early stages.

We begin in the next section by describing our model of interdisciplinarity before discussing what an interdisciplinary dissertation committee might look like in practice. We close by considering the possible implications of such changes to the dissertation committee, reflecting on the need to proceed dialogically—to consider appropriate changes without getting mired in either-or propositions rooted in suspicion or oversimplification.

Beyond Apprenticeship: Diversity, Interdisciplinarity, and Collaboration

We argue that one reason the apprenticeship model remains so persistent in doctoral training is that we do not have an adequate model for understanding collaborative, interdisciplinary research and its relationship to expertise. Economist Scott Page's research on diversity helps us theorize a model of interdisciplinarity and collaboration that could harness the power of groups and diversity to create new approaches to doctoral mentorship that may better serve students, communities, and disciplines. We follow Page in thinking of diversity as signifying not only social categories of race, gender, sex, socioeconomic status and so on, although this type of diversity is necessary and brings valuable perspectives to a doctoral committee, but also intellectual differences produced through disciplinary training, attendance at different types of schools in a range of geographical locations, and the variety of perspectives generated by different life experiences, including work experiences.

In *The Difference: How the Power of Diversity Creates Better Groups, Firms, Schools and Societies*, Page argues that collections of people with diverse perspectives and experiences usually prove better at problem solving than those with homogeneous perspectives and experiences. This argument is not a particularly radical or new idea; the belief that people with different disciplinary training and heuristics will bring different perspectives to scientific and social problems also underlies recent calls by the National Science Foundation and National Institutes of Health for proposals from interdisciplinary research teams and undergirds much interest in digital humanities scholarship. However, Page offers a more surprising claim: A collection of diverse individuals with average abilities will prove *better* at solving problems than a homogenous collection of individuals with superior abilities.[2] This claim fundamentally challenges the mythos that continues to underlie the apprentice model of doctoral education in the humanities. Namely, that the best scholarship is the work of individual genius, that individual genius can be modeled and cloned, and that such cloning is the best way to produce the next generation of scholars.

Instead, Page's research suggests that groups and diversity are key to innovation. As Page demonstrates though mathematical proofs, individuals who bring different perspectives, interpretations, heuristics, and predictive models (or what Page calls diverse "tools") build on one another's insights to advance their collective thinking. While people employing similar heuristics and perspectives when attempting to solve a problem will get stuck at the same "local peaks," or local optima, Page argues that "cognitive diversity improves performance at problem solving and predictive tasks" (314).

Some may be skeptical about the language of "problem solving," but we see value in Page's broad definition of problems and solutions: "Solutions are not just answers to math questions. They're also status quo points. What you are wearing is a solution to the problem of getting dressed" (55). Although Page's discussion of solutions to problems may seem more relevant to the sciences and to business and industry than to the humanities, his insights have broad application for thinking about the wide range of problems represented by English research. For example, problems such as interpreting a literary text, understanding the rhetorical effects of a suffragette's personal essays, or theorizing genre change are better addressed through multiple, diverse perspectives, interpretations, heuristics, and models.

In particular, Page's insights suggest the potential value of interdisciplinarity and other forms of diversity to the training of the next generation of academics and public scholars in our doctoral programs. If, as Page argues, the benefits of diversity kick in when we face difficult and complex problems, then dissertation research is a prime context for applying his insights, as the ideas students grapple with and the process of writing a dissertation are both difficult and complex. Page explains,

> People with different disciplinary training naturally bring diverse understandings and tools to problems. That diversity of tools can lead to breakthroughs that would not occur, or would occur more slowly without interdisciplinary research. . . . This book provides a logic for continuing to break down the barriers that separate the disciplines. (16)

But diversity is not limited to disciplinary differences. Rather, the diversity we outline below refers to heuristic and methodological differences that may well exist *within* disciplines. It also encompasses work outside the disciplines, among non-profit leaders and other community-based specialists. As Page notes, "Being different, as should be obvious, is not the property of an individual in isolation but a property of an individual relative to others" (168). Difference is contextual, so an economist appears different when joining a group of English professors, for whom mathematical modeling is a rarity. As much as we all contain multitudes, a person by oneself cannot be diverse.

We believe relational difference is a key point for considering how to integrate interdisciplinarity into graduate training. When we locate difference in the individual, it is difficult to imagine effective graduate programs that are both interdisciplinary and sufficiently specialized to prepare disciplinary agents who are well grounded in the discourse of several fields. Mastering the disciplinary frameworks and heuristics of multiple disciplines is both time consuming and work-intensive. However, if we locate interdisciplinarity not in the individual but in the group, the requirement for individual expertise in multiple disciplines shifts. Focus on the diversity of the group or committee allows us to (re)configure interdisciplinarity not as the individual student mastering or working in multiple disciplines but as harnessing different disciplinary perspectives and heuristics embodied by the dissertation committee and offered collaboratively by multiple mentors.

Other scholars have similarly advocated multiple mentors based on a broad understanding of intellectual community (Damrosch; Rose and Weiser; Walker et al.). As George E. Walker et al. propose in *The Formation of Scholars*, we might consider "a shift of prepositions: from a system in which students are apprenticed *to* a faculty mentor, to one in which they apprentice *with* several mentors" (91). That is, we might dispel the myth of the independent scholar—and, perhaps, the notion of "original," "independently produced," and "individually owned" scholarship—and the traditional apprenticeship model it undergirds, and instead embrace the power of groups and intellectual community to train future scholars for a changed and changing intellectual landscape, one more collaborative and future-oriented.

The incorporation of additional perspectives requires that faculty mentors understand their roles differently—as Walker et al. suggest, faculty should shift from mentoring "to" to mentoring "with." Such a shift is already underway in organizations such as the National Center for Faculty Development and Diversity, where Kerry Ann Rockquemore has promoted a model of networked mentoring for new faculty that acknowledges the role of collaboration and interdisciplinary support in the development of junior faculty. Working against the idea of what she calls the "guru" mentor, Rockquemore instead encourages us to see mentorship in terms of developing a network of people who each support discrete aspects of professional development and personal needs.

This call for diversity is not an argument for making all projects, much less all students, interdisciplinary. We would do well to craft flexible program guidelines that make room for different experiences and products, even as we preserve more traditional forms of inquiry and delivery, as not all committees should be different in the same way. Indeed, as Page acknowledges, "Successful organizations...maintain balance if some people move slowly, if they do not leap to the next new idea along with everyone else" (369). But we would do well to expand the available professional development models, as the intellectual and institutional contexts around us continue to shift. In what follows, we supplement Page's model by outlining a few examples that demonstrate how interdisciplinary and community collaboration has catalyzed doctoral research experiences in our field, preparing students for a variety of careers following graduation.

Reimagining the Dissertation: Focusing on the Process rather than the Product

In order to describe graduate education as a collaborative enterprise preparing students for a diverse range of career outcomes, we focus on the working processes of the dissertation committee to emphasize the perspectives, heuristics, interpretations, and models learned by being part of a diverse team—lessons that apply to both academic and non-academic appointments.[3]

Recent recommendations from Smith are one place to start. Smith has been at the forefront of the conversation about rethinking doctoral education and the dissertation in English, and we align with her vision of this process as intersecting fruitfully with conversations about public scholarship and alt-ac careers.[4] And, though she tends to focus on the form of the dissertation, Smith's recommendations actually underscore the importance of a shift to process as we think about doctoral work in our field. For example, in "Rethinking Doctoral Education," she outlines a series of "other forms" for the dissertation, which include "[u]ndertaking a collaborative project with other students or a faculty adviser" and "[p]ursuing a project of public scholarship, as sketched by Julie Ellison and Timothy K. Eatman, possibly undertaken in a community external to the academy or addressed to issues of public policy" (24). As Smith points out, the models of public engagement in the arts, humanities, and design provided in Ellison and Eatman's "Scholarship in Public" could readily support diverse doctoral projects and committees. Similarly, recent collections and other volumes dedicated to community-engaged scholarship are awash with examples of innovative projects that draw on a diversity of perspectives to prepare students for a wide range of careers. See, for example, the projects featured in the volume *Collaborative Futures*, which posits publicly active graduate education as a path to diverse careers. This collection includes work from our own field, including a chapter by Linda Bergmann, Allen Brizee, and Jaclyn Wells. But we wanted a better sense of how publicly engaged research was being taken up in the discipline.

To find additional models of innovative dissertation work we reviewed approximately four-hundred of the rhetoric and composition dissertations published in the last five years and found (with a few notable exceptions) little evidence of alternative dissertation uptake or publicly engaged scholarship. However, this apparent absence could also be a function of the ProQuest Dissertations and Theses database limitations. To get a more localized picture of the work being done, we solicited examples from networks of publicly engaged scholars like Publicly Active Graduate Education (PAGE), the Higher Education Service Learning listserv, the journal *Reflections*, and the CCCC SIGs for Community Literacy, Service Learning and Public Rhetorics. We sent emails to these various groups and listservs requesting current and recently graduated students or mentors involved in publicly engaged research projects to contact us to tell us about their work. We received about a dozen responses to this request and arranged Zoom meetings with those individuals so we could learn about their experiences and projects.[5]

The informational interviews we conducted with students and faculty who had engaged in this work in graduate school provided insights that help us to address the concerns and hesitations mentors in the academy have voiced about transforming the dissertation process. Without a lot of programmatic support, the transformative practices we uncovered were a result of students' own drives to engage: These scholars brought varied interests and commitments with them to graduate school and saw engaged public work and the prospect of alternative careers as a given, and they believed the work they were already committed to doing would lead to significant scholarly products. The comments of these trailblazing scholars provide insights into the kinds of work students are already doing so that we can better understand how we might build on existing models and structures that support the diverse intellectual practices to which we aspire.[6]

For instance, one current student with whom we spoke, Sarah Moon, described her non-profit background as providing the foundation for her scholarly ambitions. Moon recognized that a PhD was necessary for the kind of research she aspired to do, though she also remained open to the idea of doing such scholarship from outside the university upon graduation. She described her experience as "moving between worlds" and expressed fear of getting sucked into the "other world" of academe entirely (personal interview). At the intersection of these "worlds," though, Moon was consciously drawing on the diverse experiences and perspectives of a range of faculty and community partners to think about her work; Moon had what Page might call a diverse "toolkit." For example, her community writing and performance project, Write Your Roots, was a collaboration with a sociology professor who was co-founder and board president of a community kitchen organization. This collaborator's perspectives were foundational to Moon's developing understanding of food justice issues, even though she did not serve on Moon's committee.

Within her own department at the University of Connecticut Moon found faculty support for this work, constituting her committee with a faculty member who does community writing scholarship, a supportive chair with a background in rhetoric who does not have community engagement experience herself but "sees what [Moon wants] to do and supports it," and an ethnographic researcher (personal interview). Nonetheless, for Moon the dissertation did not appear to be a space where her two worlds could be brought together, and thus the work she conducted with the sociology professor and her other community partners remained outside the scholarly work she was doing in her dissertation. If the dissertation and the dissertation committee were more flexible, she could have built upon the different perspectives brought to bear by the sociologist and by practitioners in the community. Thus, while students can (and do) make connections between their scholarly work and their personal commitments to social issues, the lack of institutional recognition for the expertise that such community members bring to a project sends a message about the value ascribed to work outside of the academy.

The stories of recent graduates with community engagement experience echoed Moon's, both in terms of the importance of collaborating with experts outside the academy as well as with departmental faculty and the difficulty of integrating community-based commitments with degree requirements. Take, for example, Allen Brizee, a 2010 graduate of Purdue University's rhetoric and composition program and associate professor of writing at Loyola University Maryland. At Purdue, Brizee wrote a dissertation on building college-community partnerships through the Online Writing Lab, with Linda Bergmann as his director. Brizee describes his dissertation work with the Purdue Online Writing Lab and local community literacy organizations as a collaborative experience informed by insights from a wide range of stakeholders (personal correspondence). In a recent book on the experience, *Partners in Literacy,* Brizee and coauthor Jaclyn Wells, who also worked at the lab, discuss the integral role of community members to such research, and each discusses at length the previous experiences that informed their commitments to community work in graduate school. In their preface, Brizee and Wells write, "The relationships fostered were just as significant, if not more so, than the products created" (xi).

Brizee notes that his faculty mentors were supportive of the impact these community partners had on his project, particularly on the iterative design process of the research (personal interview). In this way, Brizee's project was deeply informed by diverse perspectives and knowledge domains. This diversity produced a big, complex project that did not conform easily to the standard dissertation product and was, according to Brizee, a "mess." Such messiness may characterize the work of heterogeneous groups working together on complex research tasks. But the important thing for him was the process and what he learned through this big messy project where the non-faculty contributors played a significant role, even if they were not on his actual dissertation committee. Thus, though he did ultimately compose a fairly traditional dissertation as a point-in-time product of this work, the collaborative intellectual project far exceeded the dissertation product (as it so often does) and involved many collaborators and stakeholders whose work may well be obscured by the dissertation signature page. How might we reimagine the dissertation, process and product, in order to encourage the diversity of perspectives that Brizee obviously benefitted from as he began his scholarly career?

Sylvia Gale's scholarship on publicly engaged projects and partnerships helps us further explore this question when she emphasizes the messiness of publicly engaged work and the desirability of that mess. During her time in graduate school, Gale developed the Free Minds Project, a partnership between University of Texas at Austin and local organizations to offer college-level humanities programming to low-income adults. This work remained largely separate from her dissertation work, which examined the historical intersections of literacy education and vocational education in the United States. In an article on her own professional "trajectory" (a term she resists) as a publicly engaged scholar, Gale expresses a sense of being divided and overwhelmed, referring to her graduate experience as a "crazy-making muddle of projects, programs, and plans" (315). But she also emphasizes the positive synergies produced by her historical scholarship and her publicly engaged work during graduate school and encourages publicly active graduate students and their advocates to "relish the engaged and artful multiplicity of our roles" (327). Perhaps it is true, as she argues, that "innovative public scholarship resists integration and unification" (323). Perhaps innovative scholarship of any kind resists integration and unification.

Instead of a unified professional identity or project, Gale suggests a model of multiple roles to understand the work of public scholarship in and beyond graduate school:

> As a graduate student with public roles and commitments, I acquired the skills I needed to carry out the projects at hand as I needed them, learning from and with those around me. Commitments and projects unfolded one from the other. . . . All of this involved less a progression from one phase or stage of engagement to another than a constant shifting of the weight among the various concurrent roles I inhabited. (320)

The way Gale picks up on this idea of multiple roles, or what she calls "roles thinking," resonates with our notion of diversity; just as the "juice" of "roles thinking . . . lies in the intersections themselves" and "in the spaces between roles," innovative dissertation projects might similarly take shape in the intersections between diverse individuals and their expertise (322). In this way, then, we might follow Gale's observation that "perhaps the highest goal of the engaged public scholar—the end state of the professional trajectory—is not the integration of roles but an ongoing and dynamic multiplicity" (322).

Gale's experience raises the question of how we might build on the many roles experienced by graduate students by embracing "an ongoing and dynamic multiplicity" in our conception of expertise. Brizee and Wells, too, mentioned the importance of drawing on diverse, community-based expertise, particularly about "adult education and local literacy issues" that the students and their university faculty advisors lacked. "If necessity is the mother of invention," they write, "it's perhaps also the mother of collaboration" (128).

These multiple conceptions of expertise lay the groundwork for diversifying our dissertation committees to include community experts, and they also model a variety of career outcomes for our students. Gale herself serves as an example: Building on her publicly engaged work during graduate school, she secured an alt-ac job as associate director (now director) of the Bonner Center for Civic Engagement at the University of Richmond. In a more traditional academic career himself, Brizee acknowledged that he had likewise considered applying for a range of other positions, including non-academic jobs in information architecture and usability studies. Thanks to his intensive work with a range of mentors and collaborators within and beyond the university, he felt confident that he would have been successful in a non-academic job search and happy doing that kind of work (personal interview).

Each interviewee has worked with faculty from different disciplines and community partners whose perspectives have informed the students' projects fundamentally, although the intellectual contributions of these non-disciplinary experts are not recognized by the academy's structures. As Ellison and Eatman suggest, such projects ultimately ask us to "[enlarge] the conception of who counts as 'peer' and what counts as 'publication'" as part of "the democratization of knowledge on and off campus" (Ellison and Eatman iv). Though Ellison and Eatman are discussing this shift in relation to tenure requirements, their points invite us also to reconsider the dissertation committee in this regard—its constitution and its work. The fact is, even as students have found their own ways to make their research collaborations successful, our current structures too often ask students to keep their worlds of experience apart, as Moon describes, and devalue the expertise of community contributors. This failure to acknowledge the expertise of those not in the academy impoverishes our scholarship and limits our audience to those in our own disciplines. Expanding our conception of expertise allows students to engage with multiple professional role models and mentors who can shape their scholarly identities and research questions, leading to rich and innovative research in and outside of the academy. And that research, in turn, serves the needs of those community stakeholders who benefit from the research to which they contribute. Reciprocity is a key consideration, one for which these examples and others provide a strong model.

But these examples, of course, represent individual projects, not ongoing initiatives with the sustainability needed for wide-ranging reform. If we were really interested in harnessing the power of groups and diversity to disrupt the apprenticeship model of graduate education, we might go further to refashion the dissertation committee. One conception might be to think of the dissertation committee as equivalent to a lab experience, with several students focused on similar problems or projects working in a team with faculty members from different disciplines and professionals from outside the university, as appropriate. Borrowing the educational model of the sciences, these labs would be working towards the same research and programmatic goals that we already pursue but would be doing so with a conscious foregrounding of the necessity of collaboration and a recognition that this work can enable research projects for our students. Such a team could work to map the necessary research, to carve out different parts of the project for each student, and to meet regularly to comment on drafts and share progress; when one student is "stuck," to use Page's term, the team could bring its diverse perspectives to the issue to suggest ways of moving forward. And the diffusion of labor within the collaborative structure of a lab setting makes space for a diversity of contributions and models of expertise.

Even if such team-based work is not prevalent in the humanities, there are a few models for such work. Linda Flower's Community Literacy Center serves as a notable and successful example of community-based work supporting dissertations and career development for a great number of graduate students. Brizee pointed out that the Online Writing Lab in which he and Wells worked was specifically termed a "lab" to suggest this association of research labs on campus as sites of research collaboration (personal interview). As Bergmann and others have persuasively argued, writing centers serve as spaces of interdisciplinary and extra-institutional engagement that can support the development of publicly engaged research. Such projects, Bergmann notes, are an effective way of "establishing and maintaining long-term relationships between university programs and community institutions, because research projects can last for a long time, drawing new faculty and graduate students into the work" (171). Because of longevity (for faculty) and turnover (of graduate students), the lab model could prove particularly effective not only for community partners but also for the graduate students who wish to pursue community-engaged or social action research with faculty members from their institution.

This lab model is similar to the many "collaborative, publicly oriented research centers" that Brian Gogan and his coauthors have reminded us "do exist in the humanities and in our own discipline" (338). Gogan et al. identify more than 50 research centers that they argue "function as change agents by emphasizing collaboration and conducting research focused on publics" (336). These are organizations—"centers, laboratories, studios, institutes, collectives, and environments"—that allow "faculty and their associates from varied backgrounds and expertise to come together to solve common problems that could not otherwise be addressed" (qtd. in Gogan 338). These centers institutionalize the interdisciplinary lab model and are thus a powerful (if often overlooked) model for interdisciplinary and even extra-institutional collaboration mobilized in the humanities to produce excellent research—and, significantly, excellent researchers—for a variety of publics.

Stacey Pigg, Kendall Leon, and Martine Courant Rife discuss Michigan State University's WIDE center in this regard. Building on their own diverse experiences there, they argue that "[g]raduate students whose professional training is centered in the work of a functioning research center are well prepared to work outside of typical academic research models," in part because they "acquire practical experience in collaboration and group dynamics, navigating institutional structures, and working contextually across multiple rhetorical situations" (192). Through their experience working with a multiplicity of projects and partners, students "shap[e] their own diverse career paths and their learning for future work within or outside the university" (192).

Applying this lab or research center model to the dissertation committee pushes against the apprenticeship model in that the doctoral candidate is expected to synthesize diverse perspectives and ultimately learn different tools from other members of the committee, tools not part of the primary mentor's kit. Collaboration is central. But the resulting dissertation, whatever form it takes, is the student's unique response to and distillation of the committee's diverse disciplinary and professional expertise. The resulting researcher is not a clone of any one member of the committee but has successfully learned from all of them and incorporated various heuristics and perspectives into her mental toolkit. Likewise, being accountable to a team through regular meetings to share progress will help graduate students avoid long periods of unproductivity and will prepare them to collaborate with other researchers and community members in their post-graduate careers. And whether particular students are focused on entering academe or exploring alternative careers, all team members are likely to learn to think of the ways in which their knowledge and research skills could contribute to the world outside academe. Unlike current faculty who say they are not prepared to help their students imagine alternatives because they were not trained to think this way, graduates who have such team-based experiences are likely to be far more able to prepare their own students for multiple career outcomes.

Conclusion: Reimagined Committees for Reimagined Careers

Although we begin with the end—with the creation of more diverse dissertation committees—we know that changes to the dissertation committee would also very well entail a transformation of other aspects of doctoral education, from recruitment to the dissertation product and beyond. We assume a curriculum flexible enough to allow students to pursue some interests outside English, a curriculum that would allow them to take a public policy course, for instance, or a finance or entrepreneurship course, or to participate in a social action research project, or to travel abroad as part of an international, interdisciplinary service learning team. To take just one example, Lara Smith-Sitton and Lynée Lewis Gaillet describe an innovative internship program that operates as an "alternative classroom" that "prepares students for a range of academic and mainstream employment" (211). We need to take seriously the proposition of expanding these opportunities within our graduate programs, as such flexibility allows students not only to explore their own extra-disciplinary interests but also to begin thinking of how their disciplinary work could contribute to those areas outside of the discipline (see also Krebs). The particular courses, structures, and requirements must be determined by each program to suit the needs of their institution and their students, but we can imagine curricular changes that would make programs more flexible and better able to serve the needs of students, not all of whom want to be carbon copies of their mentors.

Helping our graduate students imagine the various contributions their research can make to society is key to them discovering the possibility of a fulfilling future outside of the academy. While the value of the humanities should not be judged by its practical utility to society, it remains true that humanists *do* have much to offer in this way, and our perspectives as advanced disciplinary specialists might provide the diversity to enrich other intellectual endeavors across sectors. We believe the dissertation process is a good place to address academic labor issues and the future of humanistic study.

This should not be seen as demoralizing or capitulating to market forces. Rather, we should imagine doctoral study as leading to both academic jobs where PhDs are required and to careers outside academe where PhDs are an advantage—where scholarly thinking is engaged in public contexts. In this same way, some students might constitute committees more clearly aimed at disciplinary work, while others might more purposefully incorporate community or public engagement, while all are harnessing the benefits of diversity to forward their thinking. And, ironically, we believe that students who are urged to think of how their advanced training can be applied outside the academy will actually have an advantage on the academic job market as well, as they are likely to help future students—undergraduates and graduates alike—think of how they can contribute to diverse teams to improve our future. These graduates, who can teach classes on professionalization, build community connections, oversee internships, etc., will build the pipeline for future work of this kind. That is how change happens—not necessarily with those of us already in the field, but through our students: the faculty of the future.

A major part of what holds us back may be our own skepticism and resistance. If, as faculty and as a discipline, we are averse to changes to doctoral education, such changes will necessarily fail to gain momentum. While we can't control a great many aspects of our institutions, we might follow David Laurence in recognizing that we *do* have control over our academic cultures and our definition of success for graduates (6). As Page points out, "If we want diverse groups to work better, it helps to believe that they do. . . . There's still hard work to do: belief in diversity's benefits alone is not enough. . . . But we need to believe in the value of diversity. Belief may be a necessary condition" (352). Knowing there is a long way to go, then, we are choosing to believe in the possibilities of a reimagined dissertation and a broadened future for humanities doctorates.

Notes

1. Scholars in technical and professional writing have also explored the notion of expertise and distributed expertise, particularly in connection to activity theory. We envision rich intersections between our arguments here and that disciplinary conversation.

2. In Page's model, an agent's problem-solving ability is represented by coordinates representing her perspective and heuristics. The agent's expected performance on a problem is what is referred to as her "ability." While this mathematical modeling necessarily flattens the complexity of ability in real human agents, it remains a useful model for thinking about ability and diversity in complicated real-life scenarios as well.

3. See Isaiah Simpson's 1987 article in this journal for an early, kindred exploration of using team teaching to prepare graduate teaching assistants.

4. See, for example, the MLAs Connected Academics website. Note: We come at the areas of public and community engagement somewhat from the side. That is, as we considered the value of rethinking the dissertation committee and its processes and products, we found that publicly engaged scholarship was a space where this conversation was already well underway. While we draw on this robust and valu-

able foundation, we simultaneously see the significance of rethinking the dissertation processes and products as transcending existing publicly engaged and alt-ac conversations.

5. Thanks to Keri Mathis for these suggestions.

6. Because we did not seek the generalizable knowledge about the field that a full research study would offer but instead sought anecdotal examples to illustrate our argument, the IRB representative at our institution advised us not to pursue IRB approval for this research. Though we did not conduct a full IRB study, we obtained permission to quote from and discuss these anecdotal conversations with each participant, each of whom also read and approved a draft of this article prior to publication. All names are real names, and opinions and experiences are shared in their capacity as scholars in the field. We spoke to a number of other students as well and, though we could not include all of their responses here, we are grateful to each interviewee for their generosity and interest in this project.

Works Cited

Bergmann, Linda. "The Writing Center as a Site of Engagement." *Going Public: What Writing Programs Can Learn from Engagement*, edited by Shirley Rose and Irwin Weiser, Utah State UP, 2010, pp. 160-76.

Brizee, Allen. Personal Interview. 14 Nov. 2016.

Brizee, Allen, and Jaclyn Wells. *Partners in Literacy: A Writing Center Model for Civic Engagement*. Rowman & Littlefield, 2016.

Cassuto, Leonard, and Paul Jay. "The PhD Dissertation: In Search of a Usable Future." *Pedagogy: Critical Approaches to Teaching Literature, Language, Composition, and Culture*, vol. 15, no. 1, 2014, pp. 81-92.

Connected Academics. *Modern Language Association*, https://connect.mla.hcommons.org.

Damrosch, David. "Vectors of Change." *Envisioning the Future of Doctoral Education*, edited by Chris M. Golde and George E. Walker, Jossey Bass, 2006, pp. 34-45.

The Dissertation Consortium. "Challenging Tradition: A Conversation about Reimagining the Dissertation in Rhetoric and Composition." *CCC*, vol. 52, no. 3, 2001, pp. 441-54.

Ellison, Julie, and Timothy K. Eatman. "Scholarship in Public: Knowledge Creation and Tenure Policy in the Engaged University." *Imagining America*, 2008, http://imagining america.org/wp-content/uploads/2015/07/ScholarshipinPublicKnowledge.pdf.

Gale, Sylvia. "Arcs, Checklists, and Charts: The Trajectory of a Public Scholar?" Gilvin, Roberts, and Martin, pp. 315-27.

---. Personal Interview. 1 Sept. 2016.

Gale, Sylvia, and Evan Carton. "Toward the Practice of the Humanities." *The Good Society*, vol. 14, no. 3, 2005, pp. 38-44.

Gilvin, Amanda, Georgia M. Roberts, and Craig Martin, editors. *Collaborative Futures.* Syracuse UP, 2012.

Gogan, Brian, Kelly Belanger, Ashley Patriarca, and Megan O'Neill. "Research Centers as Change Agents: Reshaping Work in Rhetoric and Writing." *CCC*, vol. 62, no. 2, 2010, pp. 336-63.

Goodburn, Amy, Donna LeCourt, and Carrie Leverenz, editors. *Rewriting Success in Rhetoric and Composition Careers*. Parlor Press, 2013.

Krebs, Paula. "A New Humanities Ph.D." *Insider Higher Education*, 24 May 2010, https://www.insidehighered.com/views/2010/05/24/new-humanities-phd.

Lang, Susan. "Electronic Dissertations: Preparing Students for Our Past or Their Futures?" *College English*, vol. 64, no. 6, 2002, pp. 680-95.

Laurence, David. "From the Editor: What's Next For Graduate Education?" *ADE Bulletin* vol. 152, 2012, pp. 3-6, doi: 10.1632/ade.152.3.

MLA Task Force on Doctoral Study in Modern Languages and Literature. *Report of the MLA Task Force on Doctoral Study in Modern Languages and Literature*. New York: MLA, 2014.

Moon, Sarah. Personal Interview. 13 Sept. 2016.

Moore, Cindy, and Hildy Miller. *A Guide to Professional Development for Graduate Students in English*. NCTE, 2006.

Olson, Gary A., and Julie Drew. "(Re) Reenvisioning the Dissertation in English Studies." *College English*, vol. 61, vol. 1, 1998, pp. 56-66.

Page, Scott E. *The Difference: How the Power of Diversity Creates Better Groups, Firms, Schools, and Societies*. Princeton UP, 2007.

Panel on Alternative Approaches to Graduate Education. *Scholarship for Society*. ETS, 1973. Pigg, Stacey, Kendall Leon, and Martine Courant Rife. "Researching to Professionalize, not Professionalizing to Research: Modular Professionalization and the WIDE Effect." Goodburn, LeCourt, and Leverenz, pp. 191-208.

Rockquemore, Kerry Ann. "A New Model of Mentoring." *Inside Higher Education*, July 22, 2013, https://www.insidehighered.com/advice/2013/07/22/essay-calling-senior-faculty-embrace-new-style-mentoring.

Rose, Shirley K., and Irwin Weiser, editors. *Going Public: What Writing Programs Learn from Engagement*. Utah State UP, 2010.

Simpson, Isaiah. "Training and Evaluating Teaching Assistants Through Team Teaching." *Composition Studies*, vol. 15, no. 3, 1987, pp. 4-13.

Smith, Sidonie. "Beyond the Dissertation Monograph." *MLA Newsletter*, vol. 42, no. 1, 2010, pp. 2-3.

---. "From the President: An Agenda for the New Dissertation." *MLA Newsletter*, vol. 42, no. 2, 2010, pp. 2-3.

---. "Rethinking Doctoral Education." *ADE Bulletin*, vol. 150, 2010, pp. 13-31.

Smith-Sitton, Lara, and Lynée Lewis Gaillet. "Bridging Town and Gown through Academic Internships." Goodburn, LeCourt, and Leverenz, pp. 209-26.

Sullivan, Patricia A. "Revising the Myth of the Independent Scholar." *Writing With: New Directions in Collaborative Teaching, Learning, and Research*, edited by Sally Barr Reagan, Thomas Fox, and David Bleich, SUNY Press, 1994, pp. 11-29.

10 Humanities Scholars. "Don't Capitulate. Advocate." *Insider Higher Education*, 24 June 2014, https://www.insidehighered.com/views/2014/06/24/essay-critiques-mla-report-graduate-education.

Walker, George E., et al. *The Formation of Scholars: Rethinking Doctoral Education for the Twenty-First Century.* Jossey-Bass, 2008.

Welch, Nancy, Catherine G. Latterell, Cindy Moore, and Sheila Carter-Tod. *The Dissertation and the Discipline: Reinventing Composition Studies.* Heinemann, 2002.

Whitson, Roger. "DHSI 2014 Day 1, or Why We Need the MLA Report." *Roger Whitson,* 3 June 2014, http://www.rogerwhitson.net/?p=2942.

Good Things in Threes: Long-Term Effects of Literate Dwelling

Steve Lamos

I investigate here the personal and professional significance of "literate dwelling"—that is, processes whereby individuals learn to acquire and use literacy within initial spaces and times of comfort in order both to move beyond such comfort and to promote productive change in the larger world. Such significance became especially clear to me during a return to my alma mater, the University of Illinois at Urbana-Champaign, and my adopted hometown, Champaign, IL, during one particular week in April 2014. Aided by work from Nedra Reynolds, Julie Lindquist, Kevin Roozen, and others, I analyze the ways in which three events that took place during this particular week—a successful academic homecoming of sorts, an unexpected reunion with a former musical group, and a welcoming of a new family member into the world—have helped me to understand how literate dwelling experiences from as long as twenty years ago continue to shape my present life in profound ways. Furthermore, I argue that narrative reflection on the effects of literate dwelling, both long-term and short-term, can help us to understand, theorize, and cultivate worthwhile life-making over time and across spaces and domains.

In late April 2014, I was invited back to my longtime home, Champaign, IL (hereafter Champaign) at the request of my undergraduate and PhD-granting institution, the University of Illinois at Urbana-Champaign (hereafter UIUC), to give a keynote at its annual graduate student symposium. After having lived in Champaign for nearly fifteen years, from 1992 until 2005, and after having completed a BA, MEd, and PhD at UIUC, I had not been back either to my alma mater or my adopted hometown in about a decade. My return for this event was thus both a personal and a professional homecoming of sorts. It would also end up illustrating rather vividly to me a number of educational and personal instances of what I'll be calling "literate dwelling": that is, the process whereby individuals learn to acquire and use literacy within initial spaces and times of comfort and safety such that they can ultimately move beyond those spaces and times in order to promote productive change in—and hopefully transformation of—the larger world.

This particular week in April 2014 helped me both to see and better understand the importance of at least three kinds of literate dwelling that I had been doing in Champaign and UIUC for anywhere between ten and twenty years previously: dwelling related to my professional work in rhetoric and composition, dwelling related to my extracurricular life as a drummer in rock bands, and dwelling related to my personal life as a spouse and, eventually, a father. Each of these types of literate dwelling started out as things that I did as I went off to school in Champaign without any kind of plan or endpoint in sight: I studied rhetoric and composition largely because I liked reading and writing, but I didn't see the immediate utility in pursuing further graduate study in English Literature; I played drums in many rock bands in Champaign because doing so both allowed me to make music and to make friends; I ended up meeting a woman in Champaign (a fellow UIUC undergraduate in English, in fact) with whom I would fall in love because, I suppose, falling in love happens to people sometimes.

However, the events of that particular week have ultimately helped me to see that each of these dwelling activities has had a profoundly important effect on my life, literate and otherwise, in ways that defy easy characterization or simplistic labeling. Specifically, that week has helped me to understand three key facets of dwelling:

1. that dwelling can take years and years to manifest in ways that are not easy to predict ahead of time;
2. that various forms of dwelling are inextricable from each other, rooted in and folding back onto one another in multiple ways, especially with respect to notions of comfort, discomfort, and identity; and
3. that past dwelling can be—indeed, must be—prologue for present and future dwelling work, a kind of preparation for future movement beyond initial spaces of comfort into a sort of engagement with the larger world.

I ultimately see these related facets of literate dwelling as driving what Elizabeth Kimball, Emily Schnee, and Liesl Schwabe characterize as the "emergent and unpredictable outcomes" (117) resulting from literate dwelling of various types. While these outcomes may be "difficult to measure and chart on an assessment rubric" (130), they lie at the very core of what it means to compose a literate life—past, present, and future. I believe that these long-term outcomes of literate dwelling are important to understand as scholars, teachers, and students of both writing and literate activity more generally, especially in an educational age that increasingly puts a premium on speed, scalability, and (often overly simplistic) outcomes assessment measures.

Literate Dwelling as Comfort and Movement beyond Comfort

The notion of literate dwelling that I want to put forward here relies first and foremost on the combined work of compositionist Nedra Reynolds and critical geographer Peter King (themselves each referencing key notions from Martin Heidegger). Reynolds defines dwelling as a process by which writers become enmeshed within, across, and beyond an initial space or set of spaces: "Writers dwell in ideas to make them their own; they squat, intellectually, before moving on. This idea of 'inhabiting' discursive spaces . . . invites us to revisit the connections between habits and places, between memories and places, between our bodies and the material world" (141).

Such dwelling-based occupation, she says, is "sedimented within structures of feeling" (141) that can become more or less comfortable as bodies and spaces interact:

> Bodies and places impact upon each other; a body becomes marked with the residue of a place, but places are also changed by the presences of bodies. Those changes can't happen, however, if people won't cross borders, won't engage with a new place, or can't overcome their fear or aversion to a particular location. (143)

Reynolds thereby insists that dwelling requires writers to begin from a space of comfort but, ultimately, to cross borders, to engage with newness, and to overcome fear of difference as part of their overall literate activity.

King similarly stresses both comfort and movement beyond comfort within dwelling processes, literate and otherwise. He contends that initial comfort is foundational to one's ability to engage with the world, writing that "to insist on our own comforts is not purely out of selfishness, but a necessary prerequisite for dealing with others, for establishing and then exercising a capability" (83) to do work in the world. Crucially, however, he insists that too much comfort can invite complacency, resulting in the creation of a "place where we can get lost, where no exit is visible, and from which we fear we may never escape" (93). As a result, King insists that effective dwelling requires a sense of "acceptance"—acknowledgement, that is, of a simultaneous need for comfort and for moving beyond it: "What we need is some balance between looking in and looking out. We need to find some accommodation, and this is ultimately an acceptance of the needs and care of others" (96). In this way, King similarly emphasizes that one must dwell only long enough within a particular space to be able to acquire the life skills necessary to move beyond that space and to impact the larger world positively.

The notion of literate dwelling that I posit here also requires a critical consideration of time. Reynolds argues that "it is important to challenge the idea of a single and objective sense of time or space against which we attempt to measure the diversity of human conceptions and perceptions" (20) as they manifest in the context of dwelling. Such critical examination is crucial, she says, in light of the kind of "time-space" compression that theorists of neoliberalism (e.g., David Harvey) attribute to processes of privatization and profit-making—that is, the sense that the world seems to be simultaneously "sped up" and "disemplaced" as a function of technological and cultural changes ranging from computer technology to cell phones to distance education platforms (20). Indeed, the understanding that I seek here requires the traversal of decidedly long periods of time—up to twenty years, in some cases—in the hope of better understanding simultaneous impulses of speed and disemplacement. This focus ultimately resonates with Julie Lindquist's focus on "slow research" into writing processes and literate activities that, she says, attempts to account for the "critical affordances of time" (655) within literate lives—that is, the idea that extended periods of time allow particular effects of various literate practices to manifest. Lindquist remarks, too, that such a slow research paradigm is essential to understanding the "wonderfully generative inefficiency" (662) of written and literate development over time. The decades of hindsight that have been afforded me when I think about my own literate dwelling constitute a kind of slow research focus, and I believe that my experiences qualify as examples of generative inefficiencies (wonderful, at least from my perspective).

Furthermore, I stress throughout my account here that different types of literate dwelling are inextricably intertwined, thereby extending a point made repeatedly by Kevin Roozen and Joe Erickson in their discussion of literate activity. They insist that we recognize the holistic nature of literate life, including both that which we might typically associate with disciplinary work (such as obtaining a PhD) and that which we might typically associate with extracurricular and/or other sorts of informal literacies:

> We don't become who we are, write how we write, represent how we represent, by cutting ourselves off from all other domains of our lives and living evermore purely in some disciplinary center. We become who we are and engage in disciplinary activity by tying together and connecting all the resources we have developed in ever surer and richer ways. If the rhetoric of modern disciplinarity has called on us to downplay those connections, the practices of modern disciplinarity have called on us to connect more intensely and precisely. (1.05)

Roozen and Erickson's stress on holism, on connections between and among types of literate dwelling, feels crucial to my consideration of the particular events of this particular week that I am discussing. Indeed, my literate dwelling in Champaign and at UIUC involved a large amount of educational, disciplinary, and literate work, but it simultaneously involved many other "surer and richer" connections between and among other kinds of literate dwelling as well.

Finally, working from the ideas expressed by Reynolds, King, and Roozen and Erikson, I want to stress that the notion of literate dwelling upon which I focus here concerns itself not just with the past but with the present and future as well. I reflect on past dwelling as it was manifest during this particular week as a means to better understand and negotiate new locales with new challenges over new spans of time. Or, to put things differently, I hope to recognize the three good things referenced in my title as a means to dwell more effectively and more responsibly in the present and future.

Part I: Dwelling, Dissertation, and Disciplinary Space

The first good thing that my week in April 2014 helped to underscore for me is most directly related to my educational dwelling in Champaign and at UIUC for nearly fifteen years. I first arrived in Champaign and at UIUC as a college sophomore in 1992, but I didn't ultimately leave for any extended period of time again until 2005, with a PhD in hand and an assistant professor position at my current institution, the University of Colorado-Boulder, on the horizon. During this period, I taught composition courses; I worked in a writing center; I administered a writing center; I held an assistant professor position at Illinois State University in nearby Bloomington-Normal for one year, commuting three to four times a week for about an hour each way.

I could talk about many ways in which I dwelled both at UIUC and in Champaign through the discipline of rhetoric and composition during this period. For the sake of space, though, I will focus on my dissertation as a key product of these dwelling processes. My dissertation focused on the ways in which writing instruction for first-generation students at UIUC, especially students of color, was directly influenced by the history and evolution of one of its longstanding writing programs—initially named the Educational Opportunity Program and later renamed the Academic Writing Program (or AWP)—that was developed as a tool for university desegregation in the immediate wake of the assassination of Martin Luther King, Jr., in April 1968. Specifically, my project attempted to understand how the interests of various stakeholders (particularly program faculty, program administrators, and campus upper administrators) alternately converged and diverged within this program over time. (The term "interest convergence" refers to critical race theorist Derrick Bell's assertion that efforts to promote racial justice typically only achieve success when they converge—that is, when they simultaneously serve the interests of the powerful racial mainstream in addition to the interests of less powerful racial minorities (213).) During times of interest convergence, I argued, such processes promoted race-conscious and change-oriented writing instruction; in contrast, during times of interest divergence, I demonstrated that the program saw an increase in color-blind and status quo-oriented writing instruction; finally, I argued that we can use an understanding of UIUC's institution-specific convergence and divergence dynamics as a means to think through present and future writing program policy decisions with respect to issues of race and racism.

My dissertation afforded me the chance to engage in substantive educational dwelling on a number of levels. On the positive side of things, it met a rather immediate practical desire: I aimed to understand more fully the history and evolution of the writing program that I most liked to teach in, the AWP program of the late-1990s. As I taught, it seemed to me that AWP functioned as a *de facto* support program for first-generation and underrepresented minority students on our campus, and I was deeply interested in understanding how and why this apparent function came to be. The dissertation thus afforded me an opportunity to learn about my immediate institutional and programmatic surroundings, their relationships to race, racism, and region, and the sorts of dwelling that they did and did not promote.

This dissertation also arose in some sense from my long-standing interest in some of the racialized educational dynamics that I had experienced while growing up near Chicago. My family lived in the predominantly white suburbs, but my father taught in the so-called "inner city" at a school serving a majority of students of color. He started his career in the early 1960s and retired from the same high school in the early 1990s. I can remember asking him, when I was a young age, how and why he taught in the city while we lived in the suburbs, whether I could ever attend his school, and whether his students ever went to college where I wanted to go to college. Furthermore, my mother is a Polish immigrant, and the ways in which she did or did not speak her native language in our home raised early questions for me about the personal and family politics of language and language use—another foundation of what I would come to study. In these ways, my dissertation served as an opportunity to think about my own educational dwelling history and its relationships to issues of race, racism, and language politics.

As a third positive result, my dissertation forced me to come to terms with dwelling as a kind of writing and research methodology. I had to think at great length about how best to analyze localized writing program dynamics with an eye on several decidedly non-local disciplinary audiences: my advisor and committee, to be sure, but also those whom I would be trying to reach through future publication and those whom I would be contacting about jobs after graduation. The process of writing was thus very much a process of learning how to translate personal and local concerns into broader ones—a process, that is, of working from a space of disciplinary and institutional comfort, through writing, to impact other spaces with wider and potentially much more skeptical audiences.

Importantly, though, I don't want to make the dissertation and the dwelling processes that it involved seem too rosy. There were many times when I disliked both graduate school and dissertation-writing immensely. Such feelings resulted in my taking seven years to finish my PhD, even with a MEd already in hand, which proved to be quite a bit longer than any of my peers. This period included a couple of years when I openly "took a break" from graduate school to teach and, fortuitously, to administer the campus writing center full-time. I felt as though working directly with students to promote diversity was more relevant than theorizing it; I also felt like the promise of a full-time, non-tenure-track position and its paycheck was more important than pursuing the dissertation itself. However, once I decided to return to full-time PhD study, I then began to worry that this deviation from the standard PhD timeline would leave me looking less prepared and less serious than my peers, and thus less likely to help me get a so-called good job—a tenure-track position—for which I was ostensibly being groomed. In this sense, I was not sure that the dwelling I was doing through my dissertation was truly going to lead to success in the traditional ways. But even once I managed to finish my dissertation, I felt significant anxiety about the prospect of its being good enough to help me earn tenure in a tenure-track faculty position. The prospect of having to transform this localized dissertation into a series of well-placed national articles and a well-placed national book, especially while under the pressure of a tenure clock, was extremely daunting. I was not convinced that the results of my earlier types of dwelling in and through the dissertation would effectively translate beyond the spaces in which I initially wrote. Much of my educational dwelling through the dissertation thus did not feel particularly good in terms of either my anticipated short-term or long-term success.

By the time April 2014 arrived, however, I had begun to experience a marked shift in my perception regarding educational dwelling via the dissertation. To begin, in 2011, I had been able to publish a book version of the work in the dissertation, recasting the story of race and racism within the EOP/AWP rhetoric program as a story of race and racism within the field of basic writing more generally: the final publisher's acceptance letter, and especially the actual book arriving in the mail, felt incredibly good. In 2012, my colleagues at CU-Boulder granted me tenure, largely based on the publication of this book and on the recommendation of disciplinary peers beyond the immediate Champaign and UIUC contexts who found this work to have merit. Tenure felt awfully good, too, I must say. It signaled that I had both passed an important professional milestone and had been granted the kind of academic freedom and protection that fewer and fewer of my colleagues receive in our neoliberal age. In the wake of all of this, I read my invitation to return to UIUC for this keynote as something of a note of congratulations from my old teachers and mentors. I supposed that, in their eyes, I had achieved at least some level of success, transforming the localized work of the dissertation successfully into something that was circulating within and across broader spaces.

It wasn't really until arriving on my old campus, however, that I would realize just how important this recognition would be for me in an affective sense—just how good it would actually *feel* to be invited and to be validated by those whom I looked up to for so long during what was a trying professionalization period in graduate school. These good feelings began to unfold with increasing intensity, day by day, during that week. I arrived for my visit late on the Wednesday night during that particular week. After touching down in Champaign for the first time in nearly a decade, I was surprised at the airport by a couple of old friends who still live in the area and who took me to dinner. The next day I spent my time meeting with former mentors and teachers, speaking with the graduate students in small groups, and otherwise wandering around on a campus that paradoxically seemed exactly the same and completely different than it had a decade earlier. Finally, on that Friday, I gave my talk (which, incidentally, also focused on issues of dwelling and neoliberalism, although it did so by exploring for-profit institutional practices and their potential relationships to our own practices at not-for-profit institutions). I was warmly introduced by my advisor; I gave the talk itself; finally, I engaged in an extended Q&A session with my audience concerning dwelling and its significance to our collective work, including a bit of friendly back-and-forth with another mentor by whom I had previously been somewhat intimidated. By the end of that talk, itself coming at the end of that week on campus, I felt truly wonderful in both a professional and personal sense—perhaps the best I had ever felt as a scholar while physically present at UIUC or in Champaign. After many years of worrying that my dwelling through the dissertation was going very wrong, I had received an affirmation from home that, at least in some sense, it had actually gone somewhat right.

Here, then, is the first good thing that that particular week yielded for me: after years of feeling rather bad as a professional-in-training throughout the dissertation writing process, I felt decidedly good. Although I had dwelled educationally in Champaign and at UIUC for years, I would not really know about whether such dwelling could be considered successful for many more years—an extended time frame not typically valued within present-day schemes for understanding education. This week also helped me to understand a bit more about Lindquist's "critical affordances of time" as they relate to notions of discomfort as characterized by both Reynolds and King. Whereas I had felt decidedly uncomfortable for long stretches of time during the dissertation process, and whereas I had felt frequently unsure regarding whether I would succeed in my dissertation writing, this week reminded me that I had endured the vicissitudes of the research process long enough to reach a reasonably positive conclusion. I was, this is to say, dwelling both in and through periods of discomfort toward a more positive and more comfortable outcome. This experience further underscores the wise advice that Laura Micciche offers with respect to cultivating an academic (and administrative) mindset rooted squarely "in the moment" (87). She argues, in particular, that "we should empower ourselves to slow down sometimes, grant ourselves enough agency to defer action in cases for which we need to be in the moment rather than racing against moments or believing that every request or problem requires an immediate response" (87). Given my frequent academic discomfort, it was definitely difficult for me during my graduate career to practice being in the moment or to grant myself the agency and time necessary to think about problems deeply—especially if such thinking resulted in time-consuming mistakes. But, with the benefit of time and experience, this particular week in April 2014 reminded me that things can turn out well enough even after much uncertainty. It has also since reminded me that I do possess the option to "defer action" as a literate dweller when confronted with academic activity that feels uncomfortable or uncertain.

Part II: Dwelling, Music, and Record-Making

Another kind of dwelling that would lead to a second very good thing for me during that week in April 2014 stemmed from the kinds of musical literacies that I used while playing drums in indie rock bands. Since my late undergraduate days, about 1994 or so, I had been playing drums in Champaign and around UIUC as a centerpiece of my social and extracurricular life. In all honesty, I applied to graduate school at exactly one place—UIUC—because I wanted to stay in Champaign to continue playing drums in the local music scene. In this sense, my initial interest in entering graduate school was much less about learning to write for people beyond my immediate environment than it was about finding an excuse to stay in town to pursue a seemingly different kind of dwelling entirely. PhD-oriented educational dwelling and musical dwelling were clearly enmeshed for me from the get-go, all part of the same combined decision-making process.

My participation in the Champaign and UIUC music scene also ultimately helped me to develop a number of literacies that, although not directly professional or disciplinary per se, were nonetheless central to my overall sense of self and place in the world. Principal among these was the literacy of the recording studio. I had started playing with two guitar player friends, Mike and Steve, beginning in about 1997. Mike was already rather famous in Chicago for his contributions to the sub-genre of indie music called "emo" (which is generally known for its mix of punk aesthetic, catchy melodies, and heart-on-the-sleeve lyrics about love and life and relationships); Steve was his high school friend and college roommate. The three of us met to play original music a couple of times a week, calling the band American Football as a kind of send-up of mainstream culture in general and mainstream sports culture in particular. As part of this experience, Mike and Steve would bring over intricate, off-time, and mesmerizing compositions to a small house I was renting; I would then sit down with them to write drum (and occasional trumpet) parts. We did this consistently, recording versions of these songs on a cassette-tape boom box at the end of each practice. On two occasions, we also visited a proper music recording studio together. In 1998, we recorded a three-song release; in 1999, we recorded a nine-song album. Within days of recording the 1999 album, however, we decided to stop playing together entirely. Both Mike and Steve were moving to Chicago after having graduated with BAs, and I was staying to run the UIUC writing center and try my hand at playing in some other bands.

Despite our breakup, the American Football album was eventually released by Polyvinyl Records, selling a few thousand copies in its first year. These sales figures were certainly above-average for a band that didn't exist anymore, but I figured that this number was due much more to Mike's past reputation and his growing popularity as a solo artist than to the music itself. The situation felt like a bit of a blip in the universe—one that had not translated into other musical successes for me. If anything, I grew decidedly disillusioned with what I felt I had failed to gain from my years of attempting to dwell musically: I had put forth lots of effort, but I felt as though I had achieved little in the way of payoff, whether musical, cultural, or economic. And so I suppose that I focused my intellectual efforts first and foremost on the business of trying to get tenure and becoming an associate professor. I did play drums here and there for the next decade or so in pick-up bands, cover bands, and in jam sessions in and around Boulder and Denver. But I didn't do so for any other reason than personal enjoyment, or perhaps a low-grade sense that it would be a shame to let my drumming atrophy entirely.

By April 2014, however, my perspective on the success of this strain of musical dwelling began to change drastically. Specifically, in early winter 2013, Steve found a box of the practice tapes that we used to make together. He sent these tapes to Polyvinyl, figuring that someone might want to hear them. This was an understatement. The label was so excited by what was on these tapes that they decided to reissue the original album with this so-called bonus material included. The LP was approaching its 15th birthday, and so they guessed that people might have an interest in hearing where it came from. This proved to be more of an understatement. On the day that this reissue was announced, Polyvinyl's website experienced enough traffic to crash its server; then, over the subsequent several days, our long-defunct band would receive multiple offers to play various "reunion" concerts across the U.S., accompanied by monetary figures that were many more times what we had typically made to play in the past.

We accepted two of these offers initially. One was for a music festival in Champaign, where we would be a Sunday night headliner; the other was for a well-respected club in New York City. As it turned out, tickets for both events would go on sale at the end of that exact week in April when I would be in Champaign and at UIUC for my talk. Indeed, at precisely the same time on that Friday that I was behind a podium talking about my research, tickets for these concerts first went on sale. And sell they did. A first show in NYC, with a capacity of 1500, sold out within minutes, a second within hours, and a third within a week or so. (Hundreds of tickets for the big Champaign festival sold during that weekend as well.) Given that we had been used to playing for 50 or maybe 100 people on a good night in the past, these were incredible numbers for us. All of a sudden, I was feeling pretty good about the outcome of my musical dwelling after years and years of feeling very much the opposite.

In the midst of this good news, I woke up bright and early on the Saturday immediately following my UIUC talk and headed up to Chicago. My old bandmates and I had previously decided that I should extend my homecoming by one day in order to practice for the first time in fifteen years. I got there, buzzing with excitement from both the great professional welcome that I had received at UIUC as well as from the great news about these gigs. We played for a few hours and, despite some initial awkwardness stemming from the fact that we had not played together in well over a decade, enough of the music was there to feel comfortable about playing again. We finished up the day talking about the gigs to begin three or four months later, about our excitement and nervousness, and about plans to meet up again in a month or two for more rehearsing.

Here, then, was a second good thing revealed to me during that particular week, contemporaneous with the first. After having dwelled musically for many years with no sense of progress or payoff other than a bit of personal satisfaction, musical dwelling started to pay off to a degree that neither I nor anyone else could have predicted ahead of time. Typical music industry measures would have almost certainly deemed our band's situation a failure: we recorded a record, broke up immediately, and watched very little happen for years and years. Educational measures, meanwhile, would likely have ignored this musical aspect of dwelling outright. Because it did not seem immediately related to my ostensible discipline or job, it likely would not have registered as anything positive at all. That week proved, however, that this musical dwelling had managed to transcend its initial spaces and comforts, a process that continues even as I write. During what is presently more than four years in a second incarnation, American Football has played about eighty gigs to upwards of 90,000 people at clubs and festivals on four continents, while offers for more gigs worldwide continue to emerge. We have also sold somewhere around 125,000 albums over what is now more than twenty years since the release of our first music together, and seen these sales coupled with literally millions of plays on various internet sites. Meanwhile, the LP that we recorded in 1999 just before breaking up has rewritten its initial history with the help of internet circulation. *Rolling Stone*, *New Musical Express*, *Pitchfork*, and others have named it as one of the most influential emo records of all time.

This week thereby reminded me once again about the wonderfully generative dwelling dynamics that can manifest with time in some of the ways that Lindquist mentions. My friends and I had achieved a kind of musical success that no one saw coming, and this success arose in large part because we dwelled musically as a way to compose music together and socialize and have fun. This week has also since reminded me that my musical success has always very much been intertwined with my educational dwelling: it has helped me to recall that musical literate dwelling regularly served throughout my time in Champaign and at UIUC as a way to let off steam when school was going poorly—a means to boost my overall sense of self-worth and value when school was making me question them. I can remember, for instance, the excitement that I felt driving to play shows in Chicago after a tough week of teaching: both the calm of the actual drive and the thrill of performing helped me to reboot mentally. I also remember the many Thursday nights that I saw music at the Blind Pig in Champaign or at the Rose Bowl in Urbana, drinking beers and decompressing about teaching and classes and dissertation chapters. I had clearly been using music (and, less productively, beer) as a foil for the difficulties that I associated with education in ways resonant with Roozen and Erickson's assertion that literate persons regularly need to "navigat[e] tensions" that arise between different varieties of literate activity (8.02.02). Whereas Roozen and Erickson tend to focus on how people negotiate tensions when one sort of literate practice might conflict with another (e.g., when an argument technique learned in a journalism class conflicts with a technique taught in a composition course), my experiences suggest that literate dwelling also requires the ability to shuttle between and among different sorts of tensions. When one type of literate dwelling (say, dissertation writing) became decidedly uncomfortable, I would pivot toward another (say, drumming); when the latter became frustrating, I might return to the first, or even perhaps pivot toward a third (say, hanging out with friends or family). My experience suggests that literate dwellers necessarily move and shuttle, that they navigate and negotiate different (and often uncomfortable) dwelling situations across space and over time as they seek larger positive engagement with the world.

Ruminating on this week has also helped me to realize that my educational dwelling enabled my musical dwelling in some important ways. Pursuing my PhD at UIUC also served as a kind of mental grounding, providing a sense that I was doing something "real" with my life even as I did music. Although I would often tell people that I wanted to be a professional musician, it has become clear to me in retrospect that I wanted to have a "real" job in academe while playing music in a way that gave more depth to that "real" job. I must have internalized the advice that both my father (himself a high school math teacher and part-time musician) and my favorite high school English teacher gave me right before I went off to college: do not confuse music as an *avocation* with music as a *vocation*. With this in the back of my mind, I have found myself increasingly content to identify first and foremost as an academic who drums rather than as a would-be drummer stuck in academe. I also realize that I can enjoy the novelty of periodically travelling to places to play music in no small part because my academic job operates as a kind of grounding for me.

In short, I feel as though I have developed a composite literate identity out of these two varieties of literate dwelling. This certainly seems in keeping with an assertion that Roozen makes in another of his articles about the seemingly "extracurricular" writing practices of the undergraduate student Angelica. After demonstrating how Angelica draws on a variety of literate practices (including journal writing, writing for the newspaper, writing for classes, and other activities) in her effort to craft a sense of herself as a literate person in the world, Roozen concludes that "even the most ordinary of writing can do the extraordinary work of serving as the basis for forging academic and professional identities" (566-67). My own experience similarly suggests that the combined literate dwelling work of academics and music, both ordinary and not, has comprised for me a kind of holistic self-identity over time in which the sum has been greater than its parts.

Part III: Dwelling, Love, and Family

Having noted the good things afforded me by academic and musical dwelling, I must insist that both of these things ultimately pale in comparison to the good things afforded me by a third type of dwelling—that in which I engage with my family. My present-day family life began to take shape back in the mid-1990s when I first met Tracy, the woman who is now my wife. She had also arrived in Champaign and at UIUC in 1992, although we didn't actually meet and start dating until 1995. She walked in the front door one day as I was working at a take-out restaurant, my first full-time job after graduating college. We hit it off immediately, talking both about a recent American literature survey that we had taken and about the trumpet playing of Chet Baker. Things moved along quickly from there. About three months after first met, we took a month-long road trip to California together in a car that I had borrowed from my parents. After learning that I would be going to graduate school and would be able to teach composition to cover tuition and (most of) my bills each month, I quit the restaurant to take the trip. Tracy, meanwhile, was routinely under-scheduled during the summer months at the coffee shop where she worked, just a few doors down from my restaurant. She had enough money to cover bills as well, and so she came along.

We spent almost a month together in that hot car and even hotter youth hostels. These experiences started to teach us something basic about literate dwelling as a couple right off the bat: how to get comfortable with each other; how to move through space together; how to get over disagreements about, say, how high the air conditioning in the car could go while driving through Death Valley before the car would overheat. But we also learned quickly about the tougher aspects of dwelling, perhaps more quickly than some young couples might. Within a few days of our return from that trip, Tracy's father passed away unexpectedly, and she went home to Chicago to grieve. There, she learned firsthand the pain of losing a parent as well as the ways in which such pain fundamentally changes family dynamics and their spaces. As the youngest of seven siblings, she would soon witness her mother, brothers, and sisters move away from the neighborhood where she grew up, yielding significant changes to the ways that they have dwelled collectively ever since. And while I watched Tracy grieve at that time, I would come to know related grief and some of its spatial implications myself about a decade later when my own father died suddenly and tragically in the house where I grew up in the Chicago suburbs. Tracy actually moved back into his house for a while to help settle his affairs while I finished out my first year as an assistant professor at CU-Boulder, 1000 miles away. I will never forget Tracy's kindness in doing that for me, nor will I ever forget how our distance during that time of stress and sorrow has redefined my sense of family, love, and commitment. Together, over time, Tracy and I have learned and re-learned the joys and pains of dwelling together: how to create spaces of comfort, to move beyond them, to go back to them, and even to watch them transform in unpredictable (and sometimes painful) ways. These dynamics are not part of the traditional stuff of composition research, perhaps, but they strike me as central to living life as fully as one can.

Jumping ahead many years later to April 2014, our family dwelling situation had begun to change again. By this date, Tracy and I had been together for just under twenty years, living in the sunny mountain foothills of Front

Range Colorado for almost ten. Tracy was also pregnant with our second baby. I had initially been invited to return to UIUC for my talk just after Tracy's first trimester, and so she and I discussed whether I should take the trip at all. We—or at least I—felt as though this trip would not prove to be a problem. Our first child, a boy, had arrived one day before his due date in 2011, and this baby, a girl, wasn't due until the third week of May. I reasoned that, because this trip was a special invitation that was unlikely to come again soon, because it would afford the chance to swing up to Chicago and play with the re-formed American Football at least once before the baby came, and because there was no possible way that this second baby could ever come a month early after the precedent her brother had set (ha ha), I should go. Tracy (somewhat reluctantly) agreed, although she wisely decided that her mother should come to stay with her and our son before I left, just in case things did not ultimately go according to my imagined schedule.

That week in April 2014 quickly became even more interesting. After having left Champaign and UIUC on that Friday, and after having played with my old bandmates in Chicago on that Saturday afternoon, I went to my brother's home in the Chicago suburbs to spend that Saturday evening with him. I went to bed around 11:00, noting that my flight home was scheduled for noon the next day. But around 1:30 in the morning, my phone rang: I knew what was coming before I even picked it up. "My water broke," Tracy said, with some panic. "You need to come home now." I sprang up, got dressed, and jumped into my rental car. Off to the airport I sped. After rushing up and down to various ticket counters asking for any possibility of an early flight, a woman whose name I have forgotten (but whose kindness I have not) bumped me to the front of a stand-by list for a 5:45 am flight. I was back at home and at the hospital by about 9:00 am that morning. Our daughter arrived about five hours later—just over three weeks early—at just under six pounds. And, so, within seventy-two hours of returning to the site where Tracy and I had first begun to dwell twenty years earlier, and about twenty-four hours after experiencing these other striking manifestations of literate dwelling, the best of the three good things occurred. My daughter was born. She came early, she came small, and she came with a bit of drama—but it was, as I have learned to say after living near the mountains for so long, "all good."

My daughter's birth at the end of an already-eventful week underscored dramatically for me just how much literate dwelling at UIUC and in Champaign was ultimately concerned with much more than a degree or a job or drumming in rock bands. Her birth impressed on me how it was that literate dwelling helped me to find my life's partner; how this dwelling gave us a grounding and a place from which to start a life together; how it has served as a touchstone in the lives that we have led together since; and how it ultimately helped us, years later, to bring new life into the world.

I should also note, however, that my harried plane ride back to the Intermountain West found me thinking intently—obsessively, even—about big-picture literate identity issues. Whereas there were many times earlier in that week when I felt first and foremost like a professor, or a drummer, or even a college student again, those other aspects of identity were thrust into the background as I raced home. Instead, I found myself dwelling (in a different sense of the word) on many things that I don't think that I had ever said to Tracy out loud before: that I absolutely would not have finished my degree without her, as she offered a kind of encouragement again and again that I could not have lived without; that my musical dwelling would never have been as meaningful without her encouragement and support and willingness to endure late nights and absences and the like; that I was sorry that she was experiencing such physical and mental discomfort, exacerbated many times over by her worries about whether or not I'd make it home in time for our daughter's birth. (And, to be honest, I felt more than a little selfish for having taken the trip in the first place.) I thought, too, about just how grateful I was that Tracy's mother was watching our three-year-old boy while Tracy was in the hospital and while I was running around the country experiencing good things related to other aspects of life. I thought as well about my own mother—how she helped my brother and I to dwell while we grew up as kids and how excited she'd be to meet our new daughter. I even found myself missing my father (gone for eight years at that point), especially saddened that he was never able to meet my kids or to share in these kinds of moments. These thoughts and feelings stick with me vividly, even as I write them down four years later. They reflect, I think, the kind of baseline life-making capacity that King stresses when he talks about dwelling processes:

> Dwelling is about the general relation we have with the world...it is about us as beings that stay awhile in between their wanderings over the earth. But it is also about the specificity of this relation to place, of *me* in *my* house with *my* family and *my* things.... And we should not see this as a problem, or as something to remedy or rectify. It is precisely as it should be. (25)

As I have continued to ruminate on that powerful week, I believe that I was being forced to develop a new sense of a *me*—a *my* that is more explicit in its recognition of others whom I love, to whom I am indebted, and for whom I am grateful. This new and more explicit me-ness and my-ness stands as an amalgamation of many powerful facets of literate dwelling—many good things simultaneously—that I have been lucky enough to call my own.

There is, however, one last piece of the family dwelling puzzle worth mentioning here quickly as well. The last four years since this week have reminded me regularly that we are able to live as we do as a family in a material sense (i.e., in an actual town in an actual house with actual food on the table) in no small part because of the good things that literate dwelling with both the PhD and with the drums have afforded us. I continue to work in my dream career in a way that allows us to live in the increasingly expensive Front Range, where real estate prices are climbing at what feels like astronomical rates. The very fortuitous supplemental income that the reunited American Football provides for us helps out a great deal, too—to the point where it has enabled Tracy to stay home full-time with our kids longer than we had initially imagined her doing. Her time with our kids has been absolutely foundational to helping them both become the little literate beings who they are—nascent readers and writers and makers of meaning in school, in music lessons, and in their day-to-day lives. All of this leads me to Reynolds one final time as she speaks at length about the importance of the material to dwelling activities: she argues that we must "find ways of keeping the material and the metaphorical interconnected, acknowledging that the real and the imagined are dependent upon one another" (46). In my case, the at-times metaphorical work of learning to write dissertations or of learning to record the drums in a music studio have, in fact, folded back on the material reality of our daily family dwelling at a fundamental level.

Conclusions: Dwelling and Its Long-Term Effects

Looking back at this eventful week in April 2014 has enabled me to make decidedly more sense of what dwelling at UIUC and in Champaign has done for, with, and in some ways through me for nearly two decades now. I went to school in a particular place across a particular span of time many years ago. Once there, I got an education (on many levels) that didn't necessarily have either the clearest sense of purpose going in or the clearest sense of what I was doing in the moment. But I nonetheless managed to dwell—educationally, musically, and with my growing family—in ways that I think have fundamentally defined the life that I have come to live as a professor, a drummer, a husband, and a father. All at once. These activities have occurred within, across, and (far) beyond the initial places and times where they began. And they have created a life for me in three dimensions.

I must conclude here, however, by noting that literate dwelling continues to pose plenty of challenges for me and for my family moving forward. Working as I do—in a flagship state institution, in a "purple" state, in the age of Trump—I find myself focused on all sorts of questions related to academic dwelling. I have wondered especially about what it means to do academic research in rhetoric and composition in this day and age and institutional context: Whom does such work serve? When? How? Still further, I recognize that I am able to do this sort of work as a tenured, privileged member of an academic workforce that is otherwise increasingly casualized through non-tenure-track teaching and service-only faculty appointments. Indeed, my own program's faculty is more than 95% non-tenure-track, and these faculty members are not, contractually speaking, recognized for doing any kind of research. I have certainly found joy in writing about my movement toward a holistic literate life in essays like this one, and I certainly hope that such writing offers insights that are valuable to others. Nonetheless, I wonder what it means to do this sort of research work when so many of my fellow faculty are discouraged from the pursuit of such work so that they can teach more course sections without the benefit of tenure.

I've also been thinking a great deal lately about musical dwelling. My bandmates and I have been reunited for about four years now, and it's been tremendous fun. Playing music with the band has been and remains a source of profound energy and pleasure for me, perhaps more than ever before. At the same time, we collectively find ourselves working to redefine musical dwelling for a band that is no longer in "reunion" mode: we've recently made a third record that will enable us to continue playing together, but we're also trying to figure out the best way to do so before hitting diminishing returns with respect to time and effort and money and family commitments. It can be quite tiring, both for us and for our families, to work all week at our "regular" jobs (which for two of the members means full-time parenting) and then to travel on the weekends for the band. And so we're all very much grappling with how best to balance avocation and vocation as middle-aged men with families.

My family's dwelling poses plenty of current and future challenges, too. To date, Tracy and I have been living in the Intermountain West for fourteen years, and our kids (now seven and four) have known no other home. We love it here—so much so that we have just bought an older house in our dream location even though it needs extensive renovation. (It sits in a valley in a quiet part of a wonderful little town that is home to mountains and bike trails and even Grammy-winning bluegrass musicians.) We have lately started each day by noting how lucky we are to be here. But we have also ended many nights discussing where and how we can obtain additional income in order to make things work in the long term (especially as we realize that we're going to have to figure out a way to pay for our kids' higher educations in about a decade or so). Our desire to make a life in this new home—in the actual material dwelling in which we reside—requires that we attend to still more questions involving literate dwelling: Do I teach extra classes next summer to make additional money? Should I seek out an administrative position for more pay? Or, perhaps, should I make more musical income somehow? Tracy is asking related questions about her own personal literate dwelling activities, too: whereas she was trained at UIUC as a secondary language arts teacher, and whereas she had worked as such on-and-off for nearly 15 years across a number of institutions, she is no longer interested in teaching. And so she finds herself wondering what she will be doing next as a literate person: What sorts of (re)education will she require? How will she dwell in a literate sense, both now and in the future, in ways that are necessarily different from the ways in which she dwelled personally in Champaign more than two decades ago? What will it mean for her to pursue these things as part of her own sense of career and family after nearly seven years at home with our kids? These big questions are all of a piece with literate dwelling across multiple dimensions—spatial, temporal, metaphorical, and material.

Clearly, then, past forms of dwelling are themselves tied to the present and future challenges of continuing to dwell. And there are certainly no guarantees moving forward—for me, for us, or for anyone else. Indeed, if Kimball, Schnee, and Schwabe are correct about the "emergent and unpredictable outcomes" of phenomena like literate dwelling, then none of us can ever fully know ahead of time when, or even whether, good things will happen. We may well even have to accept (in King's sense of the word) that bad things might happen instead. But we can certainly work to notice, to analyze, and to take advantage of the varieties and combinations of literate dwelling that we have performed in the past with an eye on the present and future.

It seems to me, furthermore, that both experienced scholars and new ones can be encouraged to reflect on their literate dwelling—past, present, and future. Certainly, those of us who have been working in this field for a long period of time should be encouraged to think back, in slow research mode, in order to tell our stories of literate dwelling. Many of us have good things to celebrate as academics and as people, including things that have taken years or even decades to manifest. Many of us also have tales of perseverance in the face of dwelling difficulties that need to be heard. Kimball, Schnee, and Schwabe say as much about their own work, suggesting that they seek to narrate their own "intensely local stories of teaching the personal in academic writing… out of concern to preserve them as narratives of our own lived journeys … not—as the ever-more-present [educational assessment] discourse would have us believe—as tickets to the place called success" (130). People who have worked for years or decades are well-positioned to illustrate both that there are no guaranteed tickets to the place called success and that we can seek out good things despite this fact.

Younger scholars and students also seem poised to benefit from a focus on literate dwelling activities, even if their focus is necessarily more in-the-moment. For instance, I have recently been assigning teaching and learning journals to graduate students that are focused squarely on their research and teaching activities here at CU-Boulder. Such work requires them to provide something of a current account of how they dwell as scholars and as teachers and as people; it can, for some students, also serve as a reminder that they possess the ability to endure in the face of struggle. I similarly find myself assigning more and more work to both lower- and upper-division students that asks them directly to make arguments about their educational goals and values, their future academic and career aspirations, and their specific experiences as students at CU-Boulder. Some of these take more personal narrative forms (e.g., "How does one of the readings (or one of the posters) help you to understand more fully your own beliefs about the significance of diversity as it relates somehow to your life at CU-Boulder—and why does this understanding ultimately matter to others?"). Others require arguments recognizable to experts in their disciplines while remaining rooted in their own ongoing research as actual students in actual labs at CU-Boulder (e.g., "Write a 2000- to 3000-word scientific argument appropriate for the disciplinary task that you have chosen and the disciplinary audience whom you have targeted."). These assignments make students' real-time dwelling the explicit focus of formal inquiry and argumentation.

Such narration, whether generated by relative old-timers or relative newbies, can make visible various types of literate dwelling that might otherwise remain hidden. It can also increase the possibility that other good things will arise as a function of the kinds of dwelling that we have collectively done and will continue to do in the future. This sort of narration, accompanied by new kinds of attunement to the dynamics of dwelling and their potential effects, can help us all to live and grow and persevere within and beyond our comfort zones—as well as to recognize and appreciate good things when they do in fact come our way.

Acknowledgments

I would like to thank *Composition Studies* editor Laura Micciche, two anonymous reviewers, Kevin Roozen, and Pete Kratzke for their incredibly helpful feedback on this manuscript. I would also like to thank Siskanna Naynaha and Wendy Olson for extensive and thoughtful feedback on an earlier version of this piece. I wish, finally, to thank all of those with and alongside whom I have dwelled as a scholar, musician, and person over the years—especially Tracy, Brendan, and Bridget; my mother, her husband, and our extended families; my mother-in-law; my father; my brother; my colleagues at CU-Boulder; the members of American Football; and Polyvinyl Records.

Works Cited

Bell, Derrick. *Race, Racism, and American Law.* 4th ed., Aspen Law and Business, 2000.

Harvey, David. *A Brief History of Neoliberalism.* Oxford UP, 2007.

Kimball, Elizabeth, Emily Schnee, and Liesl Schwabe. "Writing the Personal in an Outcomes-Based World." *Composition Studies*, vol. 43, no. 2, 2015, pp. 113-31.

King, Peter. *In Dwelling: Implacability, Exclusion, Acceptance.* Ashgate, 2012.

Lindquist, Julie. "Time to Grow Them: Practicing Slow Research in a Fast Field." *JAC: A Journal of Composition Theory*, vol. 32, no. 3-4, 2012, pp. 645-66.

Micciche, Laura. "For Slow Agency." *WPA: Writing Program Administration*, vol. 35, no. 1, 2011, pp. 73-90.

Reynolds, Nedra. *Geographies of Writing: Inhabiting Places and Encountering Difference.* SIUP, 2004.

Roozen, Kevin. "From Journals to Journalism: Tracing Trajectories of Literate Development." *CCC*, vol. 60, no. 3, pp. 541-72.

Roozen, Kevin, and Joe Erickson. *Expanding Literate Landscapes: Persons, Practices, and Sociohistoric Perspectives of Disciplinary Development.* Computers and Composition Digital Press / Utah State UP, 2017.

Where We Are

"Where We Are" highlights where we are as a field on matters current and compelling. The call for this issue's installment read as follows:

> We are seeking contributions for our Spring 47.1 (2019) issue that comment on mundane aspects of professional life in the **six-word format** made famous by Ernest Hemingway: "For sale: baby shoes, never worn." Our belief is that ordinary, mundane experiences of everyday life in the academy, and in writing studies more specifically, can reveal organizational rules, values, norms, and expected and coerced forms of participation, and much more. We also think that your collective sentences will be fun to read. No content guidelines; we're eager to see what you come up with!

The entries are loosely organized around topic and rhythmic patterns. Authors are named in bulk at the end of the section in order to emphasize collective experiences across the field. –Editor's Note

Where We Are: My Mundane Professional Life

Wake, teach, grade, research, write, repeat.
Door cracked, please—expecting students later.
Lunch is my only alone time.

RE: CFP: Your Mundane Professional Life.
So mundane, there are no words.

Email avalanche: committees, conferences, compositions, complaints.
I think I am forgetting something.

Will this count as a publication?
I wrote a book nobody read.
Reviewer B called it "utter nonsense."
Reviewer two wanted five words.
Reviewer two: "Write a different article."
Refreshes email anxiously awaiting publisher's response.

Cold coffee after an administrative rant.
Do more with less; rinse; repeat.

I thought all plans were strategic.
Aren't there men on this committee?

Let me repeat your question back.

Sorry—didn't you get my email?
Sorry for the delay in responding.
Feel free to resend your email.
I'd love to resend that email.
I dwell in the email inbox.
Email auto-reply: "Sorry for the delay."
I apologize for the delayed response.
Why wasn't this meeting an email?
Maybe we should schedule another meeting.
General education revision committee meeting today.
Very best subject line: Meeting cancelled.
Hummus doesn't make meetings more enjoyable.
Unfortunately, we need this done today.

/......................m dfssd hj ////////////////////////// ,,,,,,,,,, ,

Warning: Will grade at kids' activities.
I haven't finished grading it yet.
I grade better when baby sleeps.
I hope your grandma feels better.
B+ is a very good grade.
I grade papers, dog in lap.
Paper purgatory: always grading, never completing.
Grading, grading, conferencing, teaching, emails, meetings.
Reminder: Please submit midterm grade alerts.

The assignment should specify <insert criterion>.
Can you require [outcome] in 102?
That's an outcome, not an objective.

Adjunct life: four classes, three campuses.
Week twelve dream: on *Survivor* again.
Four sections, same class, Groundhog Day.
Do you have a few minutes?
The Kleenex box isn't for me.

Term ending: Grandmothers, pets, computers dying.
Fire alarm, nine students absent, Wednesday.

Sorry, I don't teach on Fridays.

Please submit as one contiguous PDF.
Today's request for recommendation due tomorrow.
Send paragraph explaining a writing center.
The fall schedule is due *when*!?

Volunteers needed for mandatory committee work.
Volunteers for the ad hoc committee?
Position opening: English composition, started Monday.
Dear search committee, please hire me?
Self-care doesn't fix systemic contingent strife.
Doctorate degree = over educated, under employed.
Contingent faculty member = limited horizons.
I wonder if Starbucks is hiring.

FROM Dean: RE: Raising Course Caps.
New administrative positions cut tenure lines.
New budgetary constraints will require creativity.
Your "strategic vision" undercuts our mission.
Another executive order: Fewer international students.
Student food pantry needs peanut butter.
After resource request, a sinking feeling.

Forty one-on-one conferences; antibacterial hand gel.

Just to piggyback on that comment . . .
Brought to you by Google Suite.
Writing ebbs and flows in class.
Citing scholars of color amplifies voices.
Let's write an article about this.
Writing on site thirty minutes daily.

Will make to-do list tomorrow.
Actually, we don't do that either.
Lesson planning while walking to class.
Can you quick read this over?
I don't have time to read.

Update: Humanities building elevator broken again.
The LMS is down for maintenance.
Office in concrete fortress; dropped call.
Locked out of my office again.
Forgot my dry erase marker, again.
Top research university, total crap wifi.

I tried to find the poetry in Cookeville, Tennessee.

Wanted: Big-shouldered broad for dirty work.
Graduate student life: food or heat.
Counseling services: No appointments available, again.

A booger on the marker board?
When will the grim reaper come?

Award-winning curriculum stifles dissent; goodbye.
Decision fatigue + cognitive overload = WPA life.
Replace multiple emails with phone calls.

To decrease popularity, just say assessment.

Brown face wanted; voice not required.
POC pain for white "ah-ha!" moments.
Sitting in my office just B R E A T H I N G.

Never ask about rubrics on WPA-L.
Mansplaining isn't really mansplaining, he mansplained.
If he mentions Burke again, I . . .
Out of coffee; he's still talking.

Making the case again and again.
Apparently, another justification is needed now.

Motto: There are no "composition emergencies."
Classroom: refuge; grading: requisite; service: torture.
Strangers sheepishly confess intense grammar fears.

Standing desk, arthritis in hand, neck.
Women's bathrooms are the floor below.

Picked up bus pass; missed bus.
Today I ate breakfast and lunch.

With Woolf, keep crossing the lawn.

Authors:

A. Abby Knoblauch, Kansas State University; Alissa Surges, University of Nevada, Reno; Amanda Rose Pratt, University of Wisconsin—Madison; Amanda Smothers, Elgin Community College, Harper College, College of DuPage, Waubonsee Community College; Ashanka Kumari, University of Louisville; Ashley Burchett, North Carolina State University; Brittany Roberts, Broward College; Bronwyn Williams, University of Louisville; Charlie Cat via Jenn Fishman; Christina V. Cedillo, University of Houston-Clear Lake; Christine Garcia, Eastern Connecticut State University; Christine Murphy, University of California, Santa Barbara; Christopher Basgier, Auburn University; Christopher Dean, The University of California Santa Barbara; Clancy Ratliff, University of Louisiana at Lafayette; Connie Kendall Theado, University of Cincinnati; Craig A. Meyer, Texas A&M University-Kingsville; Cydney Alexis, Kansas State University; Cynthia A. Cochran, Illinois College; Daniel Ellis, St. Bonaventure University; David Beach, Radford University; Dundee Lackey, Texas Woman's University; Edward Hahn, Inver Hills Community College; Eric Detweiler, Middle Tennessee State University; Geoffrey Clegg, Midwestern State University; Gita DasBender, New York University; Grant Vecera, Indiana University Purdue University Indianapolis; Heather Lang, Susquehanna University; Jamie M. Jones, Grays Harbor College; Jamie White-Farnham, University of Wisconsin-Superior; Jenn Fishman, Marquette University; Joel Heng Hartse, Simon Fraser University; Joel Wingard, Moravian College; Julia Bradshaw, Oregon State University; Julie Amick Cook, University of North Carolina at Charlotte; Karla Saari Kitalong, Michigan Technological University; Kate Highfill, University of Houston; Katherine Daily O'Meara, Emporia State University; Kathy Merman, University of Cincinnati; Kayla Mehalcik, University of North Georgia; Kelly Kinney, University of Wyoming; Kim Hensley Owens, Northern Arizona University; Kimberly K. Gunter, Fairfield University; Kristy Liles Crawley, University of North Carolina at Greensboro; Kyle Bohunicky, University of Florida; Lacey Wootton, American University; Lauren Brentnell, Michigan State University; Leigh Elion, University of California, Santa Barbara; Leslie Seawright, Missouri State University; Lisa Bailey, University of South Carolina; Liza Soria, University of Texas at El Paso; Mara Lee Grayson, California State University, Dominguez Hills; Margaret Price, Ohio State University; Mari E. Ramler, Tennessee Tech

University; Marshall Klassen, Kanazawa Seiryo University; Meg Mikovits, Moravian College; Megan J. Busch, University of South Carolina; Melvin Wininger, Indiana University Purdue University Indianapolis; Michael R. Moore, DePaul University; Michelle LaFrance, George Mason University; Monica Carol Miller, Middle Georgia State University; Morgan Gresham, University of South Florida St. Petersburg; Nikki Borrenpohl, Southern Illinois University School of Law; Patricia Hager, University of Southern Maine; Paula González-Álvarez, Pontificia Universidad Católica de Chile; R.J. Lambert, The University of Texas at El Paso; Rachel N. Spear, Francis Marion University; Randall W. Monty, University of Texas Rio Grande Valley; Randy Malamud, Georgia State University; Ronda Leathers Dively, Southern Illinois University Carbondale; Ryan Skinnell, San José State University; Saffyre Falkenberg, Texas Christian University; Sarah Bartlett Wilson, University of Mississippi; Shannon Finck, University of West Georgia; Shannon Harman, Illinois State University; Shannon Madden, North Carolina State University; Shelly Galliah, Michigan Technological University; Soha Youssef, Thomas Jefferson University; Stephanie Kerschbaum, University of Delaware; Valerie Ross, University of Pennsylvania; Vani Kannan, Lehman College, CUNY; Veronica House, University of Colorado Boulder; Zachary Beare, North Carolina State University; Zackary Vernon, Appalachian State University; Zandra L. Jordan, Stanford University.

Book Reviews

Composition Studies, Public-Facing Activism, and Our Continued Social Turn: A Review Essay

Performing Antiracist Pedagogy in Rhetoric, Writing, and Communication, by Frankie Condon and Vershawn Ashanti Young, editors. WAC Clearinghouse/University Press of Colorado, 2017. 258 pages.

Writing for Engagement: Responsive Practice for Social Action, by Mary P. Sheridan, Megan J. Bardolph, Megan Faver Hartline, and Drew Holladay, editors. Lexington Books, 2018. 315 pages.

Reviewed by Darin Jensen, Des Moines Area Community College

One of the articles I read while teaching at a two-year college and before taking the plunge into a PhD program was Patricia Bizzell's "Composition Studies Saves the World!" The article captured an emerging personal ethos for me as I taught in a large Midwestern community college. It is worth rereading: Bizzell's lively voice, showing that serious academic argument need not be stuffy, her arguments themselves—taking on Stanley Fish and his pronouncements about what writing studies folk ought to teach and how we ought to do it, and her own vision about the possibilities of our discipline and profession—inspired me. Bizzell details an incisive timeline of how social justice came to be embedded in our field. In the 1980s, rhetoric and composition was coalescing as a discipline; practitioners and scholars were trying to figure out how to teach writing to the "new" students entering composition classrooms—students who were more diverse in terms of class, ethnicity, and race. Bizzell recounts that she and other teacher-scholars at the time were trying to meet students where they were—not to merely flunk them out for entering postsecondary study without the necessary language, dialects, and discourses already learned. These teachers weren't "bent on saving the world," but teaching writing to all students meant learning to address their needs (174).

Her timeline moves quickly through basic writing, various cognitive and psycholinguistic methods, the nascent academic discourse movement, and her encounter with Paulo Freire's work. Bizzell points out that this work wasn't perfect, nor was it a panacea for all students. However, she asserts, "if you believe that the inequities induced by racism, sexism, and economic exploitation should be ameliorated, then I think you would have to agree that this composition research, while perhaps not saving the world, did indeed contribute to making it a better place" (177-78). I read this article as a call to action, and it let me know others were out there thinking along similar lines. Almost 30 years after Bizzell's article, this history undergirds my own work as a teacher-scholar-activist. Further, her work, in my estimation, provides context and rhetorically frames the work of writing studies as rightfully activist and hopeful.

Two recent edited collections, Frankie Condon and Vershawn Ashanti Young's *Performing Anti-Racist Pedagogy in Rhetoric, Writing, Communication* and Mary P. Sheridan, Megan J. Bardolph, Megan Faver Hartline, and Drew Holladay's *Writing for Engagement: Responsive Practice for Social Action*, are significant contributions to the arc of rhetoric and composition's social turn, which I see situated in teacher-scholar-activism. These collections, like Bizzell's article, provide a blueprint for the teacher-scholar-activism our profession and discipline ought to do. I deploy the phrase "teacher-scholar-activist" deliberately. Patrick Sullivan, in his 2015 article, "The Two-Year College Teacher-Scholar-Activist," asks two-year college English teachers to acknowledge that part of our professional identity is an activist identity—that we must "accep[t] and embrac[e] the revolutionary and inescapably political nature of our work" (327). In another article, "Meet My English 93 Class," Sullivan argues for using "public-facing activism" and for adding the voices of our students to these conversations to directly address inequitable power structures. And while Sullivan discusses the two-year college and basic writing, I extrapolate the teacher-scholar-activist identity to work across institution types. These collections operate from a similar sense of exigency and purpose. In his acknowledgements page, Young makes clear his, and by proxy the collection's, commitment to teacher-scholar-activism when he writes that he and co-editor Condon "recognize that the work we do in academic institutions will either perpetuate the status quo built on legacies of racism, sexism, homophobia, and class domination (to name an obvious few), or intervene" (ix). Like Bizzell in the 1980s, Young, Condon, and others are working to open opportunities for students and communities through writing studies. Their challenge to embrace antiracism in classrooms and communities, a challenge that Condon sees as having no "finish line," is just and intrinsic to the work of writing studies (x).

Condon and Young's collection is divided into three sections: "Actionable Commitments," "Identity Matters," and "In the Classroom." Several chapters stand out. For example, Rashab Diab, Beth Godbee, and Thomas Ferrell's thought-provoking chapter, "Making Commitments to Racial Justice Actionable," argues that enacting an "everyday educational process toward rational justice" is a means to work "against the macro-logics of oppression" (37). For the authors, this work is both "self-work and work-with-others." (37). The self-work they suggest is well-framed, calling on writing studies practitioners to look at values, emotions, relations, and conditions (27). This frame is useful for interrogating teacher-scholar practices and motivations and for creating a process for undertaking this work. Interestingly, they note that this work might only seem to have a local impact, but that over time its effect will spread. The notion of localism is significant in their chapter as the work in the classroom and the labor to enact personal change as teacher-scholar-activists working toward anti-racist pedagogies and consciousness is always and explicitly local. For the authors, the end outcome of this effort is "creating new realities that are more racially and socially just" (37). This commitment is moral and laudable, and it fits squarely within the context and history of the social turn of rhetoric and composition and with the focus on engagement in Sheridan et. al.'s book, too.

Perhaps my favorite chapter in Condon and Young's collection is Calvin Logue's "Teaching African American Discourse: A Lesson of a Recovering Segregationist." I appreciate bravery in academic writing, and this essay is brave because it examines his unexamined and unconscious acceptance of segregation and race privilege. Logue expertly relates the narrative of his experience in Birmingham on the day of the 16th Street Baptist Church bombing in 1963. His lived experience in that moment—noting that he and his children were safe, but that other children weren't—is stunning. The author's examples from his childhood in the South, his time in the military, and his own growing consciousness are examples of the power of narrative and its legitimacy as a methodology. Logue's history of his own segregationist past is haunting in that it is so plausible for human beings to let everyday injustices pass by without remark. His essay gives a terrible life to white supremacist structures.

Mya Poe's chapter, "Reframing Race in Teaching Writing Across the Curriculum," envisions interdisciplinary collaboration as a kind of activism. A compelling thesis, she argues that writing studies needs to "anticipate . . . moments where race and writing come together across the curriculum and share ways of working through these moments as we work with faculty and teaching assistants in helping them design, deliver, and assess writing" (88). Poe goes on to note research where WAC "scholars may worry about being perceived as foregrounding the values of composition studies over those of other disciplines" (88). Again, like others in these two collections, Poe turns to the local. In this way, she posits teacher-scholar-activist WAC work that feels sorely needed. She argues that by using specific student contexts, we "can move past generalizations about 'international students,' 'basic writers,' or 'transfer students'" (94). As a practitioner in a two-year college, I found that her argument resonates deeply. These labels often represent ways of othering and eventually getting rid of students—a process described in Burton Clark's landmark essay, "The 'Cooling Out' Function in Higher Education," and still relevant now, as evidenced in low completion numbers, especially for minority students. I agree with Poe that "integrating race into WAC practice has the potential to address very real teaching problems," and that this work should be grounded locally and in relation to specific students. This chapter provides essential theoretical grounding for future WAC work.

Condon and Young's introduction is a site of richness in this collection, too. They argue, "understanding that racism exists and operates beyond the academy is foundational" (4). The editors continue, "as powerful as the collective desire of Americans may be to achieve a post-racial democracy, we have not arrived. The necessity of acknowledging and resisting the historical force of racism by teaching about racism and by developing pedagogical approaches that enact and model antiracist engagement remains pressing" (10). Democracy is not possible when a rhetorical sleight of hand signaling a non-existent equality covers the silencing of many. Young and Condon's book exemplifies teacher-scholar-activism through its engagement with persistent barriers to democracy.

Mary P. Sheridan and her co-editors approach teacher-scholar-activist work from a different frame than the authors in Condon and Young's collection. In the introduction, Sheridan writes that this text addresses "more expansive understandings of where, how, and with whom we research," all toward the end of "connecting academia to the broader society" (xi). The collection's aim is teacher-scholar-activism that asserts a rhetoric of engagement—public engagement as the way we enact the social turn—as the work of writing studies. Sheridan herself takes up this idea, arguing that "engagement is one way we have embraced the implications the social turn has had on our knowledge-making practices and on how we can responsively act and learn" (xiii). The collection, which grew out of the 2014 Thomas R. Watson Conference, features eighteen short chapters that examine engagement and the ethical responsibilities it entails.

The volume's chapters are divided into three sections. The first, "Taking Positions," includes chapters about setting up public-facing activism and institution-facing activism. The first chapter, Linda Adler-Kassner's "Taking Action in the Age of Reaction: Constructing Architectures of Participation," argues that we must begin with "foundations in our position-taking" as precursor to taking broader strategic action (5). For Adler-Kassner engagement arises from what I would call located agency—what she describes as "the result of individuals working together to create and enact strategy" (6). Adler-Kassner is aware that collective engagement is difficult, especially in light of the Education Intelligence Complex. This thinking resonates with the Condon and Young collection, which theorizes and reports tactics and strategies that resist white supremacist ideologies underlying educational and societal structures. Adler-Kassner's metaphor of constructing an architecture is useful. Resilient design theory is a branch of architecture that deals with how physical structures stand up to environmental stressors. The application of this metaphor asks us to interrogate the structures we build in writing studies to ensure that they are strategic action for a more just, engaged and equitable future.

The second section of the book, "Building Relationships," moves from the foundation- setting of the first section into lived extant practices. One of the chapters that stands out is Steven Alvarez's "Practicing Confianza: Engaged Community Literacy Learning Research in Mexington, Kentucky." Confianza literally translates to "trust," but it has a deeper connotation of mutual reciprocity. Alvarez's concentration on this term and its cultural weight is a necessary contribution to community literacy work, especially the kinds of engagement, teacher-scholar-activism, and located agency to which the social turn points us. Alvarez writes that "confianza in this frame counters precarious distrust and leads to research and dialogues as sites for forming community trust and for collaborative engaged learning" (141). The care and respect Alvarez shows as he works with high school Latinx students is worth calling attention to as a practice. He notes that his approach takes time, which itself is a kind of resistance to neoliberal logics of efficiency. As I read, I felt this text and the literacy work it describes to be kindred with Freire's early critical literacy program in Brazil in that it is deeply invested in serving and listening to communities.

The final section of Sheridan et. al.'s collection is "Crossing Boundaries," including activism and teaching that happens outside of traditional classroom context. Stand outs are Steve Parks' chapter on community publishing in Palestine, Patrick W. Berry's chapter on teaching in prisons, and Stephanie Rae Larson's chapter on refugee literacy learning and the complex ideologies of literacy and not-for-profit organizations. This section is the strongest in the book because of the front-facing activism each of the chapters detail. Parks' "Writing, Democracy, Activism" details a community effort to publish a book called *Revolution by Love* in the middle of the ongoing Israeli Palestinian conflict. That the book was distributed at all "was seen as significant," Parks reported (189). He goes on to say that this work is a small example of how "writing can, perhaps, give voice to democratic activists in small but important ways" (189). Parks' chapter has value for me, not because I have worked in conflicted and dangerous situations like this, but because he tells us that he began his essay "with the dream of a moral compass" that would help teacher-scholar-activists as we step outside of our classrooms (194). He calls his work a failure. I'm not sure I agree, but I know well the feeling of failure in undertaking work to challenge structural inequalities, injustices, and violence. It is a powerful, emotionally touching chapter. In reflecting on the section title "Boundaries Crossed," I'm not sure this is the best name for this part of the book. I would argue instead that these chapters are the actionable commitments Condon and Young talk about in their collection, albeit focused on the public commitments of scholarship rather than explicit antiracist action.

Perhaps not all readers will see—or agree with—the connections I've made here. Condon and Young in their introduction tell us that "for as long as [they] have been thinking, talking, working at antiracist activism within and beyond the bounds of the academy, [they] have encountered denials and scapegoating for the most blatant racist incidents. . . . We have been asked to justify that work—to explain to our colleagues, our students, and our readers why such work is necessary," even though the answers seemed "commonsensical" to them (3). Their observation demonstrates ubiquitous resistance to anti-racist work and to labor for social change more generally. These two collections are part of a larger movement toward explicit teacher-scholar-activist work. Writing studies practitioners are taking up the moral obligations of making the world a more just and equitable place. Both collections are examples of front-facing activism.

Condon and Young conclude *Performing Antiracist Pedagogy* with a call to action, writing:

> We call on our readers and our disciplines to join with students in a multiracial antiracist struggle for justice. Let us demand of ourselves and encourage one another to do more than mouth our commitments: to make our actions match our words; to transform our classrooms, our departments, and our institutions as well as our communities; and to learn from one another as allies who possess the courage to effect change. (230)

Sheridan makes a similar claim at the end of her introduction to *Writing for Engagement*, telling readers that her chapters "share stances that make demands upon us all, that call for us to advocate for policies and practices [...] to develop a more encompassing understanding of who we are responsible to and for in our teaching and research" (xx). This signals to me a return to Bizzell, who posits three ways that composition studies changes the world in her essay—one, by doing the "proper work of teaching writing"; two, by assigning materials that raise students' awareness; and three, by having students encounter professors' "personality and values" (185-86). These two collections together form a fourth way—we join the struggle, or, as Condon puts it in an earlier book of hers, we join the band. We take on the political nature of the work of the social turn and become engaged teacher-scholar-activists. To use Adler-Kassner's metaphor, these two collections are architectural plans for how we might engage in this work.

Des Moines, IA

Works Cited

Bizzell, Patricia. "Composition Studies Saves the World!" *College English, vol.* 72, no. 2, 2009, pp. 174-87.

Clark, Burton R. "The 'Cooling-Out' Function in Higher Education." *American Journal of Sociology,* vol. 65, no.6, 1960, pp. 569-76.

Condon, Frankie. *I Hope I Join the Band: Narrative, Affiliation, and Antiracist Rhetoric.* Utah State UP, 2012.

Sullivan, Patrick. "Meet My English 93 Class." *Basic Writing e-Journal,* forthcoming 2019.

---. "The Two-Year College Teacher-Scholar-Activist." *Teaching English in the Two-Year College,* vol. 42., no.4, 2015, pp. 327-50.

Retention, Persistence, and Writing Programs, edited by Todd Ruecker, Dawn Shepherd, Heidi Estrem, and Beth Brunk-Chavez. Utah State U P, 2017. 278 pp.

Reviewed by James Clifford Swider, Indiana University of Pennsylvania

Vincent Tinto's landmark publication, *Leaving College: Rethinking the Causes and Cures of Student Attrition*, opened the dialogue for strategies universities can employ to curb students leaving the university before degree completion. Yet, three decades on, the specter of student attrition persists. At my own institution, Indiana University of Pennsylvania, the retention rate in fall 2016 for all second-year students was 71.4% (74.8% nationwide); this rate is even lower for Hispanic (63.4%) and black (53.6%) students ("Crimson Snapshot").

As an integral part of the university ecosystem, the field of composition has not ignored the retention dialogues. In 2014, Pegeen Reichert Powell's *Retention and Resistance: Writing Instruction and Students Who Leave* expanded the discussion of how composition instructors can respond to the discourse surrounding student retention. *Retention, Persistence, and Writing Programs* extends this dialogue by offering a variety of theoretical essays and empirical studies that address how the field of composition can respond to the issue of student retention.

The collection is divided into two main sections, with the first offering theoretical discussions of the role first-year composition plays in the retention dialogues, and the second explicitly detailing the steps various composition programs have taken to improve student retention along with qualitative and quantitative studies to test their efficacy.

For instance, in chapter six, Nathan Garrett, Matthew Bridgewater, and Bruce Feinstein offer evidence that success in first-year writing is strongly tied to student persistence. Their study supports Ashley J. Holmes and Cristine Busser's argument in chapter three that university writing programs must meaningfully collaborate with retention programs, stating that "when retention initiatives are employed through a top-down model, administrators are missing an opportunity to gain feedback from WPAs and writing instructors on the effectiveness of their programs" (51).

Still, a healthy skepticism on current attitudes towards retention efforts simmers across the collection. In chapter two, Rita Malenczyk criticizes the obsession universities have with retaining students, suggesting that "implemented uncritically, retention efforts can turn a university into a panopticon" (25). Similarly, in chapter four, March Scott debates the use of large data sets by universities to track students' histories to predict their success, arguing that this data, "doesn't replace the need for careful programmatic assessment and inquiry" (69). Much like David S. Martin's edited collection, *Transnational Writing Program Administration*, where many authors implied that global neoliberalism fueled American universities' international student recruitment and expansion efforts, skepticism over the intentions of modern university administrators also runs across *Retention, Persistence, and Writing Programs*. Both collections demonstrate that the field of composition does not uncritically accept the narratives spun by university stakeholders outside the discipline.

Of course, Reichert Powell contributes to the collection, appropriate considering the majority of the authors in the collection cite her work. In what may strike some readers as fatalistic and undermining the goals of student retention, in chapter eight Reichert Powell acknowledges that "some students should leave" (135); the composition instructor should instead focus on teaching skills students can use in their professional lives, regardless of whether they finish their studies.

Sara Webb-Sunderhaus's piece in chapter seven stands out in the collection by offering a glimpse into the harsh reality of a student expected to fail. A trigger warning is warranted: The chapter delves into the childhood trauma and drug use by a student. Yet this collection would be wanting without the inclusion of at least one study offering an in-depth look at the often-hidden struggles students bring into the classroom, which can contribute to their attrition.

A number of strategies by composition programs across the country are described in the second half of the collection for readers to consider using in their own contexts. Some report on the value of embedding tutors within writing courses, some on adding additional courses, and one asks instructors to reflect on the power imbalances inherent in the classroom. As a former writing center assistant director, I would have liked the collection to include an essay from the perspective of the university writing center, considering how intertwined the writing center is with writing programs.

However, while the quantitative studies of the collection are valuable for their rigorous methodologies, their results may cause the reader to question whether the steps composition programs have taken to improve student persistence is working. Sarah Elizabeth Snyder's study in chapter eleven on the efficacy of Arizona State University's Stretch Program on second language and basic writers yielded mixed results; Snyder notes that the study "supports a claim of higher retention than traditional FYC from first semester to second semester for both mainstream and multilingual students," yet "persistence from second to third semester . . . are the lowest percentages record for the Stretch Program to date" (199). Similarly, in their study in chapter fourteen on the benefits of peer advocates (PA), Michael Day, Tawanda Gipson, and Christopher P. Parker admitted that they were "somewhat disappointed that the quantitative results indicated very little difference in academic improvement and retention between PA and non-PA students" (250). Still, the inclusion of these studies is needed to provide impetus for others in the field to consider the efficacy of their own programs.

In sum, the collection reminds composition instructors that they must retain their own agency and voice in the discourse surrounding retention while simultaneously helping students develop their own agency and voice. As an instructor of basic writing at my institution, I am well aware that the faces I see during the first week of the semester may disappear halfway through; the collection has certainly instilled in me a sense of responsibility for the continued success of my students, regardless of whether they finish their degree.

Indiana, PA

Works Cited

"Crimson Snapshot Academics." *Crimson Snapshot*, Indiana U of Pennsylvania, www.iup.edu/snapshot/academics/.

Martins, David S. *Transnational Writing Program Administration*. Utah State UP, 2015.

Reichert Powell, Pegeen. *Retention and Resistance: Writing Instruction and Students Who Leave*. Utah State UP, 2014.

Tinto, Vincent. *Leaving College: Rethinking the Causes and Cures of Student Attrition*. U of Chicago P, 1987.

Bad Ideas about Writing, edited by Cheryl E. Ball and Drew M. Loewe. Open Access Textbooks, 2017. 370pp.

Reviewed by Jenn Fishman with Alli Bernard, Jessica Brown, Grace Chambers, Lorena Dulce, Ryan Higgins, Brian Huback, Saúl López, Aishah Mahmood, Shane Martin, Beth Michalewski, Madi Moster, Carly Ogletree, Alyssa Paulus, Lily Regan, Anna Story, and Haley Wasserman

Marquette University

Bad Ideas about Writing is a really good idea. This open-access digital book edited by Cheryl E. Ball and Drew M. Loewe contains a series of informed, readable rebuttals to familiar fallacies about writing. Fittingly for a publication meant for both academic and nonacademic readers, several chapters of *Bad Ideas* appeared in *Inside Higher Education* between January and November of 2017. The collection itself was published that same year by West Virginia University's Open Access Textbooks (OAT). Among additional OAT offerings—Derek Mueller's award-winning *Network Sense: Methods for Visualizing a Discipline* (co-published with the WAC Clearinghouse/Colorado State University Press), the *Scholarship of Teaching and Learning 2017 Directory*, and *West Virginia History: An Open Access Reader* (Barksdale and Fones-Wolf)—*Bad Ideas* stands out as an intervention. Born of frustration with popular discourse about writing and the limited circulation of writing scholarship, *Bad Ideas* is "an attempt by a varied and diverse group of writing scholar-teachers to translate . . . specialized knowledge and experiences about writing for a truly wide set of audiences" (2). Addressing "teachers, students, parents, administrators, lawmakers, [and] news media" (1), it is an activist work meant to provide readers with a combination of leverage and hope in the form of "more productive, inclusive, and useful ways" of conceptualizing writing (2).

As an intellectual project, *Bad Ideas* is inspired by John Brockman's annual queries to the scientific community, including his 2014 provocation: "What scientific idea is ready for retirement?" Since the late 90s, Brockman's questions have been asked and answered in his online scientific salon, *The Edge*, but they began as face-to-face deliberations, and Ball and Loewe's volume preserves that spirit, enacting a lively, Burkean parlor that I extended into the classroom by making *Bad Ideas* required reading for my advanced undergraduate composition class. In a graduate seminar, I might have assigned *Bad Ideas* with *Naming What We Know: Threshold Concepts of Writing Studies* (Adler-Kassner and Wardle), inviting students to loop recursively through discussions about what writing is and who writers are while gathering a sense of disciplinary positioning and praxes. In my advanced comp class, we read and discussed *Bad Ideas*, and then students pursued individual projects inspired by the book. Although we numbered only seventeen (including myself), our range reflected in microcosm the contributors to Ball and Loewe's collection. My students, sophomores to seniors, were mainly English majors with second majors or minors in everything from biomedical sciences and communication to education and political science. Likewise, *Bad Ideas* authors include graduate students, emerita scholars with expertise in rhetoric and composition/writing studies, and those with high school teaching, editing, publishing, and educational consulting experience.

Organizationally, *Bad Ideas* includes eight sections, which mirror "eight major categories of bad ideas . . . tied to the production, circulation, cultural use of, evaluation, and teaching of writing in multiple ways" (3). In my course syllabus, I listed a common chapter from each section, and students also read at least one chapter per section of their own choosing. Moving through the book in order, we started with "Bad Ideas about What Good Writing Is" and "Bad Ideas about Who Good Writers Are." The former section opens with a chapter by Patricia Roberts-Miller that counters the idea that rhetoric is a synonym for empty speech. Just as rhetoric plays a framing role in college composition, the argument Roberts-Miller makes about rhetoric frames confutations of bad ideas about literacy (Babb), first-year writing (Branson; Cook), knowledge transfer (Wardle; Carillo), and reading (Carillo; Barger).

The second section demystifies writers in relation to not only writing but also language itself. To begin, Teri Holbrook and Melanie Hundley call attention to an all-too-familiar contradiction: Writers represented as both "magical beings" and people so "incapable of dealing with . . . daily life" that "they drink, do drugs, need help, and occasionally slip into murderous madness" (53). In turn, Ronald Clark Brooks takes up the pervasive belief "that one has to be credentialed in order to call oneself a writer" (61), while Dustin Edwards and Enrique Paz write in collaborative defiance against the idea of the writer as an autonomous genius, and Jill Parrott soundly rejects the notion that "writing is a talent set in stone" (71). In complementary fashion, the next four chapters confront false standards to which writers are regularly held: namely, they must always succeed (Carr), and they must always speak and write Standard Written English (Pattanayak), a notion that reflects biases against African American Language (Cunningham) and home languages other than English (Alvarez). In conclusion, this section addresses bad ideas about what writers do: Confront writer's block (Carter), revise (Giovanelli), and, most fundamentally, produce writing (Butts).

The next sections challenge received ideas about style, usage, and grammar on one hand and writing techniques on the other. Section three opens with chapters critical of the authority vested in Strunk and White (Lisabeth) and more general received rules for writing (Dufour and Ahern-Dodson). The following four chapters address usage through a colloquy on voice, focusing on first-person pronouns and passive voice (Thomas; Rodríguez; Parker; Brooke). Finally, three chapters tackle bad ideas about grammar: "Teaching Grammar Improves Writing" (Dunn), "Good Writers Must Know Grammatical Terminology" (Rule), and "Grammar Should be Taught Separately as Rules to Learn" (Harris). In the section dedicated to bad ideas about writing techniques, contributors bring attention to three distinct topics. Kristin Milligan challenges the assumption that "Formal Outlines are Always Useful"; Daniel V. Bommarito disputes the claim that "Students Should Learn About the Logical Fallacies"; and Nancy Fox rebuffs an idea that teachers and students alike seem to take away from writing textbooks: namely, that "Logos is Synonymous with Logic."

The section dedicated to "Bad Ideas about Genres" is the longest with a dozen chapters that address not only particular genres and types of discourse but also related activities. This section opens with bad ideas about academic writing (Theune), creative writing (Alexis), and popular culture (Williams; Pepper). Three chapters address bad ideas about a genre that itself might be classified as a bad idea, the five-paragraph essay (FPE). Rebuking educators in particular, these chapters reject readymade claims that the FPE is rhetorically or pedagogically sound (Vieregge; Bernstein and Lowry; Bowles, Jr.). The remainder of the section examines bad ideas about research-based writing and the only school genre that may be as reviled as the FPE, at least by writing scholars—the research paper. Respectively, Alison C. Witte and Emily A. Wierszewski critique the shibboleths that research starts with answers and thesis statements, and Alexandria Lockett takes issue with the persistent notion that "The Traditional Research Paper is Best." To conclude, Susanmarie Harrington and Jennifer A. Mott-Smith address the common assumptions that "Citing Sources is a Basic Skill Learned Early On" and "Plagiarism Deserves to be Punished."

The last three sections call attention in turn to bad ideas about writing assessment, digital technology, and writing teachers. The section on assessment begins by questioning our fixation on grading (James) and grading rubrics (Leahy; Sands). Subsequent chapters bemoan "the over-graded paper" (Harris) and the overrated idea that only teachers should evaluate student writing (Friend). While peers' evaluations may have merit, Chris M. Anson and Les Perelman reject the notion that "machines can evaluate writing well" (278); Stephanie Vie rejects the perception that "plagiarism detection services are money well spent" (287); and Kristen di Gennaro nixes SAT scores as "useful for placing students in writing courses" (294). The following section singles out mostly old chestnuts about writing and digital technology. As Scott Warnock states: "We need to put to rest the idea that digital forms of writing pose a threat to overall writing ability" (301). Likewise, as Christopher Justice argues, we need to embrace the "many positive benefits" of texting (309). On balance, we need to stop trying to gamify writing (Daniel-Wariya), and we need to reconsider our unfettered embrace of digital technology along with our metaphors for people who do and do not use it (Carter and Matzke; Alexander).

The final section, "Bad Ideas about Writing Teachers," might have been titled "Bad Ideas about College Writing." It begins with a claim that almost always signals bad ideas will follow: "You're Going to Need this in College" (Hollinger). The next three chapters also concern dubious absolutes: "Dual-Enrollment Writing Classes Should Always be Pursued" (Wilkinson), "Secondary-School English Teachers Should Only be Taught Literature" (Wright), and "Face-to-Face Courses are Superior to Online Courses" (Bourelle and Bourelle). To conclude, two chapters interrogate what may be the worst idea of all: anyone can teach writing, whether online (Hewett) or off (Kahn). Within the scientific community, ideas that need to die are judged obstacles to progress. In public discourse about higher education, the notion that anyone and everyone can teach writing does more than thwart good writing instruction. It negates the combined pedagogical, scholarly, and institutional praxes on which effective and ethical formal literacy education is built and sustained. Hewett connects some of these dots when she explains: "Unfortunately, a top-down, administratively driven requirement for online writing-intensive instruction reveals an implicit, pervasive belief that to teach writing online is intuitive and therefore simple to do" (357). Kahn alludes to others when he writes: "How we got to the point where so many faculty doing such important work can be treated so poorly is a long story" (364). Offering a useful gloss on the rise of English composition, he goes on to state a widely shared desire: "I wish it were obvious that people better trained to do something would do it better than people who aren't trained as well. That feels like such a truism it's hard to know what evidence to offer to support it" (365).

The volume is full of richly informed, personally framed strong statements, which are part of the book's appeal and a source of its rhetorical oomph. In the words of my students, such moves help make the book relatable. Although "relatable" is a term I usually associate with uncritical and dangerously relativistic thinking, that is not how my students used it in their reading journals and class discussions. Under the auspices of relatability, they found *Bad Ideas* engaging because it surprised, amused, and occasionally angered them. *Bad Ideas* also introduced them to literacy practices and experiences different from their own, and it encouraged them to scrutinize their assumptions about writing along with themselves as writers. On balance, the colloquial style of *Bad Ideas* contributed to some of our most significant difficulties. For disciplinary novices, the undergirding research and scholarship may have been too camouflaged, making it too easy to read *Bad Ideas* and its authors' activism as one more opinion war. Reflecting on our overall experience as readers for this review, we talked about how next time I might assign fewer sections of the book and more of the research and scholarship behind the chapters. An opportunity to peer behind the curtain, we agreed, might help everyone better understand where contributors are coming from along with some of the challenges involved in crafting public intellectual rhetorics.

We further questioned the strategic simplicity of the book with some of our earliest class discussions in mind. For example, in the second week of the semester, we read "Formal Outlines Are Always Useful," where Milligan argues that "mandatory outlines should be given their proper burial" (164). Student-led discussion echoed this statement but, as on previous days, did not initially go much further. Listening to the group take sides based on their own habits and related failures or successes, a light bulb went off for me. Our trouble as interlocutors with *Bad Ideas* stemmed not from what authors claimed—about outlining, rules for writing, first-year composition, etc.—but from how they made their claims: in bold terms that invited us to make similar, all-or-nothing first-person arguments. Missing were explicit prompts within chapters to read critically both with and against them. When we took a step back to consider whether outlines were really the problem, discussion shifted. We focused on the word "mandatory" and the situations that might lead teachers to require outlines as well as the beliefs those teachers might hold (i.e., about writing, about learning about writing). When I asked how else students had been taught to generate ideas and organize information, the discussion deepened. We considered the purposes such assignments serve and what makes the ways they shape thinking and writing "good" or "bad."

Students also responded to *Bad Ideas* via class projects. In the second half of the semester they selected a bad idea from or inspired by the book, interrogated it via one or more modes of inquiry, delivered a presentation or lead an equivalent in-class activity, and produced a final text. A student-produced essay, "Easy to Teach, Easy to Grade," satirized the appeal of the FPE in five paragraphs written from a teacher's point of view (Chambers). Another, "Are Outlines Useful Only for Math-Minded Students," presented findings from survey-based research in a *Bad Ideas*-style chapter composed in outline form (Moster), while "Creative Writing Doesn't Belong in Science Classrooms" used interview data to reconsider assumptions about good undergraduate science writing assignments (Wasserman). "Using A Thesaurus Makes Your Writing Worse" triangulated the always changing nature of language, students' perceptions of vocabulary, and both good and bad thesaurus pedagogies (Michalewski). A chapter on workplace ghostwriting underscored the limited opportunities students have to practice writing both with and for others during college (Dulce), and "All High School Students are Literate" addressed the all-too-real literacy crisis in K-12 education (Regan). In an imagined volume, *Bad Ideas about African American English*, Alyssa Paulus conceived a study dedicated to "debunking misconceptions about AAE."

Not everyone chose *Bad Ideas* modes (i.e., chapter, book). One future teacher produced a set of lessons designed to help sixth graders explore different genres, including the FPE (Huback); another wrote a NCTE-style "Statement on Increasing Linguistic Diversity in the Classroom" (Bernard). In addition, the podcast "Cheering Them On: Student Athletes and Writing Confidence" reported on whether and how cheerleading informs high school writers' confidence (Ogletree). Two creative writers chose creative writing projects: one researched and composed a short story, "Ranch House" (Story), and one conducted a mixed methods self-study of his own NaNoWriMo efforts and compiled a set of his own rules for the annual November writing challenge (Higgins). Another pair responded to chapters on first-year writers with their own research questions. Following the format of a CWPA grant proposal, "The Writing Practices and Processes of First Year Students" outlined an ambitious project almost ready for IRB review (Mahmood), while the documentary-style video "Not All Students Need First-Year English" let students speak for themselves about the value of FYE (Brown). Two additional videos brought more student voices to the fore: "together" featured international students talking about their experiences as bi- and multilingual college writers (Martin), while "Snapshots: Creative Writers at Marquette" featured four first-generation students of color who write short stories, poetry, and rap (López).

The digital projects noted above and students' positive reception echoed the class's critique of the section on digital technology. The attention paid to texting felt dated to them, and as a group they raised important questions about the chapter on digital natives and immigrants, concepts that have been widely criticized by both digital and decolonial scholars. The digital projects also reflect students' interest in using available means to contribute to and amplify the overall project of *Bad Ideas* and bring informed arguments about writing to non-specialist audiences. This is, indeed, a good idea. We benefitted from it, and we expect others will, too.

Milwaukee, WI

Works Cited

Adler-Kassner, Linda, and Elizabeth Wardle, editors. *Naming What We Know: Threshold Concepts of Writing Studies*. UP of Colorado and Utah State UP, 2015.

Barksdale, Kevin, and Ken Fones-Wolf, editors. *West Virginia History: An Open Access Reader*. Open Access Textbooks, no date. https://textbooks.lib.wvu.edu/wvhistory/index.html.

Brockman, John. *This Idea Must Die: Scientific Theories that are Blocking Progress.* Harper Perennial, 2015.

Mueller, Derek N. *Network Sense: Methods for Visualizing a Discipline.* The WAC Clearinghouse and UP of Colorado, 2017.

Scholarship of Teaching and Learning 2017 Directory. Open Access Textbooks, 2017. https://textbooks.lib.wvu.edu/sotl/index.html.

Assembling Composition, edited by Kathleen Blake Yancey and Stephen J. McElroy. Urbana: Conference on College Composition and Communication of the National Council of Teachers of English, 2017. 246 pp.

Reviewed by Sara Austin, Bowling Green State University

Yancey and McElroy's edited collection, *Assembling Composition*, offers a "new and helpful way of understanding composing, especially in an era marked by postmodernism and postpedagogy" (3). The volume builds on assemblage scholarship such as Johndan Johnson-Eilola and Stuart Selber's 2006 article, "Plagiarism, Originality, Assemblage," Byron Hawk's 2007 *Counter-History of Composition: Toward Methodologies of Complexity*, Jonathan Buehl's 2016 *Assembling Arguments*, Dustin Edwards's 2016 *Computers and Composition* article, "Framing Remix Rhetorically: Toward a Typology of Transformative Work," and Jacqueline Preston's 2015 *CCC* article, "Project(ing) Literacy: Writing to Assemble in a Postcomposition FYW classroom." Yancey and McElroy look to both art and critical theory to define and situate assemblages; in art, assemblage is the practice of bringing everyday materials together to create a new text, while assemblages in critical theory can be combinations of bodies, concepts, and ideas, allowing compositions to be seen and traced through the assembled components. This leads to an understanding of how the components work together to generate a composition, or a second broader sense of assemblage results from a constellation of texts being understood metaphorically (3). Building on both assemblages in art and critical theory, Yancey and McElroy situate assemblage within rhetoric and composition as its own assemblage of definitions. For Yancey and McElroy, "assemblage refers to and sanctions the makingness that textuality affords and its use, reuse, and repurposing of materials, especially chunks of text, in order to make something new" (4). In other words, assemblages allow for a way of composing that combines and remixes both texts, concepts, and ideas into something new.

Assembling Composition is divided into three sections: "In Theory," "In the Classroom/On Campus," and "In the World." Alex Reid, in chapter two, "Big-Data Assemblies: Composing Nonhuman Ecology," explains how big-data analysis might be combined with assemblage theory in order to see composing as a process that involves human interaction with nonhuman objects. In chapter three, "They Eat Horses, Don't They?" Jeff Rice compares two social media posts and suggests that these assemblages create an aggregated meaning, which involves rethinking both practice and ideology. The final chapter in section one, "Beyond the Object to the Making of the Object: Understanding the Process of Multimodal Composition as Assemblage," by James Kalmbach, examines a multimodal composition course where students negotiate assemblages to create successful projects. This section offers a theory of assemblage in light of multimodality and digital technology.

Section two, which looks at assemblages in the classroom and on campus, includes Michael J. Michaud's "Assemblage Composing, Reconsidered." He argues for more instruction in assemblage composing, especially multimodal, new media, digital, and multimedia composing, to help students further develop their rhetorical skills. In chapter six, "Copy, Combine, Transform: Assemblage in First-Year Composition," Stephen J. McElroy and Travis Maynard explain the goals of a first-year composition course on assemblage along with major assignments, activities, and readings. They describe how the course helped students become better writers and how an assemblage approach to fyc might be beneficial because it engages students in composing, suggesting that the approach "makes assemblage the central theme that ties together other important concepts like multimodality, genre conventions, remediation, and rhetorical situation" (116).

In the final chapter of section two, "ePortfolio Artifacts as Graduate Student Multimodal Identity Assemblages," Kristine L. Blair examines ePortfolios and their role in building professional identities of graduate students. Overall, the section chapters provide readers with concrete ways to implement assemblage theory into their classes through examples and student perspectives on assemblages in the classroom.

Section three, an examination of assemblages in the world, begins with "To Gather, Assemble, and Display: Composition as [Re]Collection," in which Jody Shipka explores assemblages through a collection-based framework of the Evocative Objects Workshop. In chapter nine, "Assemblages of Asbury Park: The Persistent Legacy of the Large-Letter Postcard," Stephen J. McElroy analyzes the continued use of large letter postcards through assemblage thinking and argues that such thinking effects new contexts from restaurants to politics and architecture. Kathleen Blake Yancey, in chapter ten, "Multimodal Assemblage, Compositions, and Composing: The Corresponding Cases of Emigrant Cemetery Tombstones and 'A Line for Wendy,'" examines multimodal assemblages in the form of memorial compositions and argues that by looking at the composing processes of memorial compositions, we can learn about composing and compositions in general. Kristin L. Arola and Adam Arola in their chapter, "An Ethics of Assemblage: Creative Repetition and the 'Electric Pow Wow,'" argue for "good assemblages" and outline four criteria that make up a good assemblage: responsive; innovative and productive; open to new ways of thinking, seeing, and living; and benefitting the "we" rather than the "I" (211). Finally, in chapter twelve, "Conclusion: Reterritorialization," Johndan Johnson-Eilola and Stuart A. Selber place the authors in conversation with one another by re-examining the collection and re-categorizing assemblages as connections with other peoples and times, with material objects, and with performance and pedagogy. Using these themes, Johnson-Eilola and Selber call readers to continually rethink and reassemble their own interactions with text.

While assemblages are examined through four different themes in Yancey and McElroy's volume, assemblages as performance and pedagogy might provide researchers opportunities to further explore assemblages. Readers might be interested in further exploring the role of multimodal composing, especially multimodal composing in assemblage theory. Additionally, teachers might consider how a theory of assemblage could benefit transfer studies and research on transfer. Michaud's "Assemblage Composing, Reconsidered" places multimodal composing, assemblage theory, and transfer into conversation using a curriculum that focuses on rhetorically based concepts. He notes that

> For many students, just learning the form and style of a new genre can take a good deal of time and, of course, this process is sometimes hindered if a student fails to understand the larger rhetorical concerns of genre production. . . . In short, pedagogies that, borrowing the language of Douglas Downs and Elizabeth Wardle, teach students both *how to* produce a genre and *about* that genre itself are probably best suited to achieving lasting results. (91)

By emphasizing the importance of navigating the rhetorical concerns of a genre production, Michaud considers how to help students navigate the challenge of genre production within a course.

Just as reflective writing promotes transfer, critical and reflective writing is key in assemblage theory. In his chapter, "Beyond the Object to the Making of the Object: Understanding the Process of Multimodal Composition as Assemblage," Kalmbach explains that "critical reflection is an essential balance to the pleasures of technological engagement" (75). Here, Kalmbach defines engagement as "the pieces assembled during composition" (60). In Kalmbach's multimodal composition course, he suggests three steps that teachers can take to encourage them to reflect on how they are negotiating engagements: let students choose their own topics, have students choose their own tools, and use critique to make negotiation visible or to critically reflect on multimodal artifacts and the effectiveness of the artifact. By asking students to practice critical reflection on multimodal artifacts in a multimodal composition course, Kalmbach effectively uses assemblage to promote transfer.

Yancey and McElroy outline four dimensions of assemblage that the collection speaks to: (1) how theories of writing—in particular, multimodal theories of writing informed by assemblage—might be suited to current digital composing practices, (2) how assemblage might help students better understand the aliveness of writing, (3) how composing practices can be traces as assemblages, and (4) how interrogating assemblage is an ethical practice. This volume provides readers with insightful research on growing areas in the field of composition and rhetoric.

Bowling Green, Ohio

Composition, Rhetoric, and Disciplinarity, edited by Rita Malenczyk, Susan Miller-Cochran, Elizabeth Wardle, and Kathleen Blake Yancey. Utah State University Press, 2018. 355 pp.

Reviewed by Jacob Babb, Indiana University Southeast

Writing studies' status as a discipline has been a driving question for decades, resulting in the production of a significant amount of scholarship pursuing several strands of argument about the benefits and ill effects of disciplinarity. *Composition, Rhetoric, and Disciplinarity* contributes to and extends several of those strands. The contributors ask questions such as whether writing studies is a discipline, what it means to be a discipline in an increasingly corporatized university, and how writing studies' historically prominent emphasis on pedagogy and fyw affects our disciplinary status. As a whole, the collection does not seek to resolve differences regarding these questions; indeed, Malenczyk, Miller-Cochran, Wardle, and Yancey selected contributions that often challenge one another. In this way, the collection fosters conversations about what has defined writing studies as a discipline and what kinds of issues we should consider as we move forward.

The book's fifteen chapters are divided into four sections. Section one starts with a historical overview from Yancey, in which she suggests that composition has taken a disciplinary turn, much in the same vein as previous turns (e.g., the social turn, the public turn). Yancey's analysis concludes by asking what kind of a discipline we would like to be, an ethos-based question that resounds throughout the collection. The section includes Barry Maid's chapter tracing his own personal history in the discipline, from his early interactions with Lee Odell and Maxine Hairston to his experience with independent writing departments. Maid's chapter is especially powerful following Yancey's because together they show how interactions with the discipline are shaped by experiences with individuals and institutions as well as broad intellectual moments, such as the disciplinary turn. Rochelle Rodrigo and Susan Miller-Cochran's chapter calls on scholars at four-year institutions not only to acknowledge the scholarly contributions of community college scholars but also to find and engage with those contributions. The section concludes with an exploration of Kenneth Bruffee's work and legacy by Rita Malenczyk, Neal Learner, and Elizabeth H. Boquet, a powerful call to see students as collaborative members of our discipline and to apportion equal value to teaching and research.

The chapters in the second section offer compelling arguments to reconsider how we view disciplinarity, starting with Gwendolynne Reid and Carolyn R. Miller's assertion that much of our disciplinary anxiety can be traced to tensions between open and closed approaches to classifying the field. They suggest that we view disciplines as "open, networked, and continually emergent" (96), an approach that emphasizes how numerous methods and inquiries have contributed to the broad body of knowledge that we recognize as a discipline. Elizabeth Wardle and Doug Downs encourage readers to consider what we have always valued and to see those values— "inclusion, access, respecting difference, facilitating interaction, emphasizing localism, valuing diverse voices, and empowering writers to engage in textual production" (130)—as the basis for a strong discipline that can serve as an example for others. Kristine Hansen analyzes the difference between a discipline and a profession, arguing that we need to consider how to construct a profession that provides training for scholar-teachers from the undergraduate level forward and that supports better labor conditions for writing instructors.

The third section explores complications and tensions surrounding disciplinarity. Jennifer Helene Maher uses Aristotle's concept of virtue to counter arguments that disciplines inherently reinforce hegemony and a neoliberal trajectory for higher education. Drawing on her institutional experience, which required her to deny her expertise in writing studies, Maher asserts that we lose more than we gain by rejecting disciplinarity, and that we can in fact do good by demonstrating how a discipline can resist neoliberal logic. Liane Robertson and Kara Taczak argue that the content of our introductory course should be a primary concern for the discipline, a claim that rebuffs previous arguments for moving away from fyw and pedagogy in favor of a more pronounced emphasis on research. Their argument echoes Hansen's position that writing studies needs more teachers who have disciplinary knowledge, and they also claim that the discipline needs a clearer explanation of what fyw is and does for people outside the discipline. Christiane Donahue's chapter uses translingualism to show how the discipline can and should evolve in the future, moving away from English as its basis toward language, design, and rhetorical flexibility. While Donahue acknowledges that translingualism is evolving, she asserts that it can help to shape the values of the discipline productively. Whitney Douglas, Heidi Estrem, Kelly Myers, and Dawn Shepherd use their experience revising the MA program at Boise State University to demonstrate how disciplinarity is always a compromise between local needs and disciplinary values. They describe a process of mapping their individual values and making them explicit as threshold concepts as the basis for curriculum revision. I believe many departments could benefit from emulating this approach.

The fourth section begins with Sandra Jamieson's exploration of the evolution of the undergraduate writing major over the past two decades. Jamieson argues that we need to continue studying the major to determine what local social and economic needs writing majors are meeting while also seeing how the writing major can become a site for using disciplinary knowledge effectively.

Like Douglas et al., Jamieson turns to threshold concepts as a theoretical frame to help "clarify the relationship between the discipline and the major that should represent it" (262). Jaime Armin Mejia's chapter challenges the narrative of writing studies as a welcoming discipline, particularly for Latinx scholars and students, asserting that disciplines can function as sources of assimilation that is damaging to different cultural perspectives. Mejia echoes Wardle and Downs' call for inclusivity, stating that writing studies should recognize and celebrate the "tremendous willpower it takes" to sustain an ethnic identity (283). Doug Hesse's chapter argues that unless writing studies can "reembrace the teaching of writing as a central—even as the most central—core" of disciplinarity identity, that disciplinarity will not prove as beneficial in the changing environment of higher education (295). Like Hansen, Hesse suggests that we evaluate new models for faculty labor that do not dwell in nostalgia for lost institutional models of disciplinarity. Linda Adler-Kassner's chapter compliments Hesse's by looking outward and suggesting that we embrace our knowledge to forge new relationships beyond our discipline and strengthen writing studies' ability to participate in important policy debates about writing.

Across the volume, readers can trace threads that ultimately provide a sense of where the discipline is going and why it is important to think of writing studies as a discipline. Readers can see how work like writing about writing, writing transfer, and threshold concepts has impacted many of the contributors. But I will conclude this review by highlighting the collection's definition of writing studies as an open, networked discipline that has inward and outward facing obligations, outlined most explicitly in Adler-Kassner's chapter. In their conclusion, Malenczyk, Miller-Cochran, Wardle, and Yancey frame disciplinarity, whether it is inward or outward facing, as a form of responsibility. They note that we can no longer blame problems of expertise, labor, and inclusion—inward facing responsibilities—on others. Additionally, we are obliged to engage in efforts to change how writing is understood and taught outside the discipline—outward facing responsibilities. As a whole, the collection offers a vision of writing studies as an open, networked, and evolving discipline that should harness its longstanding emphasis on student learning to thrive in a shifting educational landscape that has come to see student learning as central to higher education.

The collection may leave unresolved many questions about writing studies' disciplinarity, but the emphasis on our responsibilities as a discipline provides a chance to permanently shift the conversation from whether we are a discipline to what the discipline values and what we can do based on those values. Seldom does scholarship feel so hopeful.

New Albany, Indiana

Retroactivism in the Lesbian Archives: Composing Pasts and Futures, by Jean Bessette. Southern Illinois UP, 2018. 186 pp.

Reviewed by Katie Brooks, Virginia Tech

When I was five years old, I got my first library card. That card was a vehicle through which I explored my identity in the many novels and stories I encountered. I found answers for the questions I had about life and myself. As a cisgender white female, I was and am privileged to hear my own voice repeated back to me in many books I encounter. What was a joyride for me—wandering the stacks and finding numerous books to suit my interests—can be a deeply unsettling experience for others who do not find information on or representation of their identities. When, in the 1950s and earlier, women with same-sex desire took to the library in search of information on their identities, what they encountered was a catalogue system reflecting the society in which they lived—a system that believed same-sex desire was connected to deviance, criminality, and neurological disorder.

Jean Bessette's *Retroactivism in the Lesbian Archives: Composing Pasts and Futures* responds to the need for representation by curating and circulating archival material evidence of lesbian identities: from books to boots to clothing to pamphlets. Responding to this exigence, Bessette explores the lives and work of the women who formed the Daughters of Bilitis (DOB), the Lesbian History Archives (LHA), the June L. Mazer Archives (JLMA), and historiographic queer filmmakers of the 1990s. These women developed grassroots archives—nonacademic archives—in order to create community for the women who found themselves under- or mis-represented in other archival forms. Bessette's study, comprised of four sections that cover how retroactivism allowed queer archivists and groups to respond to contextual exigencies, relies upon an expanded conceptualization of Burkean identification to understand the importance of representation. Expanding Lucas Hildebrand's definition of retroactivism—a generative methodology that shapes or re-shapes the past in order to guide "present identity formation and future politics" (11)—Bessette posits retroactivism as a twentieth century mode of activism and identity-building for both queer cultures and other marginalized groups.

Bessette begins her study with an analysis of identification in grassroots archives. The first chapter, "The Daughters of Bilitis Archive: Clearing Historical Space for Clustered Anecdotes," focuses on a rhetorical analysis of the Daughters of Bilitis (DOB) newsletter, *The Ladder*, and *Lesbian/Woman*, a collection of archived anecdotes from the years of responses to their newsletters. One of the main arguments in this chapter is that archives can prompt "archival consciousness raising" (27). DOB's *Lesbian/Woman* archival text served a validating function for women with same-sex desire, validating their identities and promoting self-acceptance, but the archives also excluded many voices. Although compiled through self-selected participation, the DOB archive was curated for a specific audience: middle-class women who adhered to middle-class values. Despite being exclusionary to most differently identifying women, Bessette's research on the DOB explores the use of anecdotes as generative. Through sharing anecdotes, women were able to see themselves like they had never seen themselves before.

In the second chapter, "Classifying Collections: Subversive Schemas as *Topoi* in Place-Based Archives," Bessette links classification to *topoi*, arguing that "reconceiving classification as a *topos* accentuates the inextricability of the *pattern* (the system of classification) and the *material* (the artifacts and records themselves) and illuminates how archival classification in certain kinds of material space can encourage certain kinds of unanticipated patterns and connections for visitors" (70). The focus of this chapter is on the Lesbian History Archives (LHA) and the June L. Mazer Archives (JLMA). These two place-based, grassroots archives both collected objects as well as texts, including clothing, boots, photographs, and home goods. Topoi, according to Bessette, guided visitors to make identity connections across the many artifacts within the archives.

Along the lines of classification, Bessette makes an interesting move, connecting Kenneth Burke's identification and *topoi*. The discussion of identification posits one of the more interesting takeaways from this chapter: Materializing Burke helps "to demonstrate how classificatory patterns interact with archival materials to generate identifications, and ultimately, to reconsider the boundaries of identity" (70). Throughout the text, Bessette uses the concept of Burkean identification to understand the roles these archives played in shaping and creating communities. However, in the second chapter, these archives take a more materialist bent by juxtaposing certain material objects to others. Materializing identification through identifying with material objects and making connections between objects highlights how rhetorical theories can be remixed for changing technologies.

Moving through the history of grassroots lesbian archives, Bessette focuses on multimodality and documentary filmmaking in her third chapter, "Remediating the Archive: Documentary Compositions of Lesbian Pasts." Bessette focuses on the emergence of New Queer Cinema, documentary films created in the 1990s that focused on both real and fictive queer people. Defining multimodal strategies used in the films, Bessette argues that the documentaries are meta-archival approaches to activism. This chapter rhetorically analyzes five multimodal strategies that are used in the New Queer Cinema documentaries: gainsaying, nonlinearity, affective impact of taboo images, manipulation/invention of archival materials, and camp historiography (130). These multimodal rhetorical strategies "demonstrate a kind of *historiographic* retroactivism," calling into question the simple strategy of recovery and "transhistoric accounts of sexual identity" (130). Gainsaying is represented in dialogues in which the subject argues with the historian on issues of identity classification. This is a call to avoid problematic scholarship that forces historical or contemporary people into categories and identities that they would not choose for themselves.

Nonlinearity highlights the nuances of collecting histories in correlation with memory. The affective effect of using taboo images, Bessette suggests, can serve to break down stereotypes within lesbian communities themselves. A particularly interesting multimodal strategy is the manipulation and/or invention of archival materials for these projects. Manipulation and invention not only work to fill in the gaps within historical archives, but also serve as commentary on what might have been if the archives were not exclusionary, while also critiquing the curation of straight archives (130). The final multimodal strategy, camp historiography, highlights the role of performativity to exaggerate cultural artifacts to both honor and critique nostalgia. Through these multimodal strategies, Bessette argues, the documentary filmmakers critique traditional archives as exclusionary spaces that leave out the possibility of the existence of different people or identities.

In Bessette's fourth chapter, "'A History of Discontinuities': On the Past and Future of Retroactivism," she examines the role of queer archives in creating community in the twenty-first century. This chapter examines a few YouTube genres as emerging archives: It Gets Better Project (IGBP), coming out videos, and long-distance same-sex relationship videos. As technologies change and grow, so does the role of technology in shaping archives. Online videos, while usurping the role of place-based archives for this age, function as community-building tools across time, space, and geographic location. YouTube, in particular, highlights the rhetoricity of archives: material both shapes and is shaped by the medium available to the archivist. Within this new medium, Bessette highlights the role of the genre in forming acceptable additions to the archive. Online media allows for more horizontal, democratic participation. At least, that is what Bessette argues in this final chapter. However, as Bessette notes, more white, homosexual men are represented in YouTube archives. Does that diminish the utopic democratic idea—that more voices can and will be heard—of the internet? According to Bessette's research, the IGBP videos created by white homosexual men get the most views. Apart from that, what about the lack of sufficient online materials for people living in rural areas? These are just a few questions that are not addressed, but Bessette does implicate the need for further research at the end of the text.

Overall, the changing technology highlighted by Bessette's case studies explores the effects that changing modes of production—YouTube Videos in particular—have on the circulation of narratives and voices. From the DOB's newsletter and subsequent anecdotal textual archive, to the use of YouTube to share experiences and give hope, grassroots archives work to give voice to those people who are under- or mis-represented in existing archives. Bessette's work is indicative of the move toward digital work in the field of composition more generally. One takeaway from Bessette's scholarship is that the means of composing has always been influenced by and has always influenced the medium available to the composer. Ultimately, her reworking of Burkean identification, examination of multimodal strategies and of current queer archival practices expands the conversation on archives in rhetoric and composition by pushing boundaries and guiding the reader to understand the role of archives in community construction and activism.

Blacksburg, VA

How Writing Faculty Write: Strategies for Process, Product, and Productivity, by Christine E. Tulley. Logan: Utah State University Press, 2018. 190 pp.

Reviewed by Emily Carson, Villanova University

In *How Writing Faculty Write: Strategies for Process, Product, and Productivity*, Christine E. Tulley details the successful writing habits of some of the most prolific academic writers. Adopting the interview format of *The Paris Review's* "Writers at Work" series, which explored how fiction writers "find ideas, struggle with writer's block, approach revision, and navigate publication venues" (ix), Tulley turns our attention to a group uniquely qualified to recount the behind-the-scenes work of faculty writers: fifteen of the most renowned rhetoric and composition studies scholars, that is, teachers of writing and top producers of writing scholarship.

Tulley's collection responds to recent attention to the distinct demands of faculty writing by those in areas like faculty development, research administration, and composition studies. Robert Boice has noted that faculty need "creative ways of moving past blocking-related feelings that they are overscheduled and too busy to complete enough writing/publication for tenure" (vii). Peter Elbow and Mary Deane Sorcinelli addressed this need through the "Writing for Professors" program they created at the University of Massachusetts–Amherst. Promoting the benefits of bringing faculty together to write in "The Faculty Writing Space: A Room of Our Own," they model the side-by-side writing their program encouraged by writing side-by-side columns to reflect individually on their experiences with faculty. For his part, Elbow suggests that lack of productivity comes from professors seeing themselves primarily as researchers and thinkers instead of writers; he recommends that faculty devote more time putting pen to paper to develop a writerly "trust" of language (19).

Tulley's book foregrounds promising insights to be gleaned from composition faculty, for whom "engaging in writing is essential to be[ing] an effective writing teacher" (4), for whom "the process of writing itself is intellectually satisfying and engaging" (5), and who, therefore, more than most, perhaps, understand "the writing that is the academic currency of most tenure-track and tenured positions" (4). The attitudes teased out through Tulley's interviews differ, thus, from "general faculty development efforts which tend to focus on productivity and don't always work" (6), usually landing on a set of trite writing guidelines: schedule regular writing time, set measurable goals, and establish a system for feedback and accountability. Indeed, many faculty reach the end of a busy academic year or open summer having been committed to such advice, but not having met their goals. This challenge became clear to me in my role assisting faculty with their writing. A junior faculty member had crafted his first-ever book proposal during a two-day writing retreat and then met with me. We worked to reorganize his draft, clarify genre conventions, differentiate book from dissertation, and pinpoint his market. As I prepared to leave his office, he considered his revision task, leaned in, and confessed, "I hear you and I get it. But *how?*"

With her introduction and conclusion, Tulley charts out patterns among the interviewees that effectively address this faculty member's formidable *how*: "how different attempts at carving up writing times into specific segments of the day....help writing faculty make forward progress" (28), how to return to writing after an interruption so that "no time is wasted figuring out how to start again" (25), and "how publishing writing faculty are moving from a draft to a publishable final product"(27).

Academics will recognize the challenges these writers depict: the practical writing tasks that actually fill their days, from emails and administrative reports to letters of recommendation, dissertation reviews, and editing tasks, such as are described by Malea Powell, Kathleen Yancey and Duane Roen; the fifteen years it took Jacqueline Royster to complete her "soul" project; the "slogging" that Cynthia Selfe describes; and the "slowness" of Jessica Enoch's writing. Such is the reality of the group's pursuit of well-crafted and accessible writing, as Thomas Rickert, Joseph Harris, Melanie Yergeau, Dànielle DeVoss, Royster, and Yancey discuss. These writers also accept the difficulty of drafting. Tulley's conversations with Yancey, Chris Anson, and Howard Tinberg about composing their addresses to the Conference on College Composition and Communication (CCCC) reflect not only the "rock star" group Tulley has enlisted for interviews (the majority of other interviewees have also chaired the CCCC), but also the recursive nature involved in striving for such well-crafted writing, even for these accomplished scholars. Harris and Anson give detailed descriptions of their revision techniques.

As senior faculty mostly at research institutions, these writers tackle multiple projects at once. The grids that Anson creates to track varied projects to completion correspond to Royster's color-coded folder system, Jonathan Alexander's "to do" document, and Rickert's "academic triage," where some projects "die out" in the face of more promising work. In fact, Enoch, Yergeau, Powell, Anson, Alexander, Selfe, and Cheryl Glenn describe being tugged toward other types of projects, such as novels, for example. To explain their productivity, Roen emphasizes good work habits and discipline, while Harris valorizes time for ideas to gestate, and Royster relies on "quick focus." To get started, Kristine Blair writes grants, Anson does "semi-drafting," and DeVoss sits right down at the exact moment an idea is proposed at a conference to chart out the project.

Many (Glenn, Alexander, Harris, Blair, Powell, and Rickert) speak thoughtfully about the privilege and responsibility of their status within the field. Harris and Tinberg describe the evolution of their attitudes about student work; they consider the ethics of incorporating student voices into research and teaching. Rickert, Yancey, DeVoss, Blair, and Selfe share how they set up, work through, and benefit from co-authorship. Nearly all of the interviewees mention the impact of technology on their writing and the multimodal options they now consider for publication. In Tulley's interviews with Glenn and Enoch—Enoch was formerly Glenn's graduate student—a dialogue emerges about the importance of mentoring; readers hear reflections from each side of this partnership about what denotes good mentoring and the positive outcomes that result from earnestly attending to the mentor-mentee relationship. Along with Anson and Roen, they describe how professors can model writing habits for students. Powell advocates for classes that go beyond individual mentoring to formally teach professional genres, such as the letter of recommendation, to graduate students.

The interview collection as a whole reveals how faculty weave writing into their roles as mentors, researchers, administrators, teachers, and disciplinary leaders. "Writing projects seldom happen in isolation from other spaces of academic life" (23), observes Tulley. As a group, Tulley determines, these successful writers employ common techniques: writing within brief moments of time available, planning the structure, scope, and audience of their text before they begin, using writing to discover and reformulate their argument as they proceed, and securing peer feedback early in the process. Readers will note additional patterns throughout the transcripts as they might not be able to resist reflecting on their own processes and goals. Such is the simple brilliance of Tulley's writers-at-work methodology: the compilation of individual testimonials shows rather than tells, collectively offering extensive personal reflection and self-disclosure so as to present a uniquely specific array of unexpected glimpses into the reality of what it means to do the writing Elbow advocates. This in-depth view effectively counters reductive advice about time management and discipline that lead faculty to underestimate the adjustments, delays, loads of laundry, minute revisions, collaborations, frustrations, hours of work on a project, hours of work off a project, and networking opportunities that lead, over time, to an extensive corpus of publications.

This backstage approach contributes to the burgeoning field of faculty productivity studies. Until now, Tulley points out, there has been a "lack of self-study" (3) among composition scholars—ironic in a field that emphasizes student reflection, but perhaps more indicative of shortsightedness within academia as a whole and the problematic lack of support for faculty writing across universities that Boice identified decades ago. The collective testimony of

Tulley's book addresses the need for innovative and practical ways individuals, departments, and supporting units can tackle the emotional challenges, time constraints, and performance pressures of writing in the academy. By probing this untapped topic, Tulley's book challenges faculty development efforts to translate the successful practices of these well-established scholars so as to operationalize their insights more broadly across the scholarly community. It likewise impels further conversation within composition studies about how looking at our own writing can help us to pursue what we mean by well-crafted writing and to better share ways of achieving it.

Villanova, PA

Works Cited

Boice, Robert. Foreword. *Working with Faculty Writers*, edited by Michele Eodice and Anne Ellen Geller, Utah State UP, 2013, pp. vii-ix.

Elbow, Peter, and Mary Deane Sorcinelli. "The Faculty Writing Place: A Room of Our Own." *Change: The Magazine for Higher Learning*, vol. 38, no. 6, 2006, pp. 17-22.

Public Pedagogy in Composition Studies: Studies in Writing and Rhetoric, by Ashley J. Holmes. National Council of Teachers of English, 2016. 201 pp.

Reviewed by Erin Cromer Twal, Embry-Riddle Aeronautical University

The public turn in composition studies set in motion institutional efforts to cultivate sustainable partnerships between university writing programs and neighboring communities. In her landmark 1996 essay, "The Rhetorician as an Agent of Social Change," Ellen Cushman urges composition instructors to renegotiate the academy's position within the local public to "establish networks of reciprocity" (7). Cushman advocated for those in rhetorical studies to take their teaching and scholarship public as a form of ethical citizenship that is responsive to public needs. Ashley J. Holmes' *Public Pedagogy in Composition Studies* builds on and extends Cushman's initial call to take our theories and methods to the streets by drawing on rhetorical theories of place and affect to conceptualize the public work of composition. In three institutional case studies, Holmes' firsthand engagement with faculty, graduate instructors, and WPAs delivers a vibrant portrait of the complex and shifting dynamics always at play between institutional and public stakeholders. Further, the book targets institutional administrators and instructors by offering readers practical next steps that advance student learning in local publics.

Public Pedagogy begins by recognizing the achievements of those in composition studies whose scholarship has made great strides in theorizing the public work of composition pedagogy—Paula Mathieu, Christian Weisser, Eli Goldblatt, Linda Flowers, Shirley K. Rose, Irwin Weiser, Nancy Welch, and Peter Mortensen. It is true that many composition scholars and instructors already practice public pedagogy; however, Holmes argues that the lack of consistent discourse used to describe this pedagogical approach in journals, conference presentations, and books (e.g., service learning, civic engagement, community literacy, social action, etc.) may lead to missed encounters to engage in generative discussions about the many ways writing programs structure public engagement (4). In response to this problem of language, she invokes the interdisciplinary term "public pedagogy" to define the contours of a public pedagogical approach that is not limited to the service imperative (5). She envisions public pedagogy as a rhetorical practice, one capable of rupturing thematic binaries that tether academics to inauthentic learning and binds "real world" contexts with authentic learning (23). In this way, public pedagogy strikes a harmony between learning through public engagement and understanding these public encounters in the space of the classroom. Inspired by

Carol P. Hartzog's *Composition and the Academy*, Holmes' research design crafts a comparative analytical method to investigate writing instruction at Oberlin College, Syracuse University, and the University of Arizona (7). Though the scope of the comparative study is limited to only three institutions, Holmes explains that these case studies allowed her "to delve deeply into a close analysis of how each program was going public and then make comparative claims about how public pedagogies function in different institutional and programmatic contexts" (9). Her research data, drawn from site visits, instructional and institutional documentation, and IRB-approved interviews with administrators, faculty, and graduate instructors, yields rich and vastly important insights about the value and place of public pedagogy in U.S. higher education.

The second chapter analyzes the ways institutions create room for students to embark on meaningful learning experiences by moving beyond the traditional classroom and going public. The chapter draws inspiration from Elenore Long's taxonomy of five pedagogical approaches articulated in *Community Literacy and the Rhetoric of Local Publics*. The five approaches—interpretive, institutional, tactical, inquiry-driven, and performative—serve as a launchpad as she contributes her own pedagogical approach that attends to the role of place in understandings of the public sphere (35). To ground her approach, the chapter cites primary research gathered from instructor interviews to trace how a faculty member and two graduate teaching assistants design writing courses around a public pedagogy at Oberlin College, Syracuse University, and the University of Arizona. Spanning scientific field-based writing, campus service-learning advocacy, and campus spatial analytical writing and research, Holmes provides readers with dynamic examples of public pedagogy *in action*. While some of these examples do not adhere to a strict *service* imperative, she broadens Long's pedagogical categories and advocates for an approach centered around public place, arguing that she wants to "teach composition in ways that prompt students to interact with unfamiliar publics, to write about issues that are meaningful within their local public contexts. . . . [T]o do this work effectively, we must be mindful of location, relocating and re-envisioning our classroom spaces in more public ways" (56-57). Perhaps the greatest takeaway from this chapter is her proposed model and complimentary illustrations that offer composition scholars and instructors a theoretical framework for understanding the dynamic interplay between location(s) and educational objectives (60-61).

Chapter three targets administrative stakeholders and offers Writing Program Administrators rhetorical strategies to navigate institutional constraints and effectively re-invent writing programs that aim to go public. Her strategies are derived from firsthand interviews with WPAs and are intended to be replicable in a wide variety of institutional contexts. Her comparative analysis of WPA strategies calls into question misguided assumptions about knowledge-making in academic and public contexts that continue to sustain toxic and unproductive tensions that pit the university against the community (66). The chapter, instead, advocates for ways WPAs may embrace "morphing" as a rhetorical administrative strategy to make adaptation a key component in curricular development that responds to emergent public and institutional demands (72). The concept of morphing implies that writing programs must continuously renegotiate and balance emerging community partner needs with shifting institutional programmatic needs, a point she observes in Steve Parks' "next step courses" at Syracuse University (84). A willingness to brave the unknown becomes, as Holmes demonstrates, a key administrative tactic for sustaining a writing program that harnesses the productive power of public pedagogies.

The next chapter describes a feminist research method to model how writing programs can revise and construct new narratives that give place to public pedagogy. She emphasizes how past institutional histories continue to hold meaning for present institutional encounters with public pedagogy. This chapter urges writing programs to consider how university mission statements and programmatic goals historically and rhetorically underwrite the present relationship between the university and local publics (97). Further, Holmes argues that "composition specialists should look to their institution's histories in order to construct narratives that carve a place for public pedagogy within the work of writing programs and courses" (99). To illustrate her proposed argument, she examines mission statements from each of the three universities in her case study and offers a thematic narrative for the historical place of public pedagogy at each institution. Further, she draws on the affordances of feminist historiography to advocate for the value of historical narratives as a catalyst for garnering institutional support for public work in composition programs (100).

The book concludes in chapter five by gesturing to the affective dimension of public pedagogy. Writing programs must pay attention to students' affective responses to their public engagement encounters, she argues. In her previously published essay, "Transformative Learning" (2015), Holmes explores case study findings similar to those presented in the fifth chapter but focuses her attention on the ways affect has been undertheorized in service-learning pedagogies, thus maintaining binaries that pit cognition against affect. Building from this premise, her fifth chapter aims to theorize the affective dimension of public pedagogies, even beyond service-learning instruction. The chapter highlights some of the unanticipated risks involved when we ask students to take their learning public. She invites instructors to reflect on how they might respond productively to these affective encounters. Perhaps most telling is her description of a University of Arizona business writing course that involved a surprising conflict between a student and community partner (142-49). Holmes untangles the layered web of emotions felt by student, instructor, and client and prompts readers to reflect on the ways affect structures public pedagogy. The chapter proposes that writing instructors adopt what she calls a feminist reciprocal model of care, which invites instructors to decenter classroom authority and remain transparent with students and partners (150). The strength of this chapter lies in Holmes' honest and careful reflection on the sometimes-risky affective work of public pedagogy, a point that often remains invisible in writing program labor.

One of the great achievements of *Public Pedagogy* is the depth and scope of the book's comparative research project. Each chapter is grounded in rich primary research that illustrates the place of public pedagogy in public and private institutional contexts. Scholars, administrators, and instructors interested in cultivating institutional frameworks that foster sustained public pedagogies will surely find this book an immensely rewarding and intellectually engaging book. The book makes strides in pushing forward new theoretical models to rhetorically respond to the productive force of affect when we situate writing instruction in public.

Prescott, Arizona

Works Cited

Cushman, Ellen. "The Rhetorician as an Agent of Social Change." *CCC*, vol. 47, no. 1, 1996, pp. 7-28.

Hartzog, Carol P. *Composition and the Academy: A Study of Writing Program Administration*. MLA, 1986.

Long, Elenore. *Community Literacy and the Rhetoric of Local Publics*. Parlor Press, 2008.

Contributors

Kara Poe Alexander is associate professor of English and Director of the Writing Center at Baylor University. Her interests include literacy studies, multimodal composition, and composition theory and pedagogy. Her work has appeared in *CCC, Composition Forum, Composition Studies, Computers and Composition, LiCS, Journal of Business and Technical Communication, Rhetoric Review*, and several edited collections.

Sara Austin is a doctoral candidate in the rhetoric and writing program at Bowling Green State University. Her research interests include first-year writing, transfer, writing program administration, and feminist pedagogy. Her dissertation places these areas in conversation by using institutional ethnography to examine transfer-focused feminist pedagogies.

Jacob Babb is assistant professor of English and writing program coordinator at Indiana Southeast. His essays have appeared in *Composition Forum, Composition Studies, Harlot*, and *WPA* (for which he is associate editor).

Beth Boehm is professor of English and Executive Vice President and University Provost at the University of Louisville. Before becoming provost in 2018, she served as dean of the School of Interdisciplinary and Graduate Studies. Beth also served as the Director of Graduate Studies in English for almost ten years.

Katie Brooks is a doctoral candidate at Virginia Tech. Her research interests lie at the intersection of rhetorical regionalism, writing, and Appalachia.

Emily Carson is a postdoctoral fellow of faculty writing assistance in the Office of the Provost at Villanova University. Her research focuses on understanding the unique needs of faculty writers. She conducts workshops on academic writing and consults individually with faculty across disciplines and ranks on their varied writing projects.

Alyssa G. Cavazos is assistant professor of rhetoric, composition, and literacy studies in the Department of Writing and Language Studies at the University of Texas Rio Grande Valley. Her pedagogical and scholarly interests include translingual writing, writing across communities, and linguistically inclusive professional development for faculty across the curriculum.

Michael-John DePalma is associate professor of English and coordinator of professional writing and rhetoric at Baylor University. His work has appeared in *CCC, College English, Rhetoric Review, Rhetoric Society Quarterly,*

Reflections, the *Journal of Second Language Writing, Computers and Composition, System,* and several edited collections. With Jeffrey M. Ringer, he edited *Mapping Christian Rhetorics: Connecting Conversations, Charting New Territories* (Routledge 2015).

Jenn Fishman, associate professor of English at Marquette University, is author of numerous publications. She has also edited the *Research Exchange Index (REx)* and special issues of *CCC Online, Peitho,* and *Community Literacy Journal.* She is the PI of three grant-supported research projects and recipient of the 2006 Richard Braddock Award.

Alexandra Hidalgo is an award-winning filmmaker whose documentaries have been official selections for film festivals in fourteen countries. She is assistant professor of writing, rhetoric, and American cultures at Michigan State University. Her video book, *Cámara Retórica: A Feminist Filmmaking Methodology for Rhetoric and Composition,* received the Computers and Composition Distinguished Book Award.

Darin Jensen teaches English at Des Moines Area Community College in Iowa. His writing has appeared in *College English, eBW, Pedagogy, TETYC,* among other venues, as well as in several book chapters. He is co-editor of the Teacher-Scholar-Activist blog and is currently working on an edited collection with Brett Griffiths.

Carolyne M. King is a doctoral candidate at the University of Delaware where she teaches courses in first-year writing, technical and professional writing, and writing center theory and practice. Her research addresses reading theory and student academic literacy practices, especially through the lens of materiality and embodiment.

Steve Lamos is associate professor at the University of Colorado–Boulder. His publications include *Interests and Opportunities* (Pittsburgh UP, 2011), essays in *CCC, College English, Journal of Basic Writing,* and *WPA,* and several book chapters. His present book project analyzes the role of affect in literate life-making.

Amy J. Lueck is assistant professor of English at Santa Clara University, where she researches and teaches undergraduate courses on rhetoric and writing, focusing especially on histories of rhetorical education and practice. She is the author of *A Shared History: Writing in the High School, College, and University, 1856-1886* (SIUP 2019). Her work has also appeared in journals such as *College English, Rhetoric Review,* and *Kairos.*

Cruz Medina is assistant professor of rhetoric and composition at Santa Clara University. Medina wrote *Reclaiming Poch@ Pop: Examining Rhetoric of Cultural Deficiency* (Palgrave 2015) and co-edited *Racial Shorthand: Coded Discrimination Contested in Social Media* (CCDP 2018). His writing has appeared in *CCC, College English, Composition Studies* and other venues.

J. Michael Rifenburg is associate professor of English at the University of North Georgia where he serves as director of first-year composition. He authored *The Embodied Playbook: Writing Practices of Student-Athletes* (Utah State University Press, 2018) and is completing a longitudinal study on cadet writing instruction.

Brooke R. Schreiber is assistant professor of English at Baruch College, City University of New York, where she teaches courses in multilingual writing and globalization of English. Her research focuses on second language writing pedagogy in ESL and EFL settings, translingual writing in digital spaces, and supporting multilingual writers across the curriculum.

Lisa Shaver is associate professor of English and Director of Women's and Gender Studies at Baylor University. She is the author of *Beyond the Pulpit: Women's Rhetorical Roles in the Antebellum Religious Press* (2012). Her work has also appeared in *College English, Rhetoric Review, Pedagogy, Peitho,* and *Journal of Business and Technical Communication.*

James Clifford Swider is a doctoral candidate in the composition and applied linguistics program at Indiana University of Pennsylvania (IUP). He previously taught composition and literature at Tsinghua University in China and was the assistant director of the writing center at IUP.

Erin Cromer Twal is assistant professor of rhetoric and composition at Embry-Riddle Aeronautical University where she integrates public pedagogies in undergraduate technical and professional communication courses. Her research and teaching give place to public rhetoric and to rhetoric in action.

Danielle M. Williams is lecturer in English and interim Director of Freshman Composition at Baylor University. She teaches courses in first-year writing, technical and professional writing, digital writing, and advanced composition. Her work has appeared in *Computers and Composition* and in an edited collection.

Dorothy Worden is assistant professor of English at the University of Alabama where she teaches courses in linguistics and TESOL methods. Her research focuses on the cognition and education of teachers of second language writing and particularly how novice teachers transform disciplinary knowledge for teaching purposes.

PARLOR PRESS
EQUIPMENT FOR LIVING

NEW, IN LIVING COLOR!

Exquisite Corpse: Studio Art-Based Writing Practices in the Academy ed. by Kate Hanzalik and Nathalie Virgintino

The Afterlife of Discarded Objects: Memory and Forgetting in a Culture of Waste by Andrei Guruianu and Natalia Andrievskikh

Type Matters: The Rhetoricity of Letterforms ed. Christopher Scott Wyatt and Dànielle Nicole DeVoss (**BEST DESIGN AWARD-Ingram**)

NEW RELEASES

Tracing Invisible Lines: An Experiment in Mystoriography by David Prescott-Steed

KONSULT: Theopraxesis by Gregory L. Ulmer

Best of the Journals in Rhetoric and Composition 2018

Other People's English: Code-Meshing, Code-Switching, and African American Literacy by Vershawn Ashanti Young, et al.

Networked Humanities: Within and Without the University edited by Brian McNely and Jeff Rice

The Internet as a Game by Jill Anne Morris

CONGRATULATIONS, AWARD WINNERS!

Strategies for Writing Center Research by Jackie Grutsch McKinnie. **Best Book Award, International Writing Centers Association (2017)**

Antiracist Writing Assessment Ecologies: Teaching and Assessing Writing for a Socially Just Future by Asao Inoue, **BEST BOOK AWARD, CCCC, BEST BOOK, COUNCIL OF WRITING PROGRAM ADMINISTRATORS (2017)**

The WPA Outcomes Statement—A Decade Later edited by Nicholas N. Behm, Gregory R. Glau, Deborah H. Holdstein, Duane Roen, & Edward M. White, **Best Book Award, Council of Writing Program Adminstrators (2015)**

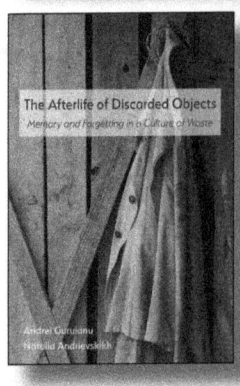

www.parlorpress.com

www.ingramcontent.com/pod-product-compliance
Lightning Source LLC
Chambersburg PA
CBHW031317160426
43196CB00007B/569